The Moral Hazards

The Moral Hazards

Police Strategies for Honesty and Ethical Behavior

Allan N. Kornblum

Lexington Books
D.C. Heath and Company
Lexington, Massachusetts
Toronto London

Library of Congress Cataloging in Publication Data

Kornblum, Allan N.
The moral hazards.

1. Police administration–New York (City). 2. New York (City)–Police.
3. Police ethics. 4. Gambling–New York (City). I. Title.
HV8148.N52K67 174'.9'3632 75-34614
ISBN 0-669-00378-6

Published simultaneously in Canada.

Printed in the United States of America.

International Standard Book Number: 0-669-00378-6

Library of Congress Catalog Card Number: 75-34614

To Helen

The problems to be met are not merely physical or academic. The moral hazards, I venture to say, are equally as great as any you will meet in the physical field.

Stephen P. Kennedy
Police Commissioner
October 1955

Contents

List of Figures

List of Tables

List of Exhibits

Foreword

This is a book about police behavior, and efforts to end police corruption in a large American city. But the relevance of Allan Kornblum's careful research is much broader. His central concerns are deviation and control in complex organizations: How field personnel alter policies and programs in order to satisfy their own needs; how top officials try to overcome such tendencies so that goals and procedures are in practice what they are announced to be. Deviation includes various forms of explicit corruption, often monetary payments, a basic problem in law enforcement agencies and in many large bureaucracies, private as well as public. Deviation also includes behavior of subordinates where money is not received from outside sources—abuse of clients, neglect, and a narrow focus on means at the cost of broader ends, where political pressure or bureaucratic convenience reshapes intended policy.

Paramount in this study is the problem of control—of how the leaders of any organization can attempt to reduce corruption and other forms of deviation, so that individual action in the field is consistent with pronouncements at headquarters. This has been a central issue in political and bureaucratic analysis at least since Machiavelli's *The Prince*, and major recent contributions have been made by Herbert Simon in his *Administrative Behavior*, Richard Neustadt in *Presidential Power*, and Herbert Kaufman in *The Forest Ranger.* For these students of social power a principal issue has been how leaders of complex organizations can, as Neustadt put it, "be on top in fact as well as name." It is a challenge and a burden shared by princes and presidents, police commissioners and school superintendents, leaders of private corporations as well as government agencies.

Using law enforcement as a focus, Kornblum concentrates his analysis on the various strategies that are significant to leadership efforts not only for police but for all organizations. And he considers the limitations of those strategies and the reasons why they often fail. Good intentions are no substitute for a clear, cold-blooded understanding of how staff members perceive and respond to organizational incentives, how vigorous control efforts from the top will generate new deceptions and other deviations, and what lessons these patterns suggest for effective leadership in large bureaucracies. Of particular note is Kornblum's model assessing administrators' use of "functional anxiety" (fear) to assure compliance from subordinates. Police officers more than ever may find themselves objects of Machiavellian schemes for control based on fear.

Kornblum's analysis of these broad issues in *The Moral Hazards* will be important to practitioners in law enforcement and a valuable contribution to the literature of administrative behavior.

Jameson W. Doig
Princeton University

Preface

This book is a study of administrative behavior, of how police executives sought to implement their directives in a highly complex and decentralized bureaucracy. It analyzes strategies used by successive administrations in New York City from the 1950s into the mid-1970s to overcome collusive resistance between policemen who were allied with gamblers. Indeed, gambling enforcement has been the bane of the New York City Police Department since the department was established in 1845.

This is not an exposé of police corruption. The existence of dishonesty and unethical behavior was incidental to my research. Nor is this a "cook book" that provides recipes for eliminating malfeasance. It is, rather, an analysis of what Douglas McGregor has described as "management by direction and control." The book is predicated on the perspective of police executives with their "top-down" approach to counter deviant behavior, because the author feels that meaningful reform can only be achieved from within.

This book will examine policies and procedures (official and unofficial) and their consequences (intended and unintended) used by officials in the NYCPD to promote ethical behavior. It will consider incentives and pressures for organizational change in light of their costs and benefits and conditions under which they are likely to be effective. It will also assess a set of drastic policies used to achieve honesty and ethical police practices during the early 1970s.

The New York City Police Department was the subject of my research because its operations shed considerable light on how large bureaucracies function and implement public policy. As a former member of the force I was acquainted with its workings; I could establish empathy and rapport with those who knew problems of gambling enforcement intimately; and my proximity to many sources of information about the department facilitated the research.

Gambling enforcement was my focus because (1) considerable data about it had been accumulated over the years; (2) dishonesty and unethical behavior were so organized and systematized that they lent themselves to analysis; and (3) malpractice was almost traditionally accepted, so that the information I sought was an open secret.

For their enthusiasm and encouragement, I am indebted to three people who read this book in manuscript form. Former New York City Police Commissioner Patrick V. Murphy, Herbert Kaufman of the Brookings Institution, and Jameson W. Doig of Princeton University. Commissioner Murphy provided me with unparalleled access to historical and contemporary records of the New York City Police Department. Professor Kaufman, whose study of the United States Forest Service, *The Forest Ranger*, served as a partial model for this book, gave me helpful recommendations. I must give special thanks to Jameson Doig, my friend and mentor, who contributed to the manuscript substantially. I am also indebted to The Daniel and Florence Guggenheim Foundation for their generous support in completing this study.

Finally, I must thank those members and former members of the NYCPD who provided me with abundant information based on their years of experience. Although I have omitted their names to preserve their anonymity, I am nevertheless grateful for their frank and perceptive contributions to the research.

From this point, my work must stand independent of help given generously by others. I accept responsibility for its limitations as well as for its possible worth to students of administrative behavior.

The views and conclusions presented herein are my own and not necessarily those of the U.S. Department of Justice.

Allan N. Kornblum
Mount Vernon, Virginia

Glossary of Abbreviations and Jargon Used in the New York City Police Department

ABC: alcoholic beverage control laws

Backstrap: procedure used by bookmakers to extend telephone wires to remote locations

Bag: policeman's uniform

Batting average: policeman's record of arrests

Blotter: official chronological record of events at a police station or other unit

Boss: commanding or supervising officer

Brooklyn number: winning digits in daily numbers lottery based on the amount of money bet (the "handle") at one race track each day

Cheese box: device used by bookmakers to relay bettor's telephone calls to remote locations

CI: chief inspector

CIIU: Chief Inspector's Investigating Unit

Clerical man: patrolman who types investigative reports and performs other clerical duties

Communication: report of a complaint from a member of the public alleging a violation of a gambling or public morals law

Complaint: official charge against a member of the force for violating departmental rules and procedures

Contract: a favor one policeman does for another, often in reciprocation for a past favor

Coop: policeman's shelter from the elements (heat, cold, rain, etc.); also *to coop:* to rest or sleep while on duty

DAR: Daily Activity Report form, which replaced plainclothesmen's memorandum books

FDC: first deputy police commissioner; also called 1 DC

FDCIU: First Deputy Commissioner's Investigating Unit

Field associate: plainclothesman who agrees to observe fellow officers confidentially and to report any malfeasance directly to headquarters

Flaking: planting evidence on arrested person

Flop (or **be flopped**): to be demoted from a desirable assignment such as detective or plainclothes

GEIRB: Gambling Enforcement Inspection and Review Board

Gold shield: detective's badge

Hard-core location: premises where violations of gambling or public moral laws have occurred repeatedly

Hook: the process, or an individual, who can influence decisions by high officials, usually to obtain a choice assignment for a policeman

IAD: Internal Affairs Division

Jump collar: procedure in which persons with arrest records are confronted, searched without probable cause, and arrested if evidence of a crime is found

ISB: Inspectional Services Bureau

KG: known gambler

Made (or **to get made**): to be promoted in rank or to receive a choice assignment such as detective

Memorandum book: personal notebook maintained on a daily basis by plainclothesmen and patrolmen

New York number: winning digits in daily numbers lottery determined by winning prices paid at one race track each day

NVO: no violation observed

OCCB: Organized Crime Control Bureau

Observation: plainclothesman seeing bets being taken or gambling records being passed on

Overhead: a superior unit in the chain of command

Overheard: an arrest based on a plainclothesman's overhearing bets being placed

Pad: an arrangement or list of people, business firms, and institutions that make regular payments to police, usually to obtain nonenforcement of some law

PBA: Patrolmen's Benevolent Association

PCCIU: Police Commissioner's Confidential Investigating Unit

Pickup arrest: arrest made for an unreported crime, usually observed during its commission

PLCL: plainclothesman

PMAD: Public Morals Administrative Division

PMD: Public Morals Division

PMDI: public morals deputy inspector

PMI: public morals inspector

Put one's papers in: to retire from the force

Quality arrest: arrest of an important member of organized gambling

Rabbi: someone, within or outside the department, who can influence decisions of high officials, usually to obtain a choice assignment

RIP: fine imposed on a policeman found guilty of violating departmental rules

R&P: manual of *Rules and Procedures*

Scratch: entry in a policeman's memorandum book

Seat: regular assignment to a police patrol car

Sheet: concise daily record of arrests in gambling and public morals made during a 24-hour period, known officially as the Daily Report for Public Morals Enforcement Activity

Shoo-fly: superior officer, usually a captain, assigned to observe patrolmen working on their posts

Shield; policeman's badge, also known as a "potsy" or "tin"

SOP: Standard Operating Procedure

Spot: premises where gambling or public morals violations are suspected

Squeal: complaint of crime from a member of the public

Stand-in: someone who is substituted to be arrested in lieu of a gambler

Standup guy: someone who is willing to remain silent in the face of charges without informing on others

Suspected premises: location of possible violation of gambling or public morals laws

TOP: Temporary Operating Procedure

Turn-around program: officers guilty of minor malfeasance allowed to remain on the force in return for undercover work to apprehend other officers guilty of more serious malfeasance

UF 128: form used by plainclothesmen to report results of gambling and public morals investigations

Work: written records of numbers plays, or bets, placed with bookmakers

Yellow sheet: a criminal's record of arrests, also known as a "rap sheet"

The Moral Hazards

1 Ethical Police Practice

The Police and Public Policy

"Nothing undermines public confidence in the police and in the process of criminal justice more than the illegal acts of [police] officers."–such were the words of the President's Commission on Law Enforcement and Administration of Justice in their 1967 report on the police.[1] And law enforcement in America is indeed troubled. During the past twenty-five years fundamental doubts concerning the credibility of police have arisen through a series of social, political, and juridical challenges. Only occasional subjects of concern in the past, police policy and practice are now under constant scrutiny. Although some issues reflect long-standing abuses–such as excessive use of force by police–as well as the historic evils generated by racial discrimination, problems of malfeasance are just now being studied seriously.[2]

The most recent chain of sociopolitical events that aroused public interest in police developed out of the civil rights movement in the 1950s. Strife resulting from campaigns for social and political equality put police, as guardians of public order, in the forefront of confrontation. Critics first condemned police mishandling of public demonstrations and acts of civil obedience, and later challenged traditional practices in dealing with blacks and other minorities. As a result the civil rights movement generated substantial political pressures to modify discriminatory police practices.[3]

Challenges to police "lawlessness" were pressed in the courts, which restricted police procedures for dealing with criminal offenders under new rules promulgated by the United States Supreme Court. In several landmark decisions in the 1960s, prearraignment detention of suspects by police was limited to ensure defendants' prompt appearance before judicial officers;[4] illegally seized evidence was excluded from criminal trials in state courts;[5] persons under arrest were guaranteed the right to consult with an attorney before undergoing interrogation;[6] and policemen were required, prior to starting interrogation, to advise suspects of their rights to remain silent and to have legal counsel.[7] These and other decisions stimulated vigorous debate about the role and character of the police service.[8]

Disturbances and riots throughout the country in the 1960s focused on police as an "occupying force" in minority communities and called into question the police's social function. Political activism in the late 1960s and early 1970s, directed against U.S. involvement in Vietnam and other issues, continued to isolate police as the most visible defenders of the status quo, alleged perpetuators of social injustice. Thus alienated, police responded to mass protest and violence with militancy of their own. Police activism included aggressive handling of demonstrations, economic demands expressed through strikes and work stoppages, and participation in the political process to influence issues related to their own concerns. More than ever, the police became the major subject in the debate over law and order.[9]

After decades of controversy, two areas of police policy emerge as major concerns in public affairs: ethical behavior and honesty. Ethical issues stem from the broad discretion of police to control crime and the tension between competing values of efficiency and "due process" that underlie law enforcement practices. Central questions about ethical behavior include:

1. discrimination in enforcement of criminal laws
2. abuses in search and seizure, interrogation, and other due process requirements
3. use of corporal punishment and deadly force
4. illicit procedures for gathering information[10]

Polarization of these issues has resulted in public alienation and police frustration. Estrangement of minorities and other groups is based on a sense of police indifference to preventing crime and insensibility to personal rights. Police, on the other hand, feel trapped between conflicting demands that they "perceive as the public's unreasonable expectations of them and even more unreasonable limitations imposed on them."[11] Many significant questions of policy were resolved through the political process and by judicial tests of police procedures. Early in the 1970s, however, violence between militants and police escalated dramatically, particularly in urban centers where each group perceived the other as a threat to its survival.

Overshadowing the controversy about efficiency versus due process, however, is a growing concern for police integrity. Involved is a variety of police malfeasance characterized by a profit motive. This kind of misconduct is criminal enterprise carried out under cover of lawful authority, whereas unethical behavior represents primarily overzealous and misguided efforts to control crime without regard for legal restraints.[12] Whereas dishonesty is a long-standing problem rather than a product of recent events, revelations of organized thievery and corruption in the late 1960s and early 1970s scandalized police across the country. Reporting the existence of "varying forms of criminal and unethical conduct" by police in several cities, in 1967 the President's Commission on Law Enforcement and Administration of Justice cited the following as the most common patterns of police corruption:

1. improper political influence in enforcement decisions

2. nonenforcement of laws relating to gambling, prostitution, and liquor offenses
3. theft
4. acceptance of illegal fees[13]

Between the two concerns in police administration—due process and integrity-integrity is paramount because corruption in police agencies creates an ethos conducive to all forms of malfeasance. Historically, the most persistent and widespread form of police dishonesty has been the nonenforcement of laws controlling gambling. Where nonenforcement exists, police forbearance is purchased by criminals providing illegal betting services, who write it off as just another cost of doing business. Cooptation by gamblers not only conveys an image of police hypocrisy, but also nourishes tolerance for myriad forms of dishonest and unethical conduct in a climate of lawlessness.[14]

Both areas of police malfeasance—dishonesty and unethical behavior—involve two practical questions: What rules of procedure and conduct should police adopt, and how can adherence to prescribed standards be achieved? Whereas police and public may clash on principles of ethical practice and the means for achieving compliance,[15] they generally agree on the continuing need for honesty as an organizational norm.

In the area of gambling enforcement, however, the question of corruption is complicated further by political uncertainty regarding legalization of gambling. The public is ambivalent. Although there is general support for honesty in law enforcement, there is no consensus regarding the desirability of gambling remaining illegal.[16] Some states have legalized gambling in limited forms, such as lotteries, bingo, and off-track betting. Although recent studies have recommended legalizing gambling, they advocate decriminalization primarily to redirect organized crime's huge profits into the public's treasury. More optimistic proponents assert that legalization will eliminate police corruption.[17] But for the foreseeable future, most forms of gambling that are now illegal will remain so, continuing the need for honest law enforcement.

Achieving Honesty as an Organizational Norm

Police are committed to enforce all criminal laws notwithstanding their personal feelings about the propriety of any prohibition. Honesty requires that within a framework of ethical standards, police diligently identify and apprehend all who violate the penal statutes. Although this definition of honesty may be the behavioral norm within police organizations, substantial evidence indicate that the generalization does not apply to enforcement of gambling laws, for organized gamblers have successfully coopted many policemen.[18] Because police executives have failed to achieve vigorous enforcement, they have had to administratively compel adherence to the supposedly voluntary norm of honesty. To this end, various strategies have been fashioned to promote compliance with officially prescribed standards of integrity. No pretense is made to secure enforcement of the gambling laws for their intrinsic social value or for "honesty's sake." Police view prohibition of gambling as an anachronism—mala-prohibita. To justify honest enforcement, administrators stress the need to eliminate the cancer of corruption and to deny revenues to organized crime.

Many strategies intended to further ethical police practice operate from outside police organizations, focusing on discrimination and failure to observe due process in enforcement.[19] Judicial challenge has been the principal approach, highlighting national patterns of police abuses. Although they do not set police policy, the courts interpret statutes and prescribe rules of procedure that indirectly govern police practice. The strategy of judicial review offers reformers important advantages. First, substantive and procedural decisions apply to all law enforcement agencies within the court's jurisdiction, obviating the need for multiple lawsuits. Second, and more significant, rulings based on constitutional standards are not subject to administrative or legislative reversal. Police resentment of court-imposed restrictions has been outspoken, and judicial rule making has been a source of recurring conflict within the system of criminal justice.[20] But the courts, never viable for promoting or maintaining honesty on a continuing basis, have been used in a case-by-case approach to punish corrupt policemen who have been discovered. Similarly, civilian review boards, which have been advocated to solve other problems of unethical behavior (excessive use of force, for example), do not seem appropriate to combat dishonesty.[21]

The most frequently used external mechanisms to end malfeasance in gambling enforcement have been investigative commissions organized at national, state, or local levels and characterized by predictable outcomes. Through a series of sensationalized but limited public hearings, commissions focus considerable publicity on illegal gambling and cooptation of police. They issue formal reports urging greater public concern and professional effort, but provide no meaningful improvement. Commissions and their recommendations are quickly forgotten.[22] Corrupt practices thus have been left to police by default because the public has offered little in the way of prevention or reform.[23]

Because honesty in gambling enforcement has remained a problem of internal management, this book studies administrative behavior—how police executives seek to promote and maintain honesty as an organizational norm. As such it probes managerial strategies used to overcome collusive resistance by policemen allied with gamblers. The challenge has proved complex, often insoluble. Police administrators understand that their organizations, although they are unique in some respects, share characteristics common to large bureaucracies. These characteristics include a social order built around a formal organizational framework, governed through a system of communication and hierarchies of authority and responsibility. Individual behavior is guided by oral and written instructions as well as by a set of indirect incentives. Because individuals often must exercise discretion in decision making, the bureaucratic organization seeks to develop attitudes through which workers voluntarily comply with official directives. Coexisting with the formal organization are informal systems for communication, status, and responsibility. A supplementary set of peer pressures also guides individual behavior, establishing work and social norms. Peer groups promote both compliance with and disregard for organizational policies. To achieve honesty and ethical behavior as an organizational norm, administrators must deal with a complex range of formal and informal pressures.[24]

Police executives thus have adopted administrative theories and techniques to improve managerial efficiency. Mechanisms of organizational influence already adopted include division of labor through specialization, use of training and indoctrination, formulation of work rules and procedures, establishment of systems of authority and supervision, and use of rewards and sanctions to encourage compliance with policy.[25] The subject of this study is the system of managerial controls used by police officials to achieve compliance with headquarter's directives—honest enforcement of gambling laws. These strategies and mechanisms are not limited in application to gambling enforcement; they apply to other areas where administrators seek to overcome collusive resistance to their goals by subordinates allied with hostile interest groups.

At this point it is necessary to dispel any preliminary assumption that "what the top officers of an organization want, the organization does."[26] This tenet is typically untrue of all large bureaucracies in which field personnel can easily disregard, modify, or contradict headquarters' directives. More often than not, policemen have ignored their superiors' orders for honesty in gambling enforcement. Also, strategies and procedures used by police officials to promote compliance in the field are not unique. Many of their approaches are used in other large bureaucracies, especially geographically decentralized organizations whose personnel must, by necessity, exercise considerable discretion.[27] As one might expect, most obstacles to achieving compliance from field personnel are common to police and similar bureaucracies. These difficulties, which are both intellectual and practical, include:

1. lack of knowledge about how to change established attitudes
2. lack of sufficient time to change attitudes
3. limitations of individuals in the organization
4. conflicting organizational goals, which confuse field personnel
5. unanticipated consequences of policies, which thwart achievement of primary goals
6. competing external incentives, which negate organizational influence
7. strategies whose costs outweigh their usefulness[28]

As this list suggests, failure is not exclusively a function of resistant subordinates and organizational bottlenecks. All too often administrators lack the managerial knowledge and skills needed to achieve goals. Police executives fall short of implementing their policies because they fail to understand the structure of incentives and other dynamics of behavior in organizations.

Underlying these administrative difficulties in controlling enforcement of gambling laws is the ambiguity of the desired behavioral norm "honesty." Indeed, the term "honesty" oversimplifies the task facing police executives; malpractice in gambling enforcement encompasses more complex patterns of behavior. "Honesty" is an inclusive term for a range of behavior more clearly defined when contrasted with various forms of malpractice in gambling enforcement. Deviant behavior of policemen falls into two broad categories: (1) extortion/cooptation and (2) corrupt practices induced by administrative incentives.

Extortion/cooptation is the more commonly known and conspicuous form of malpractice, in which organized gamblers pay police not to enforce gambling laws. Depending on location or tradition, the arrangement may be initiated by policemen offering protection—a form of extortion—or by gamblers seeking to expand their enterprise and operate more openly. In either case, gamblers ultimately coopt the police. Where such malpractice flourishes for a substantial period, the arrangements become sophisticated and standardized. In return for their "fee," police not only allow gamblers to conduct business freely, but also actively promote their clients' interests by arresting nonpaying competitors. If compelled to enforce the law, coopted policemen arrest "stand-ins" (substitutes) provided by gamblers, return betting records seized during an arrest, and warn gamblers of impending arrests or raids. To perpetuate their arrangement, policemen and gamblers collusively resist strategies for honesty.[29]

Administratively induced corruption, in contrast, encompasses a variety of unethical behavior based on policemen's perceptions of their superiors' expectations. These responses may be either lawful actions based on honest zeal or misplaced enthusiasm, or illegal practices growing out of personal frustration and cynicism. Lawful activities include making numerous unimportant arrests to give the appearance of efficiency, as well as showing token compliance with procedures for due process. Illegal practices, often abuses of legal ones, include arresting or searching without probable cause, false reporting, planting evidence on "guilty" gamblers, and perjuring to ensure convictions. Corrupt practice is not a product of collusive resistance to any initiative from management; it is an individual response, an unspoken norm of the work group.

Malfeasance, not a spontaneous development in the policeman's career, is learned through a process of socialization. Police exposed to corrupt practices in gambling enforcement are induced to participate through subtle as well as direct peer pressures. An individual does not graduate from the police academy and get offered $1000 per month the next day. He is trained and gradually conditioned so that he can handle the strain of his own immorality. Corrupt policemen and gamblers refine unethical behavior as the system of cooptation matures and expands.[30] Efforts to destroy systematized malpractice usually lead to the development of more sophisticated techniques to evade discovery. When co-opted policemen are transferred or promoted, their replacements in gambling enforcement units must join or be neutralized so that the corrupt scheme can continue. More important, policemen who have joined a corrupt conspiracy may be promoted through civil service procedures to supervisory positions, and although they may "get religion" (that is, discontinue unethical practice) they dare not act against former coconspirators.

The Case of New York City

Having set the broader analytic framework of difficulty in achieving responsiveness, I move now to my specific subject, the New York City Police Department (NYCPD). Gambling enforcement has been troubling New York City's police commissioners since the department was established in 1845. Dishonesty and unethical behavior, particularly in enforcing laws controlling gambling and public morals, have been enduring problems for police executives; indeed, scandals in gambling enforcement have a history of their own arising from a series of sensationalized investigations and public hearings. (Table 1-1 provides a chronology of corruption investigations.)

Created and funded by the New York State Legislature and occasionally by the city itself, these public inquiries have reached similar conclusions—that the enforcement of gambling and public morals laws was crippled by organized corruption. Numerous departmental investigations confirmed this finding. Following a cyclical pattern, corruption was discovered and publicized, a reform effort undertaken, and after a brief respite the illicit scheme rejuvenated—only to be reexposed in a few years as the cycle was renewed. The investigation in the early 1950s highlights the beginning of a cycle that ended in 1970, illustrates the extensive nature of schemes for cooptation, and sets the background from which this study proceeds:

Table 1-1
History of Corruption Investigations[31]

Informal Title	Years of Inquiry
Lexow Committee	1894-1895
Mazet Committee	1899-1900
Curran Committee	1912-1913
Seabury Investigation	1931-1932
Amen Investigation	1938-1942
Brooklyn Grand Jury	1949-1952
Knapp Commission	1970-1972

Scandal broke in December 1949, when the *Brooklyn Eagle* revealed in a series of articles that many policemen were working in close cooperation with a large bookmaking organization.[32] That same month, the Kings County (Brooklyn) grand jury was held over to begin formal inquiry. The high point of the investigation occurred in September 1950, when Harry Gross, head of the bookmaking hierarchy, was arrested by policemen who were working under the direction of the Brooklyn district attorney. During the next two years the press publicized organized corruption as Gross revealed details about his operation, especially its collusion with policemen.

Gross alleged that beginning in the 1940s he established a regular liaison with police, and that as a result, his business developed from a one-man "handbook" to a major enterprise centered in Brooklyn. Working from the top down, Gross first obtained clearance from police executives to operate, then negotiated "contracts" of decreasing scale with those in the enforcement hierarchy. His bookmaking expanded, and so did his conspiracy with police because payoffs for nonenforcement of gambling laws snowballed as more "spots" for betting were established. Indeed, Gross conceded later, he "couldn't have made book 24 hours" without police cooperation. He made bimonthly payoffs to policemen at every level of gambling enforcement; he paid for each "spot" in a policeman's jurisdiction and for each telephone in use. He also regularly dispensed cash bonuses and gifts. While admitting to having made payoffs for some ten years, Gross implicated the police commissioner, chief inspector, and a host of other officers, most of whom resigned from the department. Even the mayor was implicated for having received political contributions from Gross and other gamblers.

Because of Gross's disclosures, about 45 policemen, several of high rank, were convicted in criminal court or at departmental trials and were fired. Approximately 150 other members of the force retired or resigned while under investigation. During the climax of a trial of several policemen in criminal court, however, Gross proved himself a "standup guy" by balking midway in his testimony, refusing to identify policemen. Criminal charges had to be dismissed. Eventually, Gross cooperated by testifying at departmental trials, and his original twelve-year prison sentence was reduced to six years. Thus the Gross case had mixed results.[33] A corrupt scheme was apparently ended; wrongdoers were removed from the department and punished; and the Brooklyn grand jury made a public report that like its predecessors was quickly forgotten.

For twenty years after the Gross case, New York's police leadership struggled with problems of corruption as their predecessors had between previous scandals. Indeed, the NYCPD has been an experimental workshop in ethical behavior. This book will study the inner workings of the department from the 1950s to the mid-1970s, when successive administrations tried to achieve field behavior consistent with an avowed policy of honest gambling enforcement. Because of the complex pattern of corrupt behavior, and because of the transient membership in collusive schemes, departmental strategies to promote honesty and ethical behavior in gambling enforcement were shifted frequently. Procedures designed to curb malpractice prompted new counterstrategies to thwart discovery. Experimenting and groping, unsure of their success, police executives faced seemingly insoluble problems.

All available evidence indicates that in spite of concerted efforts, police administrations spanning two decades failed to achieve honest and ethical gambling enforcement. Indeed, the most recent commission investigating corruption found that the conditions that existed between police and gamblers during the era of Harry Gross were just as prevalent, *if not more so*, in the early 1970s.

The Array of Strategies

Before considering specific strategies, the reader should appreciate the difficulties of presenting multidimensional material in linear form. It is a burden shared by historians and social scientists who simultaneously describe and interpret a series of contemporaneous events. As a study of successive New York City police administrations, the materials focus on a particular set of policies and procedures but involve dimensions such as

1. description of various strategies and their intended effects
2. use and development of each strategy, and policemen's responses to it
3. evaluation of the success or failure of the strategies

Complementing the organizational problem is the need to give the reader, without staggering amounts of detail, an understanding of the strategies and how they fared. Description and analysis are combined to highlight both the nature of each strategy and its broader administrative implications. But some human dimensions of policy making—individual personalities and prejudices—have been minimized to avoid obscuring issues of organizational behavior. The reader should bear in mind, however, that strategies for achieving honesty may have originated in part from motivations other than those officially stated, as in response to a particular incident, and were only justified later in terms of managerial efficiency.

Before considering specific strategies the reader should understand the framework of their presentation and analysis. The department's leaders followed a traditional pattern for controlling behavior in organizations as they struggled to achieve honest gambling enforcement. Executives issued instructions to members of the force, allowed subordinates to implement these directives, monitored and evaluated performance, and amended their instructions depending on the extent of perceived compliance and effectiveness of the procedures. When significant discrepancies between what the force was doing and what it was supposed to be doing were discovered, officials sought to close these "performance gaps" by revising directives to eliminate ambiguities and loopholes.[34] This administrative cycle for controlling behavior depends on effective systems of communication to subordinates and accurate feedback on performance. Although this control model provides the conceptual framework for strategies intended to promote honesty in gambling enforcement, it is an oversimplified construct.

Complicating the four-step cycle were the variables of time and change. Strategies often evolved over a substantial period, several originating in procedures predating the Gross case. There were many strategies, only some of which were interdependent. Policies often resulted from pressing circumstances of the moment. Procedures were not followed continuously and uniformly; some fell into temporary disuse and were later resurrected. Because these variables made it impossible to assess the strategies in the order suggested by the simple control model, I divided them into two broad categories, which I call "directive" and "control." The reader should bear in mind, however, that in the true sense all were strategies to control behavior.

This book's analytical structure is based on both substantive and organizational considerations. Directive and control strategies are presented in a logical sequence of implementation within the framework of the traditional control cycle. Discussion begins with directive strategies that were developed to encourage honest and ethical behavior. Where directive strategies failed, administrators turned to control strategies to discover and punish malefactors. Strategies are considered as if successive police administrations were a single entity and as though policies and procedures were implemented in a rational-chronological scheme. Directive and control strategies were not implemented in the order I present them; I present them as they logically build one upon another.

Stated broadly, directive strategies sought to establish honest enforcement as the department's goal; to find officers willing and able to achieve that goal; and to provide the organizational arrangements, personal incentives, and tools necessary to do the job. To attain these objectives, four principal directive strategies evolved over the years:

1. establishing goals, policies, and procedures
2. shuffling personnel and boxes
3. changing individual incentives and attitudes
4. inducing productivity

Police commissioners played a personal but surprisingly limited role in establishing departmental goals, policies, and procedures. Commissioners made speeches to set the tone and policy themes for their administrations and frequently renewed their commitment to combat dishonesty in gambling enforcement. Generally, anticorruption policies in the 1950s were products of ad hoc decisions made in response to embarrassing incidents and occasional crises. In 1961, however, policy making for efficient and honest gambling enforcement was centralized and delegated to a single Gambling Enforcement Inspection and Review Board (GEIRB). The GEIRB, established to end reliance on ad hoc decisions, was to provide expertise and continuity, especially in efforts against corruption. Technically a staff unit, the board formulated and implemented most directive and control strategies used during the 1960s. Its decision-making process involved staff reports, special conferences, fact-finding surveys, and regular monthly meetings of administrators concerned with gambling enforcement. Though some of its suggestions for new policies and procedures were sidetracked, most of the board's recommendations were implemented. In spite of its nominal staff status, the GEIRB exercised significant de facto control over gambling enforcement through rule making and informal clearance of decisions by field units, particularly through its powers in personnel management.

Nowhere was the GEIRB's power more complete than in the two directive strategies designed to change individual incentives and attitudes: selection and training. Beginning with selection, the GEIRB upgraded criteria for appointment to gambling enforcement units. It also changed the system that previously had allowed precinct commanders to recommend candidates on the basis of voluntary self-selection to a system that required unsolicited recommendations by commanders. The board added intelligence tests and a limit on personal debts to the screening process. To overcome widespread resistance to assignments in gambling enforcement, it tried to change the motivation for those entering this field by introducing the "detective incentive." Because most of the force wanted to become detectives, the board made service in a gambling unit a formal prerequisite for the coveted detective assignment.

The concept of training was championed by the GEIRB, and throughout the 1950s and 1960s policemen selected for gambling enforcement units were required to attend a six-week investigator's course at the police academy. Instruction was oriented toward legal and technical subjects. Comparable training was provided for officers supervising gambling enforcement, supplemented with occasional conferences with the GEIRB's members.

After selecting and training new investigators, administrators sought to maintain honesty by changing individual assignments and organizational structure. Procedures for assignment and tenure in gambling enforcement were revised. Officials created a structured career ladder so that policemen in gambling units moved up gradually to positions of increasing responsibility, possibly to the detective division. Tenure in gambling enforcement was limited to four years to minimize exposure to corrupting temptations. Routine transfers of personnel were used to promote deserving officers, to punish those who transgressed departmental mores, and to banish those judged to be incompetent. As a general policy, successive police administrations relied on mass transfers of individuals suspected of malfeasance. In some instances entire units were disbanded. Most often the policemen were transferred to different gambling units or were returned to uniform duties. Mass transfer was often used in conjunction with organizational restructuring.

The organization of gambling enforcement units were changed frequently to promote both efficiency and honesty. Reorganizations were made on the assumption that structure would affect individual behavior by keeping people off balance and by altering patterns of loyalty and command influence. Several variations were used, characterized by cycles of centralization and decentralization of responsibility for gambling enforcement. Different hierarchies were established in various parts of the city throughout the 1950s and 1960s, as the lines and boxes on the department's organization chart were redrawn frequently.

Hoping to prevent cooptation, successive police administrations promulgated semiofficial production norms. Norms were based on numbers of arrests, whch created unofficial quotas for individuals and entire units. Sensitive to charges of inefficiency and corruption, officials worried that continued widespread gambling reflected poorly on them personally as well as on the department. Officials thought that a great many arrests of gamblers provided objective evidence of the department's sincere effort to enforce the gambling laws fully while simultaneously limiting cooptation. Statistics of arrests were compiled assiduously, daily and monthly, and superiors made frequent comparisons of past "achievements" to determine the efficiency of individual policemen, particularly of gambling unit commanders. When statistics were low, crash programs were instituted to increase the number of arrests and thus improve the statistical picture.

Supplementing their organizational schemes and production norms, administrators sought to provide proper tools for those enforcing gambling laws. A principal concern was policemen's use of personal funds to conduct gambling investigations. Officials reasoned that unless policemen were provided with money to pay for investigative expenses, they would either shirk responsibilities or possibly find improper sources of funds. Therefore policemen assigned to gambling enforcement were reimbursed monthly for out-of-pocket expenses to minimize financial temptation.

The thrust behind the foregoing directive strategies was to create incentives and pressures for honest and diligent enforcement of gambling laws, but the strategies often failed. When human nature proved vulnerable to temptations, police administrators relied on control strategies to close the gap between policy and practice. Their objectives were to limit opportunities for malfeasance, to increase discovery of corrupt practices, and to punish deviant behavior. Control strategies consisted of a mix of policies and procedures, principally techniques for: (1) reporting misconduct and investigative activities; (2) supervising personnel; (3) discovering malpractice; and (4) imposing sanctions.

Policemen assigned to gambling enforcement–indeed all members of the force–were instructed to report the misconduct of fellow officers to their superiors. Moreover, they were required to prepare daily a detailed chronological account of investigative work and other duties performed. Investigative reports were to be updated at regular weekly intervals so that all information got "on the record." Mandatory accounting for daily activities and current case reports was intended both to deter malpractice and to generate information that could verify integrity. To deter dishonesty through a similar process of forced accounting, officers assigned to gambling enforcement were required to complete financial questionnaires disclosing all personal and family assets.

Supervision was the department's basic strategy to promote honesty and integrity in gambling enforcement. Superiors in gambling units, usually lieutenants, were selected from the department's promotion lists of those who were awaiting appointment to captain. Selection was involuntary. The policy was based on several assumptions, principally that policemen seeking promotion were career-minded and upwardly mobile with a compelling incentive to remain honest and to see that their subordinates did, too. Supervisory procedure included both administrative and field responsibilities. Commanders were required to direct and to control gambling investigations by assigning cases and monitoring all reporting. They were to supplement these efforts by field patrols and by participation in all important arrests and raids. Through these combined efforts, supervisors were to provide the leadership and direction necessary to prevent or discover dishonest and unethical conduct.

Successive administrations did not rely on field supervision or formal inspections to ensure honesty. Instead, administrators devised elaborate techniques to discover and eliminate organized cooptation by gamblers. For information regarding malpractice in gambling enforcement, the department relied heavily on complaints from the general public. All complaints, as well as any in-house intelligence indicating cooptation or unethical behavior, were funneled to the police commissioner's office, where they were screened and forwarded for verification. Allegations with sensitive information or with significant detail indicating authenticity were handled by elite squads at headquarters, including those squads assigned to the police commissioner and other high-ranking administrators. These units, particularly the Police Commissioner's Confidential Investigating Unit (PCCIU), were generally feared because of their prominence in the department's hierarchy and because of their aggressive investigative techniques. Most complaints contained vague allegations of dishonesty and were assigned to field commanders who were responsible for checking on their subordinates. Superior officers outside the gambling unit in question were assigned these inquiries and submitted their findings to headquarters through channels.

Sanctions ranging from reprimands to monetary fines to suspension and dismissal were the department's traditional tools to deter and punish all kinds of deviant behavior. Because policemen were extremely sensitive about their rights when accused, officials had to rely on a highly legalistic and time-consuming disciplinary code. In gambling enforcement, however, sanctions used against wrongdoers were primarily informal. Intrasquad transfers or banishment to patrol work were the usual punishments. Formal sanctions were often challenged in the courts or evaded through resignation from the department.

By the early 1970s, as another cycle of corruption was completed, police administrators committed themselves to eliminating corrupt practices in gambling and other enforcement areas as their first priority. Thus many of the directive and control policies used in the past were revived and intensified. New and more coercive strategies were devised. Controversial programs included using both honest and corrupt policemen as informants, using wiretaps against policemen and gamblers, and conducting covert tests of integrity.

Before undertaking a detailed consideration of these strategies and how they fared, I will introduce the environment of gambling enforcement, including the organizational ethos in which the strategies were applied. Chapter 2 presents an intimate account of how organized gamblers operated and of the inner workings of the police department. Chapters 3 and 4 describe the directive and control strategies and assess their success or failure to achieve honesty in gambling enforcement. Chapter 5 broadens the study from the police to the difficulties of achieving responsiveness in public bureaucracies. Building on previous research in controlling behavior, I evaluate assumptions underlying directive and control strategies as well as their limitations and costs for achieving desired conduct. Alternative strategies to these external controls are explored in the concluding sections.

2 The Environment of Gambling: 1950-1975

Service Crimes

The Illicit Franchise

Historically, the sanctions of our system of criminal justice have been used to enforce standards of morality relating to sex, alcoholic beverages, and gambling. Principal beneficiaries of such proscriptive national and state legislation have been criminals who derived a franchise for the distribution of forbidden goods and services from moralistic prohibitions. As a result of recent social changes, however, only gambling remains as a principal source of illicit revenues.

Illegal gambling in United States is big business, a business controlled by a loose confederation of groups commonly known as "organized crime." Unlike ordinary lawbreaking, organized crime has unique social norms and a stringent code of discipline, and it adapts businesslike methods to maintain criminal enterprises on a continuing basis. Employing thousands of people in a conglomerate of firms, its undertakings are based on three operating principles: supplying illegal goods or services; guaranteeing profits through monopolies or oligarchic competition; and using fear and violence to maintain control of markets.[1]

Following the repeal of the Eighteenth Amendment in 1933, organized crime shifted its emphasis from production of alcoholic beverages to services, as gambling became a major source of illegal revenues. Providing betting and other services to a widespread public became organized crime's most profitable and durable enterprise. Competition for control of these profits lasted several decades and was marked not only by considerable violence but also by adoption of technical sophistication, organizational form, and corporate practices. More significant, however, has been the increasing acceptance of gambling by the U.S. public.

Once considered an aberration of human nature, gambling is now an increasingly accepted by-product of our socioeconomic development. Wagering on the outcome of a sports event and being an avid spectator are equal in respectability. The growth of legal and illegal betting stems from certain identifiable sources: increased leisure time, expanded publicity in the media, and changes in public policy.

Advances in production technology and in labor practices have given the public substantially more free time to develop personal interests. Knowledge and awareness of sports have grown with the help of the printed media, which began to report not only sports news, but also horse race and team schedules with detailed listings of competitors, unofficial odds, and betting suggestions. Radio and television helped to extend personal involvement through play-by-play coverage of the games and thus stimulated mass interest and team followings. As a result, professional sports has become a major leisure-time industry. And as the industry grew, attitudes changed.

The comparatively brief history of legalized betting in New York state and New York City, including pari-mutuel betting at public race tracks, bingo, and most recently a state lottery and off-track betting (OTB), reflects a short-term change in public policy.[2]

Originally, horse racing generated the most betting interest, until radio and television highlighted the speculative potential of baseball, football, and other team competition. Today betting on team sports dominates illegal gambling. Whereas there may be ten entries in a horse race, there are only two teams in a game, making pregame evaluation less complex. In spite of the legalization of pari-mutuel and off-track betting, it is still illegal for private individuals or firms in New York to accept wagers on the outcome of any sports event. But the state's limited bookmaking has failed to meet competition from private "bookies," who extend their services to all sports events, provide special betting arrangements, and offer the conveniences of easy credit and telephone wagering, not to mention anonymity from the Internal Revenue Service.[3]

For poor people, who until comparatively recently lacked the time and means to follow team events, the most popular form of gambling remains policy, also known as the daily numbers lottery. Like sports betting, the state lottery has similarly fallen short of the public's demand for simplified gambling. Although policy is still illegal, it is nevertheless a thriving enterprise because it offers unique individualized betting features.[4] The continued prohibition of bookmaking and numbers has helped to support an artificial market for the provision of these services to the public.

There is now a growing debate about the legalization of other forms of betting; its eventual outcome may well turn on the success of New York's lottery and off-track betting as fund-raisers for state and local government. Public attitudes toward the morality of betting seem to have shifted gradually in favor of its legalization, and one consequence of this change in attitudes is its partial reflection in the police department's enforcement of gambling laws.

Illegal gambling is often characterized as a "victimless crime," but this description is narrow and misleading. Among its principal victims are corrupted police and officials, a public treasury cheated of tax revenues, and a society exploited by other forms of organized crime (such as narcotics) that are financed by gambling profits. Indeed, the true character of organized gambling stems from its economic foundation—bookmaking, numbers, and other forms of illegal betting are actually service crimes. They are businesslike enterprises that exist only with broad public demand.[5]

Like other service industries, organized gambling completely depends on its availability to the public. To maintain accessibility, bookmaking and numbers firms must operate from more or less fixed locations where customers can obtain their services directly or by telephone. In addition, their operations depend on the daily schedule and starting times of sports competitions because bets must be placed prior to the events. Also, betting records must be collected daily at regular times to facilitate accounting and payoffs. Because organized gambling cannot conceal itself from the public and still remain a viable economic enterprise, and because it functions on a daily basis, often at the same locations and during determinable time periods, bookmaking and policy would appear to be comparatively easy for the police to suppress. Such appearances are deceiving.

Another misconception about organized gambling is that the bookmaker or numbers operator undertakes an approximately equal risk in the mutual wager. Nothing could be farther from the truth. Bookmakers and policy operators profit consistently. Through voluntary cooperation and manipulation of legitimate odds on the outcome of the wagered event, be it a sports contest or numbers lottery, organized gamblers take little or no risk of losing.[6] In fact, the bookmaker usually does not care which horse or team wins, just as the numbers operator is not especially worried about the winning number on any given day. Through a complicated process of "laying off" or balancing bets and plays, bookmakers and numbers operators are generally assured of retaining at least a small percentage of the total amount of money wagered with them. In the long run, both gambling enterprises derive enormous profits, particularly in comparison to earnings from legitimate investments.

It should be clear by now that bookmaking and policy are business enterprises in every sense. Both provide a much-demanded service to an established clientele; both have semipermanent places of operation and regular business hours; both operate as virtual monopolies because of the noneconomic costs that deter entry into the field by new firms; both provide special betting arrangements not currently available through legal betting on sports or the state lottery; and both have career personnel with substantial expertise who receive liberal pay and fringe benefits.

There are, however, important differences between bookmaking and policy. Bookmaking has undergone considerable modernization to meet pressures generated by law enforcement and to improve service to its patrons, whereas policy has changed only slightly over the years. By contracting with independent specialists for needed services and by using the telephone extensively, bookmakers have reduced their work force to one third that of the policy business. Numbers, on the other hand, remains a labor-intensive enterprise that relies almost exclusively on interpersonal relations. Because the numbers business is highly decentralized, it is more vulnerable to detection by police. Numbers operations are restricted to limited geographic areas (Harlem, for example, or Bedford-Stuyvesant) because bets are collected in person, although policy banks are usually well removed from collection points. Bookmaking, in contrast, has no geographic limitations. A bookmaker in Coney Island conducts business in Manhattan, Brooklyn, and elsewhere in the city. The most significant difference, however, is financial: Bookmaking earns three or four times as much as policy. More streamlined and sophisticated than the numbers business, bookmaking enjoys all the benefits of large-scale organization without most of its problems.

The following sections examine these service crimes in some detail to illustrate their sophistication, their appeal to bettors, and the difficulties they pose to police.

Bookmaking[7]

The cornerstone of bookmaking is the wireroom, where bets are accepted and recorded. The police were aware of approximately sixty major bookmaking organizations operating in New York City in 1973, each built around one or more wirerooms. These sixty organizations employ some three thousand full and part-time workers and have an estimated annual gross income of $1.5 billion. Although organized gambling employs thousands of people, only the few in top management derive vast profits from providing betting services (see Exhibit A in the appendix).

At the bottom of these sixty hierarchies are some 1000 to 1500 runners who gather bets from customers daily and call them in to wirerooms. (Figure 2-1 depicts the overall structure of bookmaking organizations.) Runners may be salaried employees of the organization or self-employed individuals who subscribe to services provided by a wireroom. However they work, runners provide a vital service for bookmakers by allowing wirerooms to operate efficiently yet with comparative security by not having to circulate traceable telephone numbers.

Wirerooms are usually located in out-of-the-way offices or apartments that bookmakers can lease simply by paying one or two month's rent as security. They operate from 11:00 a.m. to 3:00 p.m. and again from 6:00 p.m. to 8:00 p.m. daily, these hours being determined by the starting times of horse races and other sports events. Whether they are individual bettors or runners, all callers must use an identifying code or phrase before they can place bets with one of the two experienced clerks, or "sheet-writers," who work in the typical wireroom. Betting records ("the work") are usually transferred during the working day to minimize disruption of normal operations should there be a police raid. Seizure of the day's records is costly in terms of lost revenues from losing bettors, and also because of the bookmakers' policy to honor all seized winning bets claimed by customers.

Accounting and bookkeeping are functions of the next echelon, the figure-room, where winning and losing bets are processed to establish the day's net earnings or "bottom figure." Individual accounts of bettors and runners are

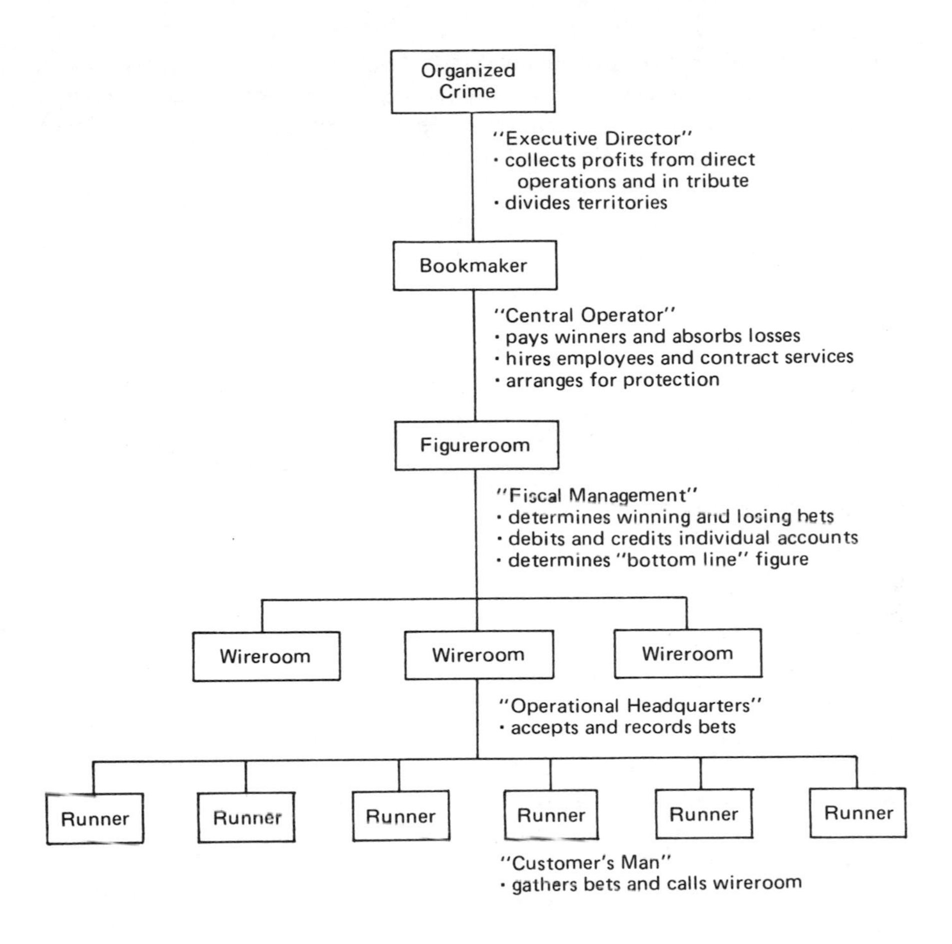

Figure 2-1. Structure of Illegal Bookmaking.

debited or credited accordingly, and this information is relayed to the wireroom before the next day's betting so that players will know their current financial status.

Bookmaking operations have several variations, related primarily to the protection and functioning of the wireroom. Usually calls are made directly to the office where bets are entered. The all-important need for security, however, has led to the creation of two or three other arrangements that differ from the "direct-number" wireroom.[8] The first of these variations was the "backstrap," an illegal extension of telephone instruments and wires from the site of their original installation over one or more rooftops to a wireroom in a nearby building. Still in use, modern backstraps apply the same principle, but they have been updated. Instead of moving the instrument and lines, a technician adjusts wires at appropriate terminal boxes so that calls placed to the wireroom are received at a location several blocks away. Modernized backstraps can be traced, of course, by telephone technicians, but the task is more complex and time-consuming than that of merely following wires over a rooftop.

A second variation of the direct number wireroom uses an even more sophisticated security system known as the "cheese box." Developed exclusively for the bookmaking industry, it provides protection through an unlimited extension of telephone lines. Bookmakers rent offices or apartments where they install two separate telephones that relay incoming calls after the cheese box is illegally connected between them. The betting public is then given the first of the two telephone numbers. At the beginning of each business day, wireroom clerks dial, from a remote location, the number of the second telephone to open up a direct voice line into the first telephone. This linkage enables them to receive all bets called in on the first number. When police learn and locate the first telephone, all they find are the two instruments and the cheese box, with no telephone lines to trace to the wireroom. Under this system bookmakers risk only the loss of the cheese box, which is worth about $1000 to $1500 (see Exhibit B in the appendix).

More recent variations in bookmaking operations also are based on security considerations. Instead of relying on backstraps and cheese boxes, which can be defeated through modern technology, bookmakers have used answering services for "call-out" wirerooms. Bettors call private individuals who operate answering services and leave code names and telephone numbers. When the wireroom calls the service, it identifies itself with its own code and receives names and telephone numbers of bettors. The wireroom then must return the players' calls to obtain their bets. Even if police raid the answering service, the employee will not know the location of the wireroom, and there are no traceable wires or electronic connections. One drawback is that players are reluctant to leave their telephone numbers in case the numbers fall into the hands of the police or the Internal Revenue Service. The principal disadvantages of the call-out wireroom, however, are extra costs in time and labor. Instead of simply accepting incoming bets, call-out rooms must place numerous calls to the service and then to customers. Although answering services enhance bookmakers' security, they also boost overhead.

In addition to their formal organization, bookmaking operations depend on several specialized services that are purchased from independent contractors. Foremost among these is the daily "line" provided by the professional odds-maker. Because bookmakers seek to minimize all financial risk in accepting bets, they are "faced with the problem of evaluating the strength of two [or more] adversaries and then, through a point spread or the assignment of odds (called the "line") evening out the two sides." To offset heavy betting on the favorites, bookmakers include predetermined odds, or a point-spread, in all bets. The "bookmaker's margin" or profit, known as the "vigorish," is built into odds or point-spread. "This is the cornerstone of bookmaking and, indeed, all other forms of professional gambling."[9] Although margins on different sports vary, the current "vigorish" in New York is 10 percent, meaning there is a guaranteed profit of 10 percent of all lost wagers booked by the sixty New York operations. For economic reasons and because they lack the ability to determine odds, most bookmakers rely on a line service provided nationally by a few professional handicappers.

Line service is vital for the profitable acceptance of bets, and it has other important implications for the bookmaking industry. It is provided by only a few firms nationally, so all sixty bookmaking operations offer the public the same betting line, thus minimizing competition and the risk of sharp bettors or other gamblers seeking some advantage through an inaccurate line of odds. More important, perhaps, is its relation to another major service needed by bookmakers, a layoff system.

Because bookmakers ultimately try to equalize amounts bet on the two contestants in any game to guarantee their profit, they need a layoff service, or a "bookie's bookie." Nationally standardized odds facilitate the transfer of bets among bookmakers. Bookmakers do not always succeed, but in the long run they come close to balancing their books by shifting excessive wagers to another bookmaking organization that is willing to accept laid-off bets for a fee or to help balance their own accounts. Often this shifting of wagers necessitates interstate cooperation when New York City bookmakers cannot absorb bets. In an emergency, some small bookmaking organizations have even laid off bets with New York City by patronizing the state's Off-Track Betting Corporation. Without a layoff service, sports betting would be too uncertain for the bookmaker-businessman who, ironically, chooses a guaranteed profit over a gamble.

To be competitive, bookmakers also need a service to provide them with the winners' names and prices immediately following each race. Prompt payoffs are made to encourage bettors to wager their winnings on subsequent races or games. Finally, many operations employ a "weatherman," who calls "associates" at race tracks and stadiums throughout the country to determine weather and field conditions. Such information can be vital to the bookmaker because it is not available to the professional oddsmaker who establishes the line several days before the game. As a result of changes in the weather and other late information—such as players' injuries—betting lines are subject to last-minute revisions. In many cases bookmakers delay publishing their line until the day before the event, and bettors often wait until one hour before game time to bet.

The Numbers Lottery[10]

Numbers is the most popular form of organized gambling in New York City, with more than 100,000 daily players. In its most common usage, this lottery allows the player to select a three-digit number and wager that it will be determined—by chance—to be the winning number for that day. The winning number is determined through horse racing events at a single track in one of two ways: by combining selected digits from the winning prices paid in successive races (the "New York number") or by using the last three digits from the total amount of money (the "handle") wagered at the track (the "Brooklyn number") (see Exhibit C in the appendix). Players can also bet on one-digit ("single action") and two-digit ("bolita") numbers. The numbers lottery is operated seven days a week and on most nights when trotting races are held. Although numbers was played in New York City as early as the nineteenth century and has been followed by many modern variations, its basic elements of an individually selected number, a wager, and daily determination of a winner remain unchanged.

The numbers lottery has a mass appeal for many reasons, particularly for its simplicity and flexibility. Betting requires no special skill or knowledge. A numbers player does not have to grapple with a complicated racing form or compare abilities of several contestants. He need only have a "lucky" number, a hunch, or a dream that a particular number will "hit" on any given day. Flexibility in the amount that can be wagered without reducing odds for payoff also makes numbers betting attractive.[11] Because any amount down to a nickel or a dime can be wagered, policy has always been popular among the city's poor and minority groups. In fact, numbers dominates all gambling in the black and Spanish-speaking areas of the city. Although the average bet is now about thirty-seven cents, plays of one to five dollars are not uncommon (see Exhibit D in the appendix).

Like the wireroom in bookmaking, the policy bank is the cornerstone of the numbers lottery. In 1973 there were some forty major numbers organizations operating in New York City, each one built around one or more policy banks. As in bookmaking, the numbers business has a hierarchical order but employs three times as many people in its operations. The overall structures of both bookmaking and policy are uniform; more variations appear in policy at its lower levels.

At the bottom of the hierarchy are collectors who accept bets directly from players. (Figure 2-2 depicts the overall structure of numbers organizations.) Anyone can be a collector—numbers knows no social, racial, or sex discrimination. The collector's job is to record the player's identity, choice of number, amount of bet, and type of play (see Exhibit E in the appendix).

Collectors vary their routines depending on territory and clientele. Some wait for customers at fixed locations such as shops or stores, freight elevators or subway newsstands—any place that has a substantial volume of pedestrian traffic yet still offers some privacy. Others move through a neighborhood, a housing development, an office building, or a factory.[12] Collectors encourage steady customers to bet on the same number every day for a week or longer, which

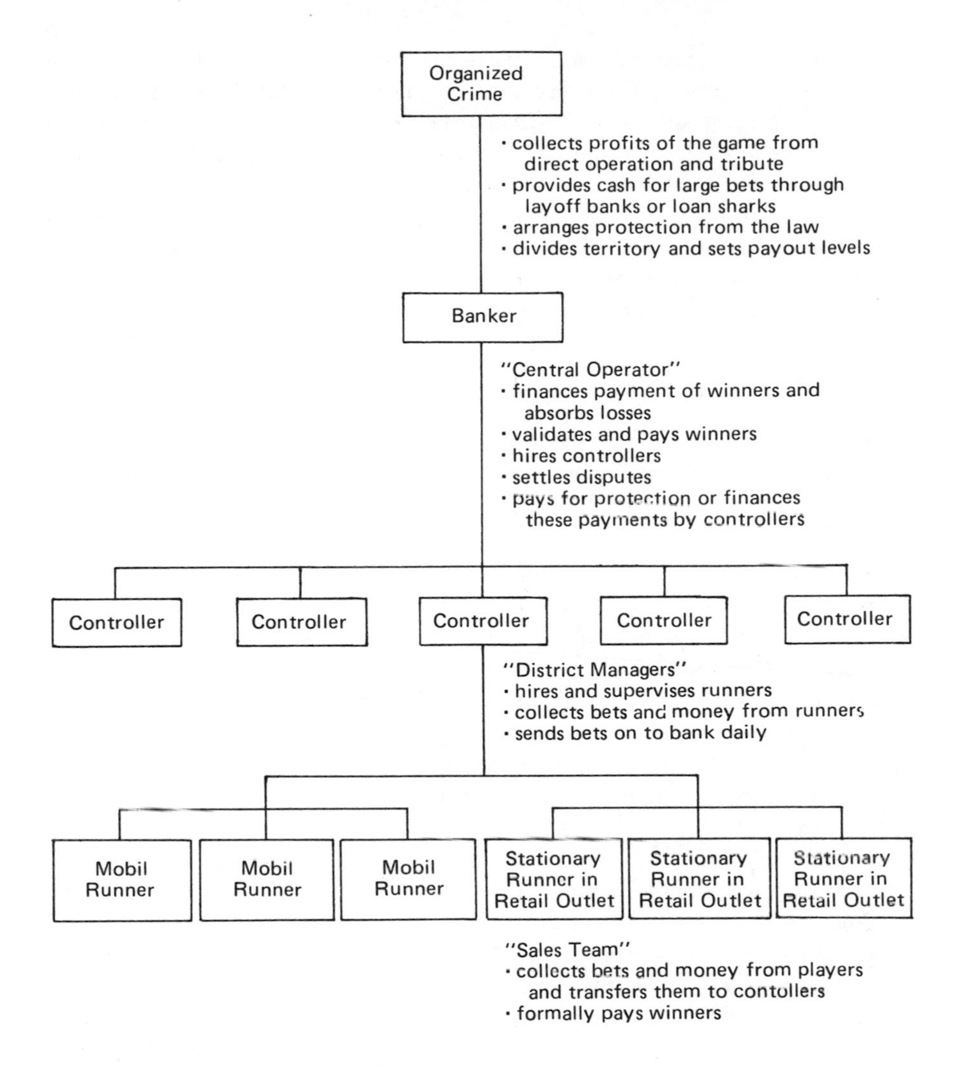

Source: Fund for City of New York, *Legal Gambling in New York* (New York, 1972), p. 29. Reprinted with permission.

Figure 2-2. Structure of Illegal Numbers Game.

helps reduce frequency of contacts, needs for daily record keeping, and exchanges of money. This precaution also reduces the chance of discovery by police and the amount of incriminating evidence. The collector's primary security measure is to accept bets only from regular players or from people introduced or recommended by reliable sources. Before turning in his work, the collector deducts his salary, 25 percent of the total amount wagered. His share is nearly all profit because collectors have little or no overhead. Using extreme caution, the collector transfers cash and bets to the next level, the controller.[13]

The controllers are on the first true management level in the policy organization. Experienced and trusted employees, they direct the efforts of subordinate collectors and pickupmen and compile their work and cash for the next higher echelon (see Exhibit F in the appendix). Generally, each controller's job involves coordinating some twenty or more collectors and two or three pickup men, the actual number varying with the size of the business and the number of banks it operates.

Controllers usually work from varying locations known as spots or drops—a basement apartment, a remote office, or the back room of a store. Lookouts in the street and by the door provide security against police raids. Once the work and monies are delivered, the controller's two or three clerks begin their accounting of the receipts, all to be finished within an hour and a half since the controller must move betting records to the policy bank or other reliable hands by 3:00 p.m. The controller, it appears, is not trusted, either, because he must relinquish the work before the third race is run and the first digit known. Like the collector, the controller also deducts his cut: 10 percent of the total amount of bets placed with all his collectors. But from this he pays salaries as well as rent, court costs, and other overhead. In some cases controllers keep only 5 percent of the gross when their bank pays all expenses. Finally, the controller repackages records and receipts for the journey upward. In most instances neither the money nor the work goes directly to the bank, because circuitous and extensive courier systems are used to prevent the police from discovering the bank's location.[14]

At the time of this writing, the known policy organizations reportedly operate sixty-seven policy banks, each one under a banker's control. Banks operate in specific geographic areas, but without fixed boundary lines. The use of separate locations for cash and records minimizes loss in the event of police seizure; thus policy banks often use multiple offices. Since the bank's security lies with secrecy of location, only the banker and one or two reliable aides know where the sites are. Electronic security devices are rarely used. The banker, who never visits banks during working hours, places subordinates in charge of operations. His only concern is the "bottom figure," or net income, for the day, which is ascertained by calling late each afternoon. Once the work and cash have arrived from the controllers, four or five bank clerks begin the final tally. One check is made to verify that 65 percent of gross is present or otherwise accounted for. Just as important, however, is the survey of the work to isolate heavy betting on a particular number. When too much is bet on a number, the bank tries to minimize possible loss by laying off some of these wagers with another bank, just as bookmakers do.[15] Cash payoffs are made that same night or the following morning, depending on how quickly money filters down through the collector to the player. Players customarily tip collectors 10 percent of their winnings. Thus the cycle is complete, to be renewed again every twenty-four hours, six days a week, year in and year out.

This concludes an overview of organized gambling, an environment where the police department has functioned for generations. Now as we begin to consider how police have enforced the gambling laws, the reader will begin to understand the organized gambler's durability and sophistication.

The NYCPD: A Decentralized Bureaucracy

Division of Labor

Large organizations such as the New York City Police Department are "fairly permanent social systems designed to achieve limited objectives through the coordinated activities of their members."[16] Police objectives traditionally include preventing crime, maintaining order, and safeguarding public morality. In response to community expectations, New York City's police have directed most of their energies toward controlling crime and maintaining order, with lesser effort expended toward enforcing standards of morality. Even so, they have lost public confidence because of problems related to morals enforcement.

In addition to enforcing prohibitions against gambling, police are also responsible for upholding statutes regulating consensual sex relations and the sale of alcoholic beverages.[17] For the most part, these proscriptive areas have generated manageable enforcement and administrative problems. Gambling, however, has posed the most enduring challenge to New York City's police administrations. Their 130 years of experience have yielded no solutions to the enigma of maintaining honest and ethical behavior in gambling enforcement. The remainder of this chapter provides an overview of police organization and the enforcement of gambling laws.

Organized along paramilitary lines, the police department reflects the traditional hierarchy of authority and responsibility. Topmost on the pyramid is the police commissioner, who, appointed by the mayor, serves a five-year term to provide continuity of administration in the event of a political change at city hall. Although chief executive of the department, the commissioner is and remains a civilian, not a member of the police force.[18] This status creates a conflict of interest because, as the public's representative to maintain civilian control over the police, the commissioner is accountable for the department's performance. The police force, on the other hand, regards the commissioner as its spokesman and defender, a role that requires him to support the force against criticism and interference. One of the commissioner's more delicate undertakings is to balance these competing interests while allowing neither to dominate his perspective and judgment.[19]

Like the head of any large bureaucracy, the commissioner's ultimate challenge is to acquire and maintain organizational control and responsiveness. To this end he fashions the department's policies and oversees its functioning, being ever wary of becoming waylaid by daily administrative problems. If he is a good executive, he delegates substantial authority and responsibility to trusted subordinates.

Foremost among these subordinates are deputy police commissioners, civilians appointed by the commissioner to serve in several functional areas. The number of deputy commissioners and their duties have changed over the years as the department's perception of its roles has changed. The first deputy commissioner is distinguished from his colleagues in that only he automatically becomes acting police commissioner in the commissioner's absence or disability. As executive aides and principal advisors on matters of policy, first deputy commissioners were traditionally concerned with the department's overall performance, and throughout the 1960s their special area of involvement was gambling enforcement. The other deputies assist the commissioner in meeting his responsibilities for administration, community affairs, legal matters, public information, trials, and—most recently in 1971—organized crime control. Deputy commissioners make up the commissioner's general staff, serving him primarily as advisors.[20]

Appointed by the commissioner, traditionally from the department's corps of senior officers, the chief inspector is the highest-ranking member of the police force (in 1973 his title was changed to chief of operations). Deriving his authority directly from the commissioner, he commands the entire force and is specifically responsible for its efficiency and discipline. An active contributor to departmental policy, his primary function is to ensure that the commissioner's directives are carried out. He exercises his authority through a pyramidal chain of command based on a military rank structure. The structure of ranks has changed over time, as shown in Table 2-1.[21]

Noncompetitive appointments (that is, all ranks above captain) are made by the commissioner from members of the force who hold the permanent civil service rank of captain. Promotions to deputy inspector and inspector, which are by tradition quasi-permanent, are stepping stones to the more prestigious ranks of deputy and assistant chief inspector. These four ranks, filled by comparatively few superior officers, form the structure that exercises de facto control over the department.[22] Whereas there is less authority and responsibility as one moves down the rank structure, as in the military model, the basic functions of all commanders are essentially the same. There are only differences in the scale of their responsibilities for law enforcement, administration, discipline, and the integrity of the force under their command.

It is not easy to advance within the police department. From the entry level of patrolman (now "police officer") there are two tracks for promotion. The first involves civil service examinations, held for the successive ranks of sergeant, lieutenant, and captain, at regular intervals. All members of the force in the

Table 2-1
Change in Structure of Ranks, 1957-1975

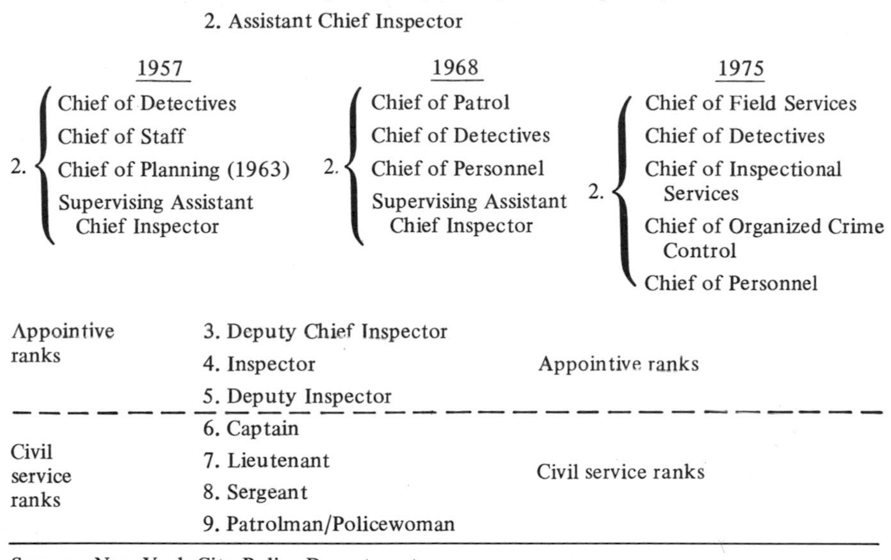

1. Chief of Operations (formerly Chief Inspector)
2. Assistant Chief Inspector

	1957	1968	1975
2.	Chief of Detectives	Chief of Patrol	Chief of Field Services
	Chief of Staff	Chief of Detectives	Chief of Detectives
	Chief of Planning (1963)	Chief of Personnel	Chief of Inspectional Services
	Supervising Assistant Chief Inspector	Supervising Assistant Chief Inspector	Chief of Organized Crime Control
			Chief of Personnel

	Rank	
Appointive ranks	3. Deputy Chief Inspector	Appointive ranks
	4. Inspector	
	5. Deputy Inspector	
Civil service ranks	6. Captain	Civil service ranks
	7. Lieutenant	
	8. Sergeant	
	9. Patrolman/Policewoman	

Source: New York City Police Department.

preceding ranks are eligible to take the tests following completion of minimum time in grade, two years. The second track for promotion involves a career in the detective force. This route parallels that of the civil service except that appointments, promotions, and tenure among detectives depend on the police commissioner's discretion. Detective sergeants and lieutenants do take competitive examinations to earn their ranks; they are appointed and they serve as supervisors at the discretion of the commissioner. See Table 2-2 for the approximate number of people in each rank in 1972.

The department is divided by function into several operating units, which were formerly called divisions but are now called bureaus. (Table 2-3 reflects changes in the branches of the department from 1957 to 1975.) Although their numbers and titles have changed in response to departmental needs and responsibilities, these units have retained their essential character in spite of some consolidation over the years (see Exhibits G and H in the appendix).

Patrol remains the core of crime prevention and law enforcement. The Patrol Services Bureau (since 1973 called the Field Services Bureau), under the command of the chief of patrol (now called chief of field services), has always been the department's backbone. Most patrolmen are assigned to the patrol force, now called the "uniformed service," performing foot and radio-motor-car patrol (RMP) throughout the city. Even sophisticated technical advances have

Table 2-2
Approximate Number of Members in Each Rank, 1972

Rank	Number
Chief Inspector	1
Assistant Chief Inspector–Bureau Chief	4
Assistant Chief Inspector	14
Deputy Chief Inspector	22
Inspector	43
Deputy Inspector	101
Captain	362
Lieutenant	1,032
Sergeant	2,210
Patrolman	27,548
Policewoman	332

Source: 1970 Police Department's *Annual Report* and *New York Times*, November 17, 1972, p. 30.

Table 2-3
Changes in Branches of the Department, 1957-1975

1957	1968	1975
1. Patrol Force	1. Patrol Bureau	1. Field Services Bureau
2. Detective Division	2. Detective Division	2. Detective Bureau
3. Safety Division	3. Personnel Bureau	3. Inspectional Services Bureau
4. Emergency Service Division	4. Technical Services Bureau	4. Organized Crime Control Bureau
5. Youth Division	5. Division of Licenses	5. Personnel Bureau
6. Communications and Records Division	6. Administrative Units	6. Support Services Bureau
7. Division of Licenses		7. Criminal Justice Bureau
8. Police Academy		
9. Headquarters Division		
10. Administrative Units		

Source: New York City Police Department.

not modified the patrolman's essential functions: to deter and apprehend criminals, to enforce all laws and ordinances, to maintain public order, and to deal with emergencies and social problems as varied as human nature.[23]

The Detective Bureau is the department's second major operating unit and its oldest specialized force, dating back to the 1890s. Assignments to detective are coveted as much for their challenge as for their prestige. Historically, detectives were investigative generalists who worked in small decentralized units throughout the city. Although considered specialists vis-à-vis the patrol force, they handled all serious crimes, regardless of their nature. The generalist approach was modified in the early 1970s, when the department, in its effort to invigorate the patrol force, simultaneously sought to enhance detectives' performances through across-the-board specialization in investigating crimes.[24]

The remainder of the force works in myriad functional units both administrative (for example, personnel, training, crime lab) and operational (for example, tactical patrol, emergency service, traffic). Civilian employees complete the department's basic structure, serving in clerical and administrative capacities that do not require police skills or training. There has been a continuing effort to civilianize the department to release patrolmen for field duties where their training is needed.

Fixing Responsibility

In establishing accountability for performance, the department follows two basic approaches: It assigns people to fixed territorial areas of responsibility, and it provides detailed procedural instructions. Although subdivided into fixed geographic jurisdictions, the department integrates its operating elements into a workable system. On each level of subdivision one finds a microcosm of the overall police department that preserves in every detail this bureaucracy's essential character—the hierarchy of authority, functional specialization, and command responsibility. The department resembles a patchquilt of fiefdoms that are tightly woven into one overall design. New York's 365 square miles are broken down into seven major geographic areas, called borough commands, which include Manhattan North, Manhattan South, Bronx, Brooklyn North, Brooklyn South, Queens, and Staten Island (see Exhibit I in the appendix). Borough commands are headed by assistant or deputy chief inspectors, supported by staffs of superior officers and clerical personnel.[25]

Each borough command is divided into several units called divisions, controlled by an inspector and his staff.[26] Divisions, in turn, are subdivided into patrol precincts, each led by a captain. Precincts are the foundation of the department's organizational structure (see Exhibit J in the appendix). Most policemen work in patrol precincts under the direct supervision of lieutenants and sergeants. Precincts are further divided into a series of radio-motor-car patrol sectors that overlay the ultimate geographic jurisdiction—the "foot beat" (see Exhibit K in the appendix).

The police department functions through procedures described in the *Rules and Procedures* (R&P), which is recognized informally as the policeman's bible. Few bureaucracies can boast of the thoroughness of detail found in this exhaustive series of rules and proscriptions. It originated within the department in 1853 and has since undergone substantial modifications in form and detail though not in essential character.[27] It contains descriptions, prescriptions, and admonitions regarding the who, what, when, where, and why of every conceivable responsibility relating to the functioning of the department and the individual officer. The conduct of New York's finest is regulated on and off duty by this paper tyrant.[28]

The *Rules and Procedures* is updated through periodic issuance of new General Orders and a continuous flow of limited directives known as Standard Operating Procedures (SOPs), Temporary Operating Procedures (TOPs), and Chief Inspector's Memos (CI Memos). In addition, each of the major functional bureaus now issues its own memoranda, which include Chief of Patrol Memos, Chief of Personnel Memos, and the like.[29] This unceasing paper snowstorm, intended to direct field personnel, also may excuse noncompliance because of the resulting but not unexpected confusion regarding the most current version of a particular policy or procedure.

Supplementing the department's internal guidelines are New York's penal statutes, which give police a mandate to preserve public morality. Over the years the statutes prohibiting gambling have been narrowed–first to distinguish bettors or players from those employed in organized gambling, and second to meet the increasing sophistication of these enterprises. As in other parts of the criminal law, gambling statutes often provided as much confusion as they did guidance. Imprecise words in the statutes were subject to disparate interpretations. Moreover, standards of evidence and proof remained ill defined. The statutes were interpreted through case-by-case court decisions that established guidelines used by police and gamblers alike, each in their own way. Organized gamblers responded with policies and procedures designed to evade the letter of the law and to minimize possible liability. Gambling enforcement was also affected by several landmark Supreme Court decisions reinforcing constitutional safeguards over police practices in the seizure of evidence and in interrogation.

Prior to 1967, gambling statutes were scattered throughout more than fifty different sections of the New York Penal Law. These statutes dealt with five varieties of gambling, treating each separately "in great detail, specifying numerous ways in which one committed lottery offenses, bookmaking, and so on."[30] The revised statutes bear few substantive changes but have undergone "considerable revision with respect to form" so that all prohibitions are listed in but ten sections of a single article. These simplified statutes avoid the pitfall of enumerating every possible type of conduct that would be illegal, no longer allowing gamblers to structure their operations to evade the more stringent prohibitions.[31]

Overcoming the Bureaucracy

In a rational effort to avoid sanctions of the criminal law, to limit liability if apprehended, and to minimize business disruptions, organized gambling adjusted to changes in the law and in court decisions to eliminate weaknesses in its operational procedures. Through self-imposed restrictions and a series of evasive maneuvers, bookmakers and numbers operators seek to nullify police interference, while police, in turn, counter organized gambling's ingenuity with new investigative techniques.

Possession and/or presence are still the basis of any arrest and conviction for bookmaking and numbers. The gravamen of the offenses has not been changed. Common elements such as receiving, forwarding, or possessing betting records or money wagered, regardless of the nature of the gambling scheme, must be proved. Objective standards, such as the number of bets or plays received and/or their total value, are used to differentiate between degrees of offenses. Generally, arrests for either bookmaking or numbers are predicated on actual possession of bets or monies, or on being present when such bets and monies are being accepted, forwarded, or tabulated. It is understandable why those at higher echelons of bookmaking or policy follow one cardinal rule: Avoid personal involvement. Bookmakers and policy bankers work in a "never-never land"—they never accept bets, never handle work or money wagered, and never visit wirerooms or banks. All these responsibilities fall to trusted subordinates who direct daily operations. Personal contact by the bosses is limited to meetings with employees at times and places unrelated to the gambling enterprise, usually on Sundays, when they receive the week's receipts. Almost all risk of arrest is borne by members in the intermediate and low levels of the organizations—particularly those on the low level, who are the most visible.

To limit the liability of arrested employees, bookmaking and policy organizations try to keep the amounts of work and cash on hand below statutory minimums for felonies. Runners periodically call their bets into the wireroom instead of letting them accumulate. Similarly, betting records are moved from wirerooms to figure rooms several times a day, depending on the number of bets. As mentioned before, rapid transfer of bets minimizes disruption caused by police raids.

Numbers organizations, on the other hand, rely primarily on subdividing work to limit criminal liability and reduce interruptions. Being high-volume cash-and-carry enterprises, they cannot afford to limit their operations. Instead they use separate couriers to transport betting records and cash and if necessary, in large policy banks, they subdivide the work into branch banks, or "legs." Although these operational policies are somewhat inconvenient, they reduce the likelihood of serious felony charges and severe dislocations of business. On the whole, then, bookmaking and numbers organizations have adapted themselves to statutory restrictions without substantially reducing their efficiency.

The Supreme Court decisions in the mid-1960s—particularly *Mapp* v. *Ohio*—were unanticipated but welcomed supports for gamblers because new requirements made law enforcement more difficult and costly. No longer could runners or numbers collectors be stopped at will, searched, and summarily arrested if they were found in possession of bets or numbers plays. Similarly, wirerooms, controllers' spots, and policy banks no longer could be raided arbitrarily. Arrests, search warrants, and wiretap orders required probable cause for any lawful seizure. Stricter standards for admissibility of evidence, although they strengthened personal liberties, gave gamblers more room to maneuver free of ad hoc enforcement and harassment by police.

Where they were not able to eliminate weaknesses from within nor to exploit statutory loopholes or advantageous court decisions, organized gamblers sought to shore up their enterprise by undermining police efforts. Contradictory as it may seem, the attempt to obtain police protection has been a significant strategy for organized bookmaking and policy. Although they are vulnerable because of their exposure to the public, their heavy reliance on internal communications, and the scale of their operations, organized gamblers are anxious to pay for police forbearance. It is another expense, with several compensating dividends, for once police have been coopted, bookmaking and numbers services can be provided in a more businesslike climate, free of fear. Employees can operate more openly, increasing accessibility and income as well as acceptance by the local community. Operators can substantially reduce expenditures for security in time, energy, and money, and they can save on related overhead costs such as bondsmen, lawyers, and legislative lobbying. It matters little to organized gambling who initiates police cooptation; police participation is essential to the continuance of the gambling enterprise no matter how it comes about.

For police executives, gambling enforcement is a costly investment of their resources and energies. There are essentially two ways they could approach gambling investigations. The first is to obtain evidence by infiltrating bookmaking and policy organizations using undercover agents, paid outside informants, or employee-informers. The second relies on evidence garnered by police externally through wiretaps and surveillances. Undercover agents have placed bets with wireroom runners or policy collectors and have gained entry to horserooms or numbers spots prior to raids. Rarely, if ever, have undercover agents penetrated gambling organizations to the point of becoming trusted employees with access to higher echelons. Until very recently, police made extensive use of outside informants in gambling investigations, but the information they provided was generally limited to low-level street operations such as wireroom telephone numbers and identities of runners or collectors.

Employees of organized bookmaking and policy have never been a productive source of information because their "company loyalty" is a distinct obstacle. Not only do they receive generous salaries, but they know that the organization absorbs all expenses resulting from arrests, including legal fees and bail bonds. Even if convicted, employees are assured that the organization will pay fines imposed and salaries during any thirty-to-ninety-day jail sentence. Such fringe benefits mitigate fears of punishment. They also leave police with little bargaining power because their suspects, who have minimal incentive to cooperate anyway, are buoyed by the organization's benevolence. Even so, organized gambling does not take its employees' allegiance for granted. Indeed, the "need to know" requirement of bookmaking and policy precludes all but a handful of reliable employees from knowing anything significant, such as the location of a wireroom or bank. The gambler's loyalty and security have compelled police to use external investigative approaches such as wiretapping and surveillance.

Wiretapping, an efficient and productive investigative tool, is particularly useful in bookmaking investigations because wirerooms use the telephone night and day. The equipment outlay requires a comparatively small capital investment, and one policeman can monitor many tape recorders simultaneously at low operating cost. Before wiretaps can be used, however, the police must obtain the wireroom's telephone number and caller code, information usually available from a careless bettor or informant. Police can then call the wireroom to place bets themselves, resulting in tape recordings that serve as probable cause for a search warrant.

Wiretaps have less value against numbers organizations because they use the telephone infrequently. Here police must identify important people in the hierarchy and establish sufficient probable cause before the court will issue an order for a wiretap. Even if secured, wiretaps are productive only when employees are careless or lazy enough to call the policy bank. In most investigations of numbers organizations, the police must rely heavily on personal observations, the difficulties of which are legion. Practiced pickup men and policy-bank clerks recognize police surveillances quickly and are extremely careful. A successful tail leading to a policy bank requires many skilled policemen, inconspicuous vehicles, flexible communications, and a measure of good luck.

Gambling investigations are highly labor-intensive, requiring the investment of millions of dollars each year in police personnel. This commitment also represents a major opportunity cost because investigative efforts could be directed against other crimes, those that threaten lives and property rather than supposed moral well-being. Balancing expenditures against benefits is an important policy decision for a police administration.

Traditionally, the payoff for this investment has been measured by the number and quality of gambling arrests. Desirable "quality" arrests involve higher-echelon gamblers such as controllers, policy bankers, and bookmaking operators, while less desirable "quantity" arrests involve gamblers at lower levels—runners, collectors, and pickup men. Over the years New York City's police administrations have emphasized "quality" over "quantity" arrests but with disappointing results. Most bookmaking and policy arrests were of low-level employees, with only occasional successes in locating wirerooms and policy banks. Even in the latter case, however, bookmakers and bankers were rarely jailed. The ambiguity of the gambling statutes has led to a disappointing conviction rate, and many cases were dismissed during pretrial hearings because of insufficient evidence, illegal searches and seizures, or other legal grounds. Most cases remaining on court calendars never reached trial because, through plea bargaining, the gamblers' counsel obtained concessions such as reduced charges, small fines, or light jail sentences in exchange for guilty pleas. Measured in terms of costs and benefits, gambling enforcement appears to have been a losing investment for administrators.

Unless police can make arrests at the top of the hierarchies, and unless they can seize substantial amounts of betting records on a regular basis, law enforcement provides little or no deterrent to illegal gambling. To the gambling operator, arrests of subordinates and seizures of small amounts of "work" are mere business costs. Any fines imposed on those eventually convicted represent nothing more than a license fee that organized gambling must pay the state in order to operate. In spite of these shortcomings, which police themselves recognize, gambling enforcement remains a significant effort for the New York City Police Department. That effort will now be examined in some detail.

The Plainclothes Force

Structure

During the nineteenth century, the department relied on specialized "plainclothes" patrolmen to enforce gambling statutes and other laws regulating public morals. (In 1973 the terms "plainclothes" and "plainclothesmen" were exorcised from the department's official lexicon.) In the early 1900s this loosely knit system was reorganized, assuming a formal structure for the first time. There was no specific designation for the plainclothes force in departmental organization charts because it functioned as a unique and semiautonomous branch of the patrol force. It had its own hierarchy of authority and responsibility, which for command purposes was part of the uniformed service. Its members, neither uniformed patrolmen nor detectives, were "detailed" to plainclothes work in much the same way that others received assignments to detective.

Throughout the 1950s and 1960s the plainclothes force was staffed at approximately 2 percent of the patrol force's strength, with some reduction in the late 1960s as a result of the shift in emphasis to narcotics enforcement (see Table 2-4). Traditionally, plainclothesmen were selected by superiors at borough and division levels. They worked for these ranking officers, even undergoing transfers to stay with them in new commands. This practice was discontinued in the mid-1950s, however, following the Gross scandal. Under a new process for selection, precinct captains and other commanders recommended candidates from their units on the basis of demonstrated aptitude for and interest in plainclothes work. Formal appointments were made after interviews with Plainclothes Selection Boards.[32]

Table 2-4
Plainclothes Work Force

Year	Number of Plainclothesmen	Number of Patrolmen
1955	389	20,080-22,460
1958	470	24,112-23,636
1960	560	23,805-23,515
1961	575	23,515-24,374
1965	597	25,897-27,030
1966	597	27,030-27,429
1967	580	27,429-27,481
1968	578	27,481-29,904
1969	480[a]	29,904-31,506

[a]Decrease due to transfer of 100 plainclothesmen to the Narcotics Division.
Source: *Annual Report*, New York City Police Department (1954-1970).

Plainclothes candidates, like prospective detectives, attended the six-week criminal investigation course at the police academy, receiving instruction in enforcement of public morals laws and criminal investigation. Permanent instructors and a series of guest lecturers focused on illegal gambling–statutes, techniques of gathering evidence, and court procedures. Among the guest lecturers were municipal court judges, assistant district attorneys, and representatives of allied law enforcement agencies. Graduates were assigned directly to plainclothes units or temporarily returned to patrol until vacancies occurred.[33]

Although it underwent several structural changes, the plainclothes force remained highly decentralized, like the patrol and detective forces. Because seven patrol borough commanders had overall responsibility for law enforcement, including gambling and public morals, it was logical to create the plainclothes force out of the uniformed service. Thus plainclothes units were established as part of every patrol borough and division and as part of some Bronx and Brooklyn precincts; all were subordinate to the patrol unit commanders. They had no separate chain of command or communications, as did the Detective Division; instead they functioned as an entity within the patrol hierarchy. To enhance gambling enforcement, borough and division commanders were provided staff assistants–public morals inspectors and deputy inspectors who supervised borough and division plainclothes squads, respectively. In Brooklyn and Bronx precincts, captains were allowed to delegate some of their plainclothes supervisory responsibility to sergeants. Of course the plainclothes force was not expected to suppress gambling on its own, as every member of the force was given nominal responsibility to enforce the gambling laws.

All told, there were as many as sixty units responsible for gambling and public morals enforcement at various times throughout the 1960s. (Figure 2-3 depicts the organizational structure of the plainclothes force.) Heading the hierarchy were borough plainclothes squads, elitist units that generally consisted of a public morals inspector (PMI), a captain or lieutenant for field supervision, and five to ten plainclothesmen. Their responsibilities included "quality" gambling enforcement and supervision of the rest of the borough plainclothes force. In several borough squads, located where the numbers game flourished, exclusive policy-bank squads were created to locate and eliminate these centers.

The mainstay of gambling enforcement were division plainclothes squads,

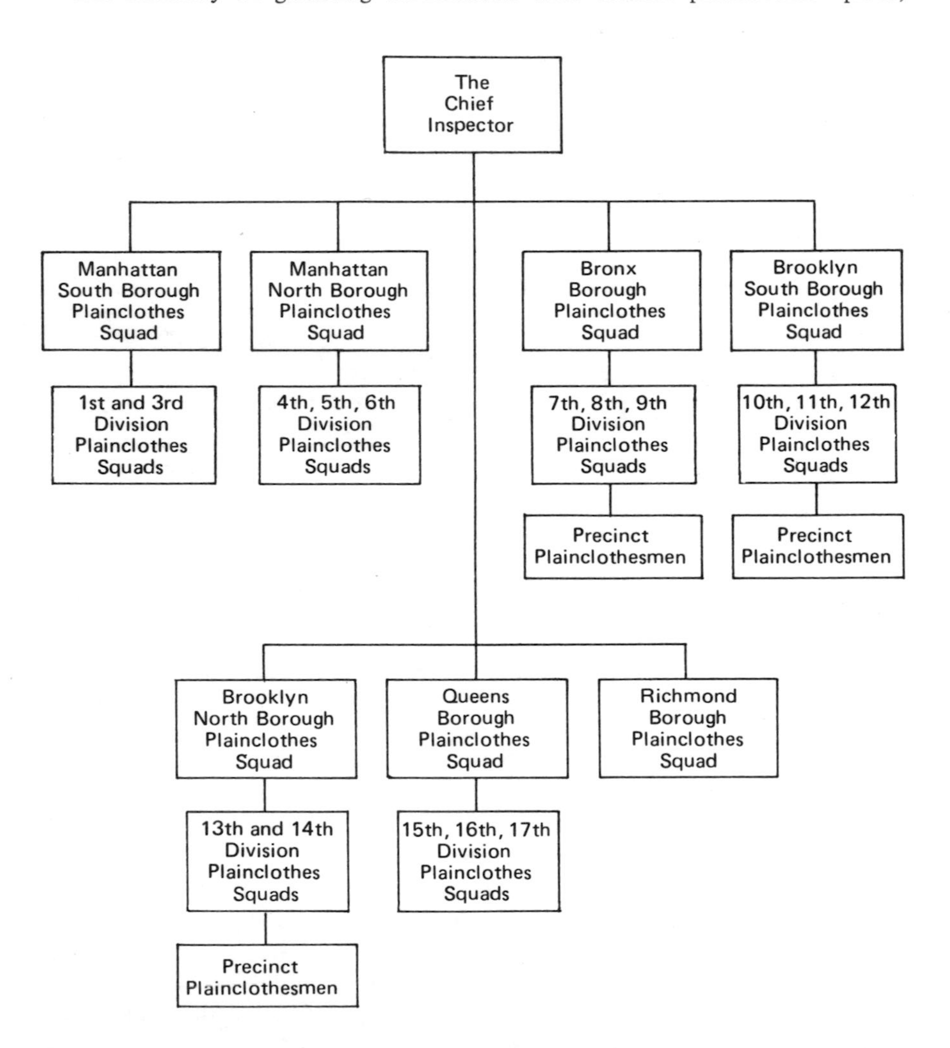

Figure 2-3. The Plainclothes Structure (1960s).

which usually were composed of one or two public morals deputy inspectors (PMDI), two lieutenants for field supervision, and fifteen to twenty-five plainclothesmen. Responsible for several precincts, division plainclothesmen conducted the majority of gambling investigations because of the decentralized operations of organized bookmaking and policy. To fix accountability for effective enforcement, the division's territory was often divided among the supervising deputy inspector and/or lieutenants, each being responsible for specific precincts. Brooklyn and Bronx precinct plainclothes squads, typically four men strong, concentrated on lower-echelon gambling within the comparatively narrow confines of their precincts.

Not part of the plainclothes force itself, but also responsible for gambling enforcement, were several headquarters units with city-wide jurisdiction. They included the Police Commissioner's Confidential Investigating Unit (PCCIU), the Chief Inspector's Investigating Unit (CIIU), and the Bureau of Public Morals. The PCCIU and CIIU investigated large bookmaking and policy organizations, particularly those that crossed borough and city boundaries, and conducted other sensitive inquiries as directed by the police commissioner or chief inspector. The Bureau of Public Morals, part of the chief inspector's staff, served as a clearing house and repository for records about gambling and public morals. All complaints were directed to the bureau, recorded there, and forwarded to the field. Reports of completed investigations were then returned for review, along with administrative data for statistical analysis.

Thus the department's approach to gambling enforcement followed its characteristic pattern of decentralization, fragmenting authority and responsibility.

Plainclothes Work[34]

Before they could enforce gambling laws effectively, plainclothesmen had to infiltrate the gamblers' environment somehow. They dressed in a style suitable to the neighborhood and to the role they played. Plainclothesmen were not cloak-and-dagger types who assumed fictitious identities as has been the strategy in narcotics enforcement. They merely adopted appearances that facilitated their movement and patrolled their territory, alert for ongoing gambling activities. They also conducted more formal investigations, interviewing complainants and suspects.

The official nature and scope of plainclothes work was elaborately described in the *R&P*, supplemented by an unending flow of orders and memoranda. Policies and procedures for enforcement of gambling laws remained constant for many years. Until recently, gambling enforcement had three primary focuses: known gamblers (KGs), "hard-core" locations, and communications. Because gambling is a continuing operation with fixed and determinable elements, plainclothesmen could concentrate efforts against specific individuals and locations. In fact, detectives minimized the difficulty of plainclothes work, claiming that the real investigative challenge lay with more serious crimes—homicide and robbery—where the perpetrators' identities were unknown. Plainclothesmen were quick to counter that detectives often had physical evidence, witnesses, or cooperative victims to work with, whereas they had to overcome public apathy, relying on ingenuity to penetrate extensive security systems used by organized gamblers and still satisfy court restrictions on their investigative efforts.

Although known gamblers were the department's preeminent focus, there never was an official definition of who was or was not a KG. Even the *R&P* failed to provide criteria. According to the plainclothesman's working definition, a KG was anyone who earned his livelihood through organized gambling. The KG program, which originated in 1946, was intended to identify major figures in bookmaking and policy hierarchies and to concentrate plainclothes investigative efforts on them. Each plainclothesman, regardless of unit or level, was assigned an average of five to ten KGs, although some case loads were much higher in jurisdictions where illegal gambling flourished. These assignments were based on one criterion—the locations or places that KGs frequented, operated, or resided. Thus KGs could be assigned, depending on their activities, to several plainclothesmen at various levels in different parts of the city. A KG who resided in Brooklyn and worked in a Manhattan organization, for example, fell under the investigative supervision of the precinct, division, and borough plainclothes squads in Brooklyn as well as under those in Manhattan. Such compartmentalization created administrative overlapping and duplication of investigative effort throughout the plainclothes force.

Because the emphasis of the KG program was on "discreet inquiries," plainclothesmen were prohibited from conducting personal interviews of KGs, their families, associates, or employers. This restriction not only protected police identities but also minimized the gamblers' opportunities to learn of the investigation. It also lessened the likelihood of compromise and corruption. Thus plainclothesmen were forced to rely on surveillance and informants as their basic investigative tools.

In further support of the program, officials created a special KG file, an index and repository of information that was maintained at headquarters units such as the Bureau of Public Morals and in borough and division plainclothes squads. Plainclothesmen were required to know those gamblers listed in their respective files. Special forms and systems for reporting designed to keep the KG file current also kept headquarters apprised of field progress. Unfortunately, with no criteria defining a KG or controlling file entries, the index burgeoned from a few hundred names in 1946 to several thousand over the next fifteen years, and hence it lost its usefulness. In 1961, officials tried to revitalize the file for a more selective drive against gamblers by dividing it into active (no. 1 file) and inactive (no. 2 file) sections. Provisions were made for periodic transfers of names of inactive gamblers to the inactive file. Even so, the no. 1 file continued to swell until it too became a repository of outdated information because inactive and even deceased gamblers were still listed as active.[35]

Hard-core locations, the second major focus of gambling enforcement, were places where gambling operations were conducted regularly. Bars, shoe-shine stands, candy stores, freight elevators, or other public places with a high volume of pedestrian traffic were suspect. Departmental regulations required patrolmen to report business establishments or premises where suspicious activities suggested the possibility of illegal gambling. The information then was referred to the plainclothes force for follow-up. Plainclothesmen investigated a number of hard-core locations in addition to their responsibility for KGs. Because bookmaking and policy involved regularized operations, hard-core locations provided more manageable investigative leads. Posing as customers, hoping to observe or overhear betting activities, plainclothesmen or their informants would frequent the sites. Even personal surveillance, however, usually failed to penetrate organized gambling's effective security shield. Results of all investigations, successful or not, were entered in an elaborate index of hard-core locations.[36]

Communications, the third major focus of gambling enforcement, consisted of written or oral complaints, usually anonymous, which alleged the existence of a violation of laws controlling gambling or public morals. A typical communication, taken from the training files of the NYCPD, follows (names, dates, and identifying data have been changed):

There is a parasite named "Manny" who preys on the low salaried employees at City hospital. I do not know his name but I think that his cousin owns the grubby little delicatessen at 419 13th Avenue. He is around the place most of the time.

This man can be seen from early morning to mid afternoon walking on 13th Avenue. His favorite stop is the delivery alley at the end of 89th St. There is always a lot of hospital employees that hang about this entrance, as well as trucks and cars using this entrance. He picks up all kinds of policy bets ranging from 5 cents bet by one employee to $1 bet by one of the technicians.

Manny is about 5'2"–125 lbs.–swarthy complexion. He not only takes money from people who can ill afford to gamble but he disrupts the efficiency of the staff by causing them to congregate about this entrance.

This man operates in such an open manner that the police of the neighborhood are either blind or corrupt. If something isn't done about this man I will write to the Mayor or the Governor.

–Angry Nurse

Communications also applied to information received from reliable sources such as the district attorney's office or another law enforcement agency. After being recorded at the Bureau of Public Morals, all communications were forwarded to appropriate field units for investigation to determine authenticity. Plainclothesmen had to act promptly, having only ninety days within receipt of information to complete their inquiries, unless borough commanders extended deadlines in the event of encouraging developments. Plainclothesmen also faced prohibitions, when interviewing suspects, against revealing the complainant's identity or unnecessarily impugning any suspect's reputation.

To intensify drives in these three focal areas, officials developed specialized "target" programs against policy banks and KGs. Harassment was the principal tactic used. Indeed, the effectiveness of policy-bank teams forced numbers operators to divide banks into several branches to minimize interruptions and losses. At first, policy-bank targets were selected by police headquarters, but this authority was later transferred to borough commanders. The converse occurred in the selection of KG targets, where headquarters subsequently made the final decisions. Targeted KGs were subjected to twenty-four-hour surveillances until they could be arrested while engaged in gambling or forced to suspend operations. By 1964 the KG program had generated a new focus of enforcement: gambling combines. Investigations were now to be conducted against higher echelons of organized gambling, based on interrelationships among KGs who formed combines, with each combine treated as a single, integrated unit. This reemphasis on quality enforcement was necessitated by certain difficulties, especially the plainclothes force's skepticism of the KG program.

Although subject to the management of squad supervisors and to prescriptions in the *R&P* and various memoranda, plainclothesmen had substantial discretion, even setting their own investigative priorities. They usually worked in teams, semipermanent twosomes, assisting each other in investigations of their respective KGs, hard-core locations, and assigned communications. Their out-of-pocket expenses were reimbursed from official funds. Plainclothesmen determined the amount of time and energy devoted to each case, relying primarily on surveillances, discreet observations, and information furnished by paid informants. Most arrests for gambling, however, were made as a result of plainclothesmen's or their informants' either placing bets directly with gamblers or overhearing others doing so. Informants were needed because runners and collectors were careful to accept bets only from known clients.

No account of gambling enforcement would be complete without mention of the voluminous paper work involved. Using prepared forms, plainclothesmen were required to keep daily records of all investigations so that their cases would be current (see Exhibits L and M in the appendix). Supervisors were expected to stay abreast of the plainclothesmen's work by reviewing case files that were maintained in each squad office, in addition to directing field efforts. Periodic reports on activities of all KGs were required, and all communications with allegations of gambling had to be "answered out" within the prescribed ninety days. Applications for search and arrest warrants required lengthy affidavits and supporting memoranda of justification. Arrests of gamblers generated a volume of investigative reports and administrative forms to be completed posthaste. Departmental regulations called for myriad daily, monthly, and annual statistical reports in addition to special ad hoc accounts required at irregular intervals.

To prepare and process the paper work, plainclothes squads relied on a small staff assigned to them from the borough or division clerical pool. Because these "clerical men," trained policemen, were experts in the department's administrative procedures and court requirements, plainclothesmen and squad commanders alike relied heavily on them. Also, clerical men became intimately familiar with the workings of organized gambling in the squad's territory. Squads floundered or survived in a sea of paper depending on their clerical men's expertise. Investigative and statistical reports flowed up and down an elaborate communications network that followed the hierarchy of the plainclothes force and played a major role in planning and policy making in enforcement of gambling laws (see Exhibit N in the appendix).

Work-Group Norms[37]

Before one can assess the behavior of plainclothesmen, one must appreciate first, what motivated them to seek the assignment, and second, the norms that governed their conduct. Underlying all dimensions of plainclothes work was one driving force–the detective incentive. Most patrolmen shared this motivation to become detectives–to "get out of the bag," or "get the gold shield." Achieving detective meant not only enhanced status and prestige but also an escape from the tedium and menial labor of patrol life to the supposed challenge and excitement of criminal investigations. By departmental decree, plainclothes was the official stepping stone to the detective assignment, since most if not all detectives were to be selected from this force on the basis of demonstrated aptitude for investigative work. Demonstrated aptitude usually hinged on a high volume of arrests. Because there were limited openings in the Detective Division, it was impossible for every plainclothesman to achieve assignment, a situation that spurred competition for outstanding records of arrest. This detective incentive and its resulting strife were but the first links in a chain of events having far-reaching consequences for honesty and ethical behavior.

Personal incentives and peer pressures were inextricably interwoven and formed a pattern of behavior unique to the plainclothes force. Just as the department had a set of unofficial work norms, the plainclothes force, like other subgroups, developed and enforced its own standards of behavior, which were reflected in relations with the rest of the department and in interactions of its component units. These standards regulated social intercourse and work practices, and brought rationality to the force's efforts. Plainclothesmen's attitudes and conduct were modified and molded into conformity through a lengthy process of socialization. And norms of expected behavior were based on a distinct assortment of individual and group incentives.

Socialization of plainclothesmen began with the criminal investigation course, preparatory academy instruction in official policies and procedures for work related to public morals. For most students, this was the first time that ideas and attitudes formed during their prior experience on patrol were exposed to formal policies of gambling enforcement. "Street-wise" policemen presented a challenge in training because, having worked a beat or radio car, they knew the discrepancies between policy and practice. In spite of the patrolmen's varied experience, the course skirted realities of plainclothes work, emphasizing procedural materials. Plainclothesmen thus emerged unprepared for the temptations awaiting them.

When reporting to their first assignment, newly graduated plainclothesmen traditionally faced skepticism and suspicion from experienced squad members. Kept at arm's length, tyros underwent a period of on-the-job training, a spell that allowed others to gauge the recruits' attitudes and values while the newcomers absorbed the squad's work norms and standards. Responsibility for these initiation rites fell to the recruits' permanent partners, who were assigned by the squad commander. New plainclothesmen had much to learn. It took six months or so to digest the hierarchy of gambling organizations in the squad's jurisdiction and perhaps longer to grasp the intricacies of plainclothes investigations and administrative short cuts. In addition to gambling enforcement, plainclothesmen also had responsibility for suppressing prostitution and inspecting licensed premises. It is not surprising that at first they were unsteady and unsure of themselves, dependent on seasoned partners for training and guidance in most things official and everything unofficial. Complicating this lack of experience was the fact that incoming recruits rarely met the people they replaced, inheriting work "cold" without any opportunity to discuss background details and the like. Initiation usually lasted about one year, by which time most plainclothesmen knew their jobs, had been assimilated into the squad, and had acquired sufficient skill to be effective investigators.

In spite of the success of individual adjustment, the plainclothes force was still permeated by suspicion and secrecy bred from the detective incentive and ubiquitous competition. Within individual squads, there were cliques of one or two teams who would not share information in case others might gain some advantage in making prestigious arrests. Occasionally, teams did work together on a major case, but only under established guidelines. Such internal fragmentation extended vertically as well as horizontally. All plainclothes squads operated autonomously with little or no cooperation, sharing of information, or joint investigative effort. Cooperation was extended only when absolutely necessary or to some squad's advantage. This atmosphere did not preclude informal communication among friends during or before their plainclothes assignments. Indeed, because of these exchanges, subordinate commands had some idea of what was happening "overhead."

Distrust was particularly directed against the next higher echelon in the plainclothes structure. Borough squads, traditionally dubbed "super-sleuths," made division plainclothesmen wary, while precinct squads were edgy about all higher commands. What caused the uneasiness? Subordinate units feared, most of all, that an "overhead squad" would make a gambling arrest within the lower unit's geographic jurisdiction. If circumstances were such that the subordinate command could have discovered the violation, their failure to do so impugned their efficiency if not their honesty. Often, a unit thus embarrassed proceeded to rearrest the person arrested by a higher squad (or someone else at the particular location) in an effort to prove its integrity. Fear of being second-guessed reached its peak with respect to the ultimate authority–the Police Commissioner's Confidential Investigating Unit (PCCIU) and the Chief Inspector's Investigating Unit (CIIU). The entire plainclothes force experienced dread and anxiety when the commissioner's or chief inspector's squads made a major arrest, which was invariably followed by tortuous explanations, transfers, and demotions. Vigilance for "overhead arrests" was not an idle preoccupation.

Individual plainclothesmen were similarly concerned with informal but nevertheless real norms of production. Although there was no official quota for arrests in gambling enforcement, each plainclothes squad prepared for headquarters a "Daily Report for Public Morals Enforcement Activity" reflecting the day's activity (or inactivity). Statistics of arrest and summons activity were compiled for individual squad members as well as for each command, resulting in the creation of unofficial quotas, the amounts and types depending on gambling activity within the territory. A typical monthly production norm for a person in an active squad was one bookmaking or policy arrest, two prostitution arrests, plus several ABC (alcoholic beverage control) summonses.

Quality arrests of organized gambling bosses meant prestige and, eventually, promotion to detective. Plainclothes investigators able to generate quality cases were treasured by squad supervisors since they too were graded and promoted according to the squad's production. To promote equity, unofficial norms regulated merit for arrest activity. A plainclothes team usually "split" the credit when they arrested two or more gamblers, correcting any imbalance in quality or number with subsequent arrests. When a major case was handled by several teams in one or more squads and resulted in multiple arrests, established practice called for the plainclothesman to whom the case was assigned to "take" arrests of KGs and parcel out lesser arrests to his colleagues. Understandably, plainclothesmen were discouraged from exceeding established quotas, except in major cases, lest norms for squad activity became too high, because administrators wanted to show increased arrest and summons activity each succeeding year. One should not assume, however, that gambling investigations were routinely successful–most plainclothes efforts languished in frustration. Plainclothesmen were demoralized further by the frequent losses of court cases through legal technicalities or the downgrading of charges in plea bargaining.

As mentioned, plainclothesmen focused on known gamblers, hard-core locations, and communications–a less vulnerable group of targets than they appear. KGs, so circumspect in their activities, were formidable subjects for successful investigation. Indeed, some were never indexed in the file purposely because they could not be arrested. Because the department required an annual report on each KG, squads divided their active KG file into quarters so that one fourth of those suspects were observed and reported on in each ninety-day period. Because it was nearly impossible to catch experienced gamblers red-handed, many KG investigations were perfunctory checks of residences and local haunts that generated unimpressive paper work. Although plainclothesmen were supposed to continue these inquiries, most investigations dwindled after reports were submitted. A plainclothesman's adrenalin would flow, however, at the thought of an overhead command–the PCCIU in particular–arresting his KG after he had reported the gambler inactive. A KG reported active should have been arrested. No wonder plainclothesmen viewed their KGs as potential "bombs," generally unproductive for arrest purposes yet sources of personal risk. Because of this dilemma, squad commanders grew reluctant to transfer names of KGs to the inactive files, there being a remote chance of superiors arresting these individuals. Too many careers were at stake. Such reasoning contributed to the proliferation of the active file until it swelled into a useless index of outdated information.

The combines program, supplanting the KG focus, suffered from the same "creative writing" problem. Administrative pressures encouraged "puffing" and even artificial combinations. Gamblers who were arrested together or who were seen frequenting the same location were suddenly reported as being part of a combine, and many combines were suspiciously located near local race tracks.

Plainclothesmen were equally skeptical of the rewards of investigating hard-core locations. The program evolved from an apparently "successful" one-time survey of gambling conditions, in which gambling activities were exaggerated in response to administrative pressure to find those locations. Citizen complaints alleging the existence of gambling at a residence or business often stemmed from revengeful or malicious motives. Also, the patrol force tended to color their suspicious premises reports, a result of a generally defensive posture regarding gambling enforcement. This attitude reflected a department-wide norm, the need to protect, or "cover," oneself. Patrolmen did not want gambling arrests made on their beats unless a report of their observations was on record. Thus some even filed fictitious information.

Beyond these detours, plainclothesmen faced precautions taken by organized crime. Gamblers would not transact business in any location when strangers were present. Plainclothesmen could make observations in bars and similar establishments where patrons lingered, but such places were usually small and poorly lighted; even informants were of limited value there. And surveillances rarely yielded evidence that supported convictions. Hard-core locations, then, had serious limitations as sources of gambling arrests.

Like the other target areas, communications were similarly unproductive. Many were "shotgun" types, wild defamations of character that included accusations of gambling as one of many crimes. Others were vague denunciations of little value. The real problem was in the plainclothes system rather than the allegation. Higher-level squads siphoned productive intelligence from all communications, passing down only worthless information or allegations that could not be substantiated. Those at the bottom of the hierarchy, division and precinct officers, viewed hand-me-downs with jaundiced eyes—the information had already been worked and "picked clean." Although plainclothesmen complained about this practice of reinvestigation, it was justified as a matter of policy on at least two grounds. First, because borough squads might draw negative results because of poor timing or human error, a second check provided needed coverage. Second, lower commands still might "take a bite" and embellish arrest records because even following a borough arrest, gamblers would be back in business within a day or so. Such reasoning appealed to some borough commanders and public morals inspectors who wanted to "produce" as many arrests as possible. Plainclothesmen, however, shared a different outlook. Every incoming communication represented a potential test of their honesty and integrity: Perhaps the overhead command, knowing that the allegation was indeed true, had sent *this* message down to see if the gambling would be suppressed. Communications were always suspect.

In summary, it is evident that plainclothesmen were frustrated, demoralized, and always defensive. They functioned in a competitive and secretive atmosphere, viewing a heavy work load apprehensively, always fearing that overhead commands might somehow squelch the promise of a detective assignment.

Determinants of Behavior

Early determinants of individual behavior, such as family values and attitudes, affected plainclothesmen's outlooks toward gambling long before they joined the force. Surely no New Yorker in this or previous generations grew up oblivious to the existence of gambling, having seen it in the media, school, neighborhood haunts, and possibly the home. In many parts of the city, gambling was an accepted fact of community life that produced no stigma of immorality in the minds of the young. For some, sports betting was a casual and socially acceptable means of vicarious participation, akin to watching television. It is thus understandable that attitudes tolerant of illegal gambling were not likely to undergo dramatic reversals because of the policeman's oath. Some new policemen did, of course, hold contrary views. In all cases the department sought to mold recruits to one mind—the denial of any legitimacy in bookmaking or policy.

Once embarked in their apprenticeship in the police academy, probationary patrolmen were exposed to a more sobering view of the relationship between organized crime and illegal gambling. As they learned about the evil consequences of underworld domination–the economic drain on the community, the diversion of gambling profits to narcotics–many young policemen reevaluated the "innocence" of illegal betting. And by the time they arrived at their first precinct, imbued with beginner's spirit, they were less sympathetic to illegal gambling.

The rookie patrolman soon learned that many things he was taught at the academy were not true. Almost immediately, he saw contradictions and discrepancies between how the force was supposed to function and how it actually operated. While learning routine short cuts and evasions of bureaucratic rules, he also became aware of the omnipresence of organized gambling, its widespread public acceptance, and its impact on the department's integrity. Few, if any, came to plainclothes ignorant of all its hazards.

Early experiences, academy training, and departmental socialization affected a policeman's preplainclothes attitudes and values. With his first plainclothes assignment, his perspective may have been modified further as a result of the gambling activity he was exposed to. Most significant, however–and a matter of pure chance–was the influence of those he was assigned to work with. His preservice experience and official training underwent new stress as a result of plainclothes mores and work norms.

The plainclothes environment had both internal and external facets. Internally, there was the detective incentive generating competition, secrecy, and self-concern. Compromised by heavy work loads, plainclothesmen often felt compelled to report investigative activity that was never conducted and to maintain high numbers of arrests, "activity" that kept them in contention for detective assignments. The pressures of supervision and overhead arrests compounded their defensiveness, disillusionment, and cynicism. The result, usually, was a group of people who, compelled to accept their own compromises as well as their colleagues', did not complain or seriously consider revealing others' misconduct. Even when not involved in wrongdoing, plainclothesmen feared that scandal could jeopardize their careers. Locked into personal limbos and unwilling to return to the uniformed service as failures, most plainclothesmen resigned themselves to holding on, ever hopeful for the gold shield.

Because of this disillusionment, plainclothesmen were perfect targets for cooptation by organized gamblers. For the most part the public was indifferent to gambling enforcement. The community was more concerned with arrests of narcotics pushers and muggers than raids on policy banks, and the police shared this attitude. Plainclothesmen thus found themselves facing personal and professional contradictions: Organized crime was willing if not anxious to pay for forbearance while the public often belittled the need for gambling enforcement. These frustrations, coupled with the formidable problems of bookmaking and policy investigations, further lowered plainclothesmen's resistance to malpractice. Such working conditions created the backdrop for unethical behavior on every level of the plainclothes force.

3 The Directive Strategies: 1950-1975

Police executives developed a mix of directive strategies that created pressures and incentives for diligent enforcement of gambling laws in order to establish honest enforcement as the department's norm; to find plainclothesmen who were willing and able to achieve that aim; and to provide the organizational arrangements, personal incentives, and tools necessary to do the job. The administrators followed four principle approaches that I call:

1. establishing goals, policies, and procedures
2. shuffling personnel and boxes
3. changing individual incentives and attitudes
4. inducing productivity

These strategies, in varying degrees, embodied two themes of behavioral control: limiting plainclothesmen's discretion by "preforming decisions" through restrictive work rules and procedures, and developing plainclothesmen's "will and capacity to conform" to official policies by changing individual incentives to foster voluntary compliance.[1]

Establishing Goals, Policies, and Procedures

The Police Commissioners

To achieve honest, ethical enforcement of gambling laws police commissioners sought organizational control and responsiveness by using traditional policy-making tools, relying on their powers to appoint, promote, and remove personnel; issue directions and operating instructions and modify them when necessary; establish organizational structure and alter it as conditions required; and allocate the department's fiscal, material, and human resources.[2] In spite of their authority, commissioners faced various obstacles in attaining responsiveness, including personal limitations, other demands on their energies, and a resistant bureaucracy. At times some of these obstacles seemed to conflict with vigorous anticorruption policies.

Circumstances at the time of appointment influenced each administration's priority and approach to ethical problems. Commissioners in the early and mid-1950s assumed leadership during periods of well-publicized scandals involving corruption in gambling enforcement. In the late 1950s and throughout the 1960s, police administrators were diverted to other concerns such as internal labor relations, civil liberties for minorities, narcotics enforcement, and violent street crime. Thus problems relating to malpractice, including corruption in gambling enforcement, were pushed onto the back burner. A new exposé of widespread institutionalized corrupt practices in 1970[3] begat another reform administration, which made honest law enforcement its highest priority. Thus the department's struggle to achieve integrity peaked and declined with the times, with many years of drift between scandals.

Each commissioner's approach to leadership and policy making reflected his experience and personal qualities. Almost all commissioners were hindered by brief tenure, which made it impractical to achieve organizational control, let alone significant improvements in enforcement of gambling laws. Of the more than thirty commissioners since 1900, over one half held office for less than two years. Since 1950, seven of the ten police commissioners held office less than three years, and only one served for more than five years (see Exhibit O in the appendix).

Most commissioners between 1950 and 1975 were career members of the department, having risen gradually through the ranks, usually coming to the commissionership from the post of chief inspector. Although versed in law enforcement and departmental functioning, none had much experience in plainclothes work; in fact, some had assiduously avoided the assignment. Steeped in departmental mores during a lifetime of service, they tended to be independent in making decisions but tradition-bound in responding to nonethical, dishonest conduct. Career commissioners did share one significant advantage—first-hand experience increased their understanding and appreciation of the department's workings. Bits of information regarding plainclothesmen's activities enabled them to imagine the complete range of deviant behavior, particularly regarding noncompliance with policies designed to increase honesty.[4] Noncareer commissioners, in contrast, knew less about the department and thus were less restricted in their view of issues in gambling enforcement. Their lack of knowledge, however, made them more dependent on career officials who served them. All commissioners must have learned, sooner or later, that although their predecessors were rarely, if ever, fired because of high crime rates, they had been frequent casualties of scandals in gambling enforcement. Understandably, police commissioners felt more vulnerable over gambling than practically any other area of law enforcement.[5]

No matter what their background, commissioners faced a common obstacle—an enormous organization burdened with most of the malfunctions possible in a large bureaucracy. Scandals generated fear and uncertainty in the force from top to bottom, increasing otherwise normal resistance to change, and complicating reform efforts. A commissioner's impact on gambling law enforcement traditionally began with his principal appointments, particularly the first deputy commissioner and chief inspector. These appointees recommended candidates for other high-ranking positions, such as deputy commissioner, chief of detectives, and borough commanders. Appointments above division level were significant for the newly installed commissioner because borough commanders were traditionally responsible for supervision of the plainclothes force. All selections were important reflections of the commissioner's use of his strongest policy-making tool—appointive power. Members of the force, distrustful of official pronouncements, looked for the commissioner's real policy in his promotions. Through his choice of senior officers, he made an implicit statement of his intention to seek honest gambling law enforcement.

As a prelude to shuffling the hierarchy, new commissioners opened their administrations with major policy statements at conferences with senior commanders. Certain themes always surfaced—the need for department-wide honesty; the unacceptability of corruption; and the intention to hold commanders accountable for their subordinates' malfeasance. These themes were reiterated opportunely at ceremonial, social, and working functions.[6] And the commissioners' annual warnings against accepting gratuities from merchants during the Christmas season were as predictable as the appearance of tinseled trees. Although commissioners urged a commitment to ethical behavior through appointive power and public statements, they were mindful of the need to support the force so departmental morale would not suffer during stressful periods. Thus they always voiced a thematic counterpoint praising individual dedication, sacrifice, and honesty. Commissioners defended their men at every opportunity. In speeches before business and civic leaders, they often condemned the public's role as corrupter of the police and directed members of the force to arrest any and all who offered bribes. They defended the department against nonspecific charges of widespread corruption made by investigating grand juries and commissions, putting the department's shortcomings in perspective by citing failures in the courts and other elements of the criminal justice system.[7]

Such was the case, for example, in the early 1970s during another corruption scandal.[8] Balancing his attacks on other agencies and commissions, the police commissioner spoke out against departmental corruption more vociferously than any police commissioner since the 1950s. Rebuking his corps of senior officers for not vigorously prosecuting corruption, the commissioner warned that he did not plan to have scandal mar his career: "I intend to leave this department with my whole skin and banners flying. . . . It will either be your hide or mine on this corruption issue, and I don't intend to get nailed."[9] With a mandate for change, the new commissioner was able to initiate controversial policies and procedures, adroitly using the situation to overcome resistance from constituencies within the department.[10]

The Gambling Enforcement Inspection and Review Board[11]

For many years prior to and throughout the 1950s, policies followed in gambling law enforcement were established, as were procedures for other areas of law enforcement. Controversial issues were usually communicated to commissioners through internal mechanisms, most often in recommendations from trusted subordinates. External sources, such as the press and district attorneys, also exposed problems, especially dramatic cases of corruption. Because there was no formal development of departmental policy in dealing with gambling enforcement, field commanders enjoyed broad discretion in making operational decisions. Thus policies in enforcing gambling laws were considered on an ad hoc basis, depending on how they emerged or were perceived by the commissioners' subordinates. Once resolved, issues tended to be forgotten. When old problems reemerged, decisions were often reversed by succeeding administrations.

Early 1961 marked the department's first effort to centralize planning and policy making in enforcement of gambling laws. The Gambling Enforcement Inspection and Review Board (GEIRB), created to replace ad hoc processes and to provide for a continuous policy-making effort, had specific objectives:

1. to review and evaluate methods, procedures, special problems, and assignments in gambling enforcement
2. to coordinate and direct units of the department for maximum efficiency in the suppression of gambling
3. to inspect and report on the effectiveness (or lack of effectiveness) of field commands in gambling enforcement
4. to cooperate with district attorneys, grand juries, and law enforcement agencies
5. to develop new methods to detect, apprehend, and convict professional gamblers
6. to research methods used in other cities that might be effective in the department's gambling enforcement
7. to make periodic reports and recommendations to the chief inspector and police commissioner[12]

The first deputy commissioner, a renowned corruption fighter, was designated chairman. Other senior officials served as permanent members of the GEIRB, and field commanders served as temporary members on a rotating basis. The board's permanent membership changed over the next several years to conform to the department's revised rank structure.

Although it was hardly unprecedented in the annals of public administration for an agency to create a central policy-making unit, the establishment of the Gambling Enforcement Inspection and Review Board was a first for the department. Through the board, officials hoped to focus continuing concern at police headquarters on strategies for gambling enforcement. Borough commanders were the first to be affected by the GEIRB's existence because although they were still responsible for enforcing gambling laws in their jurisdictions, they yielded substantial discretion. Some commanders felt that the board was an unwarranted intrusion upon their prerogative, conflicting with their responsibilities. To others, it offered welcome relief, even an alibi for malfeasance in their commands.[13]

The GEIRB gathered information through several techniques. Its permanent staff processed routine work—correspondence, statistical studies, agendas, and reports for meetings.[14] Often the first deputy commissioner raised questions of policy via memoranda to board members, requesting written opinions that would be discussed in subsequent meetings. It sought the views of junior and senior supervisors in the plainclothes force, sometimes inviting these officers to meetings to review policies and explore shortcomings of current procedures. The GEIRB also corresponded with the city's district attorneys and judges to resolve problems related to the presentation of cases involving gambling. Surveys were made of gambling procedures followed by police in other cities.

Approximately seventy board conferences were held regularly from 1961 to 1968 in the office of the first deputy commissioner. Although the first deputy commissioner dominated the GEIRB in all deliberations because of his rank, reputation, and forceful personality, he never provided the needed leadership. Board conferences were freewheeling discussions, more like brainstorming sessions that had no resolutions. Decisions were made by majority consensus as determined by the first deputy commissioner, a pattern consistent with his role as departmental watchdog. Thus the GEIRB's recommendations were for the most part a reflection of the first deputy commissioner's perspective of problems.

Contrary to one of its stated purposes, the board acted primarily as a staff and advisory unit, an advocate of new policy, and it did not "direct" operations in the field. It avoided supervisory responsibility for the plainclothes force; instead it recommended new procedures to the chief inspector and police commissioner. In spite of their status as staff, not commanders, board members did influence field units through an informal process of problem solving. They counseled commanders who requested interpretations of the board's policies or sought advice for special situations. The GEIRB's progress report of 1966 stated that there was "no hesitancy to step into the middle of 'line' operations." In addition to forming decisions for field officers, the board stimulated arrests by soliciting statistical data from plainclothes squads and by prodding commanders who lacked initiative in enforcement.

The GEIRB's annual reports prepared for the police commissioner from 1961 to 1966 outlined the board's proposals that had been accepted. The board's efforts, directed both at field and administrative procedures, were intended to promote efficiency and probity in gambling law enforcement. There were several "innovations" in field operations, including the establishment of a specialized gambling patrol car, policy-bank teams, the known-gambler target program, gambling combine structures, and revisions of the KG file. The GEIRB attempted to make its most important contributions to ethical behavior through personnel administration, especially in selecting, training, assigning, and supervising plainclothesmen. Moving from policy maker to participant, the board began by setting criteria for new plainclothesmen, and by 1965 it was spending three fourths of its time administering personnel policies in the plainclothes force.

In spite of the wealth of information available to them, board members often lacked insight in fundamentals of specific subjects, and their lack of awareness reduced their effectiveness as policy makers. Although the GEIRB recognized deficiencies in the plainclothes force (the splitting of arrests of minor gamblers, for example), it still failed to grapple with the causes of the lax, dishonest enforcement of gambling laws. Officials underestimated gamblers' ability to coopt plainclothesmen, the sophistication of collusive resistance to their strategies, and the department's own administrative incentives to corruption.

Policies and procedures were often piled one on another, lacking a coordinating theme or goal. The board's deliberations reveal that it was not only conscious of the hazards of corruption in the plainclothes force, but also was keenly aware of its own limitations and the department's inability to suppress organized gambling. Although the GEIRB was responsible for many well-conceived recommendations, most of them were implemented only partly, too late, or not at all. In particular, the board's efforts to limit plainclothesmen's exposure to the moral temptations and to change individual incentives and attitudes fell short of its goals.

By 1966 the GEIRB's activities dwindled. After formal meetings were all but discontinued in 1967, the first deputy commissioner acted alone on the board's behalf, relying on informal consultations and the continued work of the small staff. In a realignment of power during the late 1960s, the GEIRB's responsibilities were circumscribed to "the policy and administrative aspects of the total gambling enforcement program," which relegated the board's existence to a group of filing cabinets. Supervision of field operations was delegated to a new Public Morals Administrative Division (PMAD). As this division assumed authority for decision making, the Gambling Enforcement Inspection and Review Board declined. In 1972, long after its active role in gambling enforcement had ended, the board was abolished, having served a useful function without having realized its full potential.[15]

As the GEIRB was being phased out of existence in the late 1960s and early 1970s, the plainclothes force underwent a gradual metamorphosis, culminating in complete centralization of policy making and operational control. Centralizing gambling and narcotics enforcement under one head, the reform administrations of the early 1970s undertook a new commitment to promote honest, effective enforcement in these corruption-prone areas. Responsibility for integrity and efficiency in gambling enforcement was held by one deputy police commissioner. Accountability was fixed, and responsibility for the failure of anticorruption strategies could not be evaded through an obscure multimember board.[16]

While a strong anticorruption posture was not unusual for a new police administration, officials were now willing to recognize the existence of fundamental problems within the bureaucracy. They acknowledged the departmental incentives to corruption and vowed to eliminate them. Reassessing the official view of corruption, administrators rejected the "rotten apple" theory that conceded the existence of only a few corrupt policemen.[17] They were also disposed to evaluate and criticize efforts of previous administrations to promote ethical behavior, although more by implication than direct attack. More important, officials were realistic about the priorities of gambling enforcement, placing a higher premium on integrity than efficiency. They were prepared to accept a reduction in statistics of arrests. Readiness to take action was reflected in all their strategies, particularly those used in enforcement of gambling laws.

Like strategies implemented in the 1950s and 1960s, the new policies were promulgated gradually, but with a sense of urgency. Pressures generated by the independent Knapp commission's ongoing investigation of corruption weighed heavily on officials. The mix of strategies included some old, some borrowed, some new. Whatever they used, administrators made new inroads, accelerating the struggle against corruption. Many changes were actually new applications or modernizations of the GEIRB's procedures. Indeed, some policies were revivals of earlier tactics that had never been implemented although they were technically on the books. Several radical innovations were also undertaken to discover and crush organized cooptation.[18] Perhaps more important, anticorruption strategies attacked fundamental causes as well as institutions perpetuating malpractice. Instead of simply promulgating one procedure after another in shotgun fashion, programs and policies to promote honesty were coordinated to reinforce each other. Building on the policies of the past two decades that attempted to control enforcement of gambling laws, administrators in the early 1970s sought to eliminate the departmental ethos that was conducive to corruption and also to isolate corrupt policemen from other members of the force.[19]

Reducing Discretion

Throughout the 1950s and 1960s policies and procedures governing gambling law enforcement were designed, first, to fix responsibility for subsequent accountability. Their second objective was to reduce individual discretion in as many activities as practicable through explicit directions and prohibitions. Police administrators hoped to lessen opportunities for unethical practices by affording plainclothesmen little or no discretionary authority.

Rules for the plainclothes force, whether intended to promote operational efficiency or personal integrity, were implemented through the department's traditional system of communications. A separate chapter of the *Rules and Procedures* (*R&P*) dedicated to public morals and gambling enforcement set out general procedures for plainclothesmen that had evolved with the force since the early 1900s.[20] When new difficulties in enforcement were encountered because gamblers developed more sophisticated techniques—either with or without police connivance—plainclothes procedures were updated through a series of written directives known as Temporary Operating Procedures (TOPs) and Standard Operating Procedures (SOPs). Techniques that proved effective were later incorporated into the more permanent *R&P*.

To a great extent, directives affecting gambling enforcement procedures form a diary of corrupt practices in the plainclothes force. Prohibitions issued in response to discovered malfeasance of plainclothesmen, so-called "horror stories," tightened ambiguous points of procedure in departmental rules. Such instructions sought to close the barn door after the horse had bolted. The following illustrations not only reveal the illusive and diverse range of problems involved in maintaining ethical behavior in gambling enforcement, but also indicate that many directive strategies were sporadic and inconsistent responses rather than continuing policies.

Revising the known gambler file. The vulnerability of the known gambler file provides the first case in point. There was evidence that some plainclothesmen had withdrawn KGs' cards for a fee. In 1955, the size of the KG file card was changed from 4 x 6 inches to 8 x 9 inches, the larger format offering more space for entries and less likelihood of the card's removal from the file. For the same reason, the KG file's card index was replaced by a bound ledger and each KG was assigned a serial number at police headquarters. These procedures tightened control over gambling records.[21]

Eliminating stand-ins. Also in 1955, it was revealed that organized gamblers, in cooperation with some plainclothesmen, were hiring stand-ins for gamblers in arrests and court proceedings to maintain anonymity. The department responded to this practice with a new procedural rule: Gamblers had to be fingerprinted at the time of arrest and again when sentenced.[22]

Eliminating false arrest records. A related problem in court procedures involved substitution of false arrest records. Judges read arrest records before sentencing, and defendants with fewer arrests usually received lighter punishments. When the department discovered that coopted plainclothesmen were substituting false arrest records to obtain lesser sentences for convicted gamblers, it required that a special seal be affixed to each record at the Bureau of Criminal Identification prior to the record's use in court. Only one seal was maintained, with samples furnished to judges for comparison.[23]

Prohibiting KG interviews. In 1966 the department instituted an investigative policy prohibiting plainclothesmen from interviewing KGs in person. Doing so not only protected police identities and the confidentiality of investigations, it also eliminated the use of an alibi inadvertently provided by the department to coopted plainclothesmen. During some investigations of corruption, plainclothesmen suspected of having been coopted admitted that they had indeed met with KGs but only to determine the KGs' activities for official reports. The restriction against interviews precluded the use of this defense.[24]

Separating plainclothesmen from clerical staffs. In 1966, the Gambling Enforcement Inspection and Review Board prepared a model floor plan for all plainclothes squads, requiring the physical separation of plainclothes personnel and their clerical staffs in the main offices of division and borough commands. The separation was intended to increase the security of public morals reports and investigative work.[25]

Revising wiretapping regulations. Between 1958 and 1970 there were several revisions of departmental regulations governing wiretapping. The changes not only satisfied new legal requirements in the criminal code, they also tightened the department's control over use of eavesdropping equipment. Plainclothesmen were denied authority for wiretapping in emergencies without prior judicial approval. Stringent rules were imposed regarding use of equipment and procedures for reporting intercepted communications.[26]

To eliminate corruption, administrators in the early 1970s continued to restrict and control gambling enforcement by reducing individual discretion further. Through a series of new directives, which are discussed in the following sections, officials imposed more stringent procedures to limit plainclothesmen. An entirely different concept for the administration of gambling investigations was also implemented.

Concomitantly, officials sought to end the uniformed force's involvement in corruption stemming from organized gambling. In a realignment of departmental priorities, commanders in the patrol force were directed "to place gambling law enforcement in its proper perspective." The police commissioner, in an unprecedented move, revoked the patrol force's authority to make arrests: "Individual discretion by patrolmen in dealing with persons engaged in unlawful gambling operations will not be accepted under any circumstances. All enforcement efforts and contact with illegal gamblers will be on a directed basis." Thus officials sought to eliminate any unsupervised contact between uniformed policemen and gamblers to prevent a variety of corrupt practices, even though it meant foregoing arrests for violations of the gambling statutes.[27]

In summary, the strategy for controlling behavior through the establishment of goals, policies, and procedures probably had less impact than officials hoped for. Institutional weakness, such as brief tenure of police administrations and the failings of the GEIRB, detracted significantly from effective decisionmaking. Instead, the impressions and implicit understanding generated by policy makers were as important, if not more so, than their substantive decisions. Administrators relied essentially on one theme: limiting plainclothesmen's discretion. Restrictive rules and procedures were not effective in preventing corrupt practice.

Shuffling Personnel and Boxes

The department's traditional strategy to promote honesty in gambling enforcement was periodically to revise individual assignments and restructure the plainclothes force. Plainclothesmen suspected of malfeasance or lesser infractions were transferred to other gambling squads or sent back to patrol. Mass transfer of plainclothesmen was the usual crisis response during the scandals of the 1950s and 1960s. Changes in organizational structure often complemented mass transfers and were intended to establish a series of checks and balances conducive to honesty and ethical behavior. Expediency underlay much of the shuffling. The plainclothes force was completely centralized in the early 1970s as part of a campaign for reform.

Policies in Assignment

Policies in assignment, always controversial issues in the management of police personnel, had important implications for members of the force. Assignments determined whether policemen had challenging or boring work, pleasant or hostile surroundings, and opportunities to achieve promotion. Whereas advancement in rank was controlled primarily by civil service examinations, assignments were a major discretional area for police administrators. Indeed, New York policemen often relied on someone's influence to secure choice duties.

Police officials and members of the Gambling Enforcement Inspection and Review Board used assignments as an important tool to promote efficiency in gambling law enforcement. The board discontinued the custom of routinely transferring plainclothesmen with their superiors and established a structured career ladder instead. Its intention was to fix individual performance as the criterion for selection and advancement. Initially, plainclothesmen graduating from the criminal investigation course (CIC) were assigned to precinct squads in Brooklyn and the Bronx, and to division squads in other parts of the city. Promotion to division and borough plainclothes units depended on whether they performed "proficiently," which meant, of course, that they needed a high volume of arrests to their credit. In the absence of high arrest records, they were transferred back to the uniformed force. As a practical matter, plainclothesmen usually advanced to the division level, and some were promoted to borough squads. But after four or five years most were "flopped" back to patrol duties.[28]

The first career path for plainclothesmen created problems in the efficient enforcement of gambling laws. One concern was the assignment of only new CIC graduates to the precinct level of enforcement. Precinct captains complained that this policy limited efficiency because inexperienced personnel lacked the expertise needed to investigate and suppress organized gambling. They contended, moreover, that as a result of rapid turnover of plainclothesmen through promotion, there was erratic and inconsistent enforcement. These commanders wanted a mix of experienced and novice plainclothesmen. The GEIRB, apparently sensitive to trading off efficiency for integrity, was reluctant at first to make this change. Board members thought plainclothesmen would learn their jobs better at the precinct level where there was less competitive pressure for the detective assignment than in the division and borough squads. More important, they said new plainclothesmen needed to be free of corrupting influences and would be more malleable and responsive to training in the precinct. This experience was supposed to shape attitudes and improve integrity in the long run.

In the mid-1960s officials modified policy, and some experienced plainclothesmen were assigned to precincts experimentally. Concurrently, graduates of the criminal investigation course were assigned to division and borough squads, but not in active gambling areas. In the late 1960s, the GEIRB finally recommended assignment of novice and experienced plainclothesmen to all levels of enforcement, but this move was based on considerations of necessity, not ethical behavior. The transfer of 100 junior plainclothesmen to the Narcotics Bureau in mid-1969, plus the normal turnover of personnel promoted to detective or transferred back to uniform, threatened the stability of the plainclothes force. Thus the GEIRB supported new policies in assignment to ease the work load of the 480 men left in plainclothes.[29]

Periodic Transfers

Officials used voluntary and involuntary intersquad transfers of plainclothesmen as a routine tool of personnel administration. In the plainclothes force, involuntary transfers served several purposes, the most traditional being disciplinary. New assignments could impose hardships such as a longer traveling time, a less desirable environment for working, or a more authoritarian commander. Involuntary transfers were also imposed to resolve personality clashes, to satisfy personal preferences, and to deal with suspected dishonest or unethical behavior.

Generally, an official request to transfer a plainclothesman contained little or no explanation. Commanders used noncommittal statements alleging only that the individual "failed to meet the high standards" of the squad, a description that superiors routinely endorsed with "recommend approval" and forwarded to the chief inspector. Whereas there were many reasons for intersquad shifts, all transferees were regarded with suspicion. If not corrupt or inept, they must have created some other serious problem to warrant transfer according to plainclothes norms.

By the mid-1960s the Gambling Enforcement Inspection and Review Board, deeply involved in plainclothes assignments, focused its attention on the use of transfers. To reduce the shuffling of personnel and to force commanders to eliminate "rotten apples" rather than simply move them to another barrel, the board required supervisors to specify the cause for all transfers they requested. Before filing such applications, squad leaders were to discuss the difficulty with the plainclothesman in question and to record the admonition. If the individual still failed to meet his responsibilities, the commander could ask that the individual be returned to the uniformed force, providing he would not be reassigned to another plainclothes squad.

When misfits or underachievers were "flopped," they returned to the uniformed force resentful and cynical. These attitudes became widespread and undermined recruiting efforts. Some administrators suggested alternatives between the two extremes of ultimately "flopping" or promoting plainclothesmen, possibly allowing them to select precincts of their choice. No ameliorating policy was ever adopted, and only in a few cases were commanders able to influence the assignment of an individual being transferred out of plainclothes.[30]

In extraordinary circumstances, particularly crises generated by disclosures of wholesale collusion with gamblers, officials responded with periodic mass transfers within the plainclothes force. Administrators assumed that reassignment to different commands would eliminate or diminish organized cooptation by breaking up corrupt cliques and scattering conspirators throughout the city. Dispersal meant it would take substantial time for would-be malefactors to develop confidence in one another and to restructure their conspiracy with organized gamblers. Mass transfer in the plainclothes force occurred under various administrations throughout the 1950s and 1960s. In a few instances, the entire plainclothes force was "flopped," and shifts of whole divisions, including commanding and supervising officers, were not unusual. This policy was not limited to gambling enforcement. One administration routinely transferred several hundred sergeants each November to prevent their receiving Christmas gratuities from local businesses.[31]

Mass transfer had at least three serious drawbacks as a problem-solving strategy. First, it produced only an apparent reduction in corruption. The Brooklyn grand jury that investigated the scandal involving Harry Gross concluded:

The juggling of police assignments is worse than useless. It is, in fact, vicious in that it is adroitly calculated to lull the public into a sense of false security and at the same time to spread and to perpetuate the insidious arrangement which has always enabled grafting vice-squad policemen from the low to the high echelons to pursue their criminal designs with little danger of exposure.[32]

Second, because the indiscriminate nature of mass transfer affected honest and dishonest plainclothesmen alike, coopted men gained a cogent argument to pursuade others to join their conspiracy. All plainclothesmen suffered a loss in reputation when there was a shake-up. At the very least, honest men were motivated to warn dishonest colleagues of possible discovery by the PCCIU or another anticorruption unit. Thus mass transfer helped to thwart the discovery of cooptation.

Finally, mass transfer did nothing to help eliminate the resurgence of corruption that often involved clerical patrolmen. Clerical staffs often played a significant role in schemes of cooptation because they read, screened, and typed all communications, including investigative reports and affidavits for search warrants. With a virtual monopoly of knowledge about gambling enterprises within the squad's jurisdiction, clerical patrolmen were invaluable sources of information regarding current complaints and investigations. Incongruous as it may seem, they were often exempt from mass transfer, which meant that the roots of corruption were free to take hold again in a new group of plainclothesmen. Clerical men were immune from transfer because the department was unwilling to forfeit their expertise. Newly staffed squads would have floundered without experienced clerical men to provide continuity and maintain productivity. Officials rationalized that clerical men were not technically members of the plainclothes squads but instead were part of the office staff at division and borough headquarters. Although in the mid-1960s the GEIRB entertained the idea of including clerical men in mass transfer, its deliberations never crystallized into policy.[33]

Changes in Organizational Structure

Complementing transfers, the department often modified the structure of the plainclothes force, assuming that organizational structure would affect individual behavior. Officials reasoned that a revised hierarchy and new leadership would alter patterns of loyalty and command influence. Dislocation would promote honesty by disrupting the chains of communication and confidence within any corrupt conspiracy. Thus lines and boxes on the department's organization charts shifted after each exposé of corruption.

For decades the department vacillated between centralized and decentralized responsibility for enforcement of public morals. As far back as 1864, precinct captains were accountable for suppression of illegal gambling until a scandal at the turn of the century narrowed the focus of liability on a few district (division) inspectors. Further centralization occurred in 1924 when gambling enforcement was assigned to a Special Services Division. A few years later the cycle was completed when the job reverted to district inspectors, who held it for several decades. After the Gross scandal, which involved widespread cooptation in Brooklyn, gambling enforcement was centralized into a single Public Morals Squad in that borough. This reorganization was due in part to recommendations made by the Brooklyn grand jury investigating the Gross case. During the 1950s and 1960s the enforcement of gambling laws remained decentralized in patrol divisions throughout the city, except in Brooklyn, where one Public Morals Squad had borough-wide responsibility.[34]

Under the watchful eye of its grand jury, Brooklyn emerged as the department's workshop, where organizational changes were made in an attempt to alter plainclothesmen's behavior. Late in 1959, the department began an experiment in Brooklyn to determine the best format for the plainclothes force. Responsibility for gambling enforcement remained centralized in a single squad for one half of Brooklyn, while in the other half a three-tiered system was created, with plainclothes squads in patrol precincts, divisions, and borough headquarters.[35]

Following its creation in 1961, the Gambling Enforcement Inspection and Review Board evaluated Brooklyn's two structural approaches–the centralized squad and the tiered system–to determine which was more efficient. Advocates of the pyramidal structure thought it wiser to involve many commanders in enforcement because of the department's insistence on accountability. They reasoned that the more superior officers involved, the less likelihood of a successful conspiracy. More cynical supporters of decentralization felt that involvement of many policemen would make collusion too costly for organized gambling. When the board's staff analyzed the two systems in mid-1961, it concluded that in terms of arrests there was no statistically significant difference between them. Thus the staff suggested that the structure decision be based on "sound principles of organization and management." After considerable deliberation, the board recommended adoption of the three-tiered system of precinct, division, and borough plainclothes squads throughout Brooklyn. Its decision was based on the principle that "decision-making responsibility should be placed in the unit closest to the level of operation. . . . [T]he smaller the area of responsibility the tighter the control and the more justification to hold the person in charge to answer."[36] Significantly, the pyramidal scheme was not adopted throughout the city.

Officials intended Brooklyn's multilevel system to establish checks and balances and to promote honesty within the three tiers of enforcement. Precinct plainclothesmen, restricted by narrow geographic boundaries, had limited responsibilities. Their main concerns were local, low-ranking gamblers and gambling conditions on the streets. Division plainclothesmen in all boroughs were responsible for the middle levels of organized gambling. In Brooklyn, they also supervised the precincts' plainclothes squads. Borough plainclothes squads had dual responsibilities: to attack the highest echelons of organized gambling and to supervise division and precinct squads. Ideally, the structure provided horizontal and vertical checks and balances so that all levels felt tension and competition from subordinate and supervisory units.[37]

The multilayered plainclothes structure was intended to affect honesty and ethical behavior in other ways. Officials reasoned that a single unit of enforcement with one set of friendships and peer pressures would be too vulnerable a target for gamblers' collusion schemes. In contrast, supervisory and competing squads founded on mutual distrust would make cooptation of the whole system more difficult and discovery of unethical behavior more likely. Administrators believed that individuals vying with each other for arrests would be less inclined to cooperate in a conspiracy.[38] As we will see, however, other pressures and incentives eroded the checks and balances that were built into the plainclothes structure.

Under the system prevailing during the 1950s and 1960s, control of gambling enforcement remained fragmented, a nominal responsibility of patrol officials. The plainclothes force had no direct chain of command or communication. Enforcement was subject to the whims of intervening borough and division commanders who often interpreted and executed departmental policy to satisfy local conditions. The resulting lack of uniformity produced inefficiency (the duplication of effort and unnecessary competition, for example) and misdirection of personnel and enforcement.

The Organized Crime Control Bureau (OCCB)

For many years administrators recognized that lack of centralized control was a serious weakness in enforcement of gambling laws. Friction, competition, and disparate interpretations of departmental policies reduced efficiency within the plainclothes force. Early in its deliberations, the GEIRB toyed with the idea of establishing a Public Morals Division comparable to other major branches such as the Patrol and Detective Divisions, but it never acted on the idea.[39]

In 1967 officials began to centralize responsibility for gambling enforcement in the newly created Public Morals Administrative Division. Among its duties were to coordinate all plainclothes units for maximum efficiency, to conduct investigations against corruption, and to recommend new policies to the police commissioner. In spite of this variation, however, the basic structure of the plainclothes force remained the same. Although one unit now directed them, plainclothes squads were still subordinate to patrol borough and division commanders. The plainclothes force was like an old building with a new roof.[40]

Changes in organizational structure continued to be an important strategy for reform during the 1970s. Shortly after a new administration took office, the plainclothes force was again restructured–borough plainclothes squads were abolished and their investigative personnel transferred to subordinate division plainclothes squads. This modification was intended to "increase efficiency" and to establish "stricter control of investigative personnel." But the shift was only a stop-gap measure.[41]

Late in 1971, the post of deputy commissioner for organized crime control was created, and his new command, the Organized Crime Control Bureau (OCCB) was established.[42] An attempt to counter the department's fragmented efforts in enforcing gambling and narcotics laws during the 1950s and 1960s, the OCCB was a major commitment to centralization. The OCCB was designed to harness the energies of two corruption-prone functions and to increase investigative efficiency because gambling and narcotics were believed to be interrelated at the higher echelons of organized crime. For the first time, gambling and narcotics were brought under the direct control of a deputy commissioner. Not only was it unusual for members of the force to be commanded by a deputy commissioner, but at a time when problems involving gambling and narcotics were undergoing considerable publicity, such a change knowingly increased the police commissioner's risk of personal involvement in any subsequent scandal.

The OCCB was formed through an amalgamation of four groups: the Public Morals Administrative Division, the plainclothesmen still working in patrol divisions, the Narcotics Administrative Division, and all members of the Narcotics Bureau. There were four principal units in the OCCB. The Administrative Division processed all communications alleging violations of laws controlling narcotics and public morals, managed personnel and equipment, and performed myriad clerical tasks. The Narcotics and Public Morals (gambling) Divisions conducted field investigations; each division was subdivided into enforcement districts comparable to patrol divisions (see Exhibit P in the appendix). The Field Control Division, a watchdog, monitored all activities in enforcement to ensure efficiency and integrity. Because of the higher priority given to enforcement of narcotics laws, the work force in each public morals district was reduced, with many investigators transferred to the OCCB's Narcotics Division. (Table 3-1 shows the breakdown of the OCCB's work force.)

Organizational structure changed continually throughout the OCCB's early existence. The Public Morals Division diversified its efforts beyond gambling by adding specialized units to investigate pornography, loan sharking, smuggling of untaxed cigarettes, and illegal sale of firearms. By mid-1973, the entire Organized Crime Control Bureau shifted with the change of police commissioners and the new commissioner's restructuring of the department's upper hierarchy. The deputy commissioner for organized crime control was reappointed first deputy commissioner and his former post was abolished. The OCCB, however, remained under his control when the entire bureau was transferred to his new command. The irony of this reshuffling was that it created

Table 3-1
Breakdown of the OCCB's Work Force, 1972-1975

Division	1972	1973	1974	1975
Administrative	98	114	n/a	114
Field Control	68	61	n/a	54
Public Morals	652[a]	408	415[b]	279[c]
Narcotics	916	608	n/a	455
Special Services	0	143	n/a	112
	1734	1334	n/a	1014

n/a = not available
[a]452 investigators plus 200 supervisors and clerks
[b]276 investigators plus 132 supervisors and clerks
[c]169 investigators plus 110 supervisors and clerks
Source: New York City Police Department.

a structure for gambling enforcement similar to that of the 1950s and 1960s. when the first deputy commissioner held de facto responsibility.[43]

Streamlining gambling enforcement in the OCCB played an important role in the scheme for reform. Because they cut away the intermediate layers of command in the plainclothes force, directives intended to promote integrity reached their targets sooner and without dilution. One voice was heard. The existence of fewer gambling squads facilitated control of plainclothesmen, and smaller units allowed for face-to-face communication between headquarters and the field. More significant, however, the simplified command structure provided a viable framework for revised procedures in reporting, supervision, and radical programs to encourage integrity.

Thus it seems clear that the periodic shuffling of personnel and organizational units throughout the 1950s and 1960s was not an effective means of influencing individual behavior. It provided expedient but illusory results to create the appearance that corrupt practice was at an irreducible minimum. Centralization of gambling enforcement in the early 1970s was probably not as significant a change as was the new administration's commitment to achieving integrity.

Changing Individual Incentives and Attitudes

As an alternative to shuffling assignments and revamping organizational structure, which were often crisis responses, officials sought to induce honesty by altering the process and criteria for selecting plainclothesmen, as well as the incentives for individuals seeking assignment to plainclothes. Training was used primarily to improve efficiency. In the early 1970s more sophisticated but unpopular approaches were undertaken to reduce plainclothesmen's tolerance or corrupt practice and to impose accountability for malfeasance.

The Selection of Plainclothesmen

Selection of personnel can be a highly effective mechanism for influencing organizational behavior because careful elimination of people not likely to conform to established policies reduces the need for controls in the field. The department overlooked this strategy for many years, in spite of its potential. Until the mid-1950s, division and borough commanders selected plainclothesmen according to friends' and subordinates' recommendations. Once selected, plainclothesmen joined the staff of division or borough commanders and often transferred with them to new commands, a policy that nourished personal loyalties. What motivated volunteers for plainclothes assignments is not well documented, but the most typical explanation was the desire to shed the uniform, to "get out of the bag."

Most policemen shunned the assignment, fearing the sordid reputation of plainclothes that was traditional within the department. Police cynics quipped that plainclothesmen had "B numbers," identification numbers assigned to criminals. The stigma developed in part because the work thrust plainclothesmen into frequent association with prostitutes, pimps, homosexuals, and the like. Discouraged by the history of scandal and ruined careers in gambling enforcement, patrolmen avoided plainclothes and sought other avenues of advancement.

In the mid-1950s, police administrators tried to upgrade the plainclothes force by replacing previous ad hoc procedures to improve the process of selection. A series of semiannual directives from 1960 through 1970 outlined the new policy for commanding officers to recommend candidates for the criminal investigation course and subsequent plainclothes work. Prerequisite qualifications for nominees included integrity as well as (1) the ability to detect gambling violations and enforce the gambling laws as evidenced by arrests; and (2) the career-mindedness evidenced by being on promotion lists or attending an accredited college or a departmental in-service training program.[44]

Two significant points in selection were initial recommendations by precinct captains and final screening by the Plainclothes Selection Board. Recommendations went directly to the chief inspector's office (bypassing normal channels), where each nominee's personnel record was reviewed. Screening, first done on an ad hoc basis, was formalized in the early 1960s in a selection board composed of senior officers who participated in rotation. The high volume of candidates made board interviews perfunctory, with field commanders making the critical choice in their initial recommendations.

Precinct captains were never enthusiastic about the program, having been asked to select and subsequently lose their best patrolmen. In almost all cases the prerequisite for nomination was a high number of arrests. Because the patrolmen were also reluctant, commanders usually recommended volunteers who applied for the criminal investigation course. This method of selection was an open secret in the department. Recognizing the practice as a long-standing weakness, the GEIRB directed commanders to consider not just volunteers, but also those who they felt "would perform plainclothes duties in a manner reflecting credit upon the department." The shift in policy was based on the board's realization that "the man who seeks the recommendation may be the very man who should not be assigned to this type of duty."[45]

In spite of the department's efforts to improve selection procedures, recruitment problems continued throughout the 1960s. Many patrolmen were unwilling to relinquish comfortable assignments for the uncertainties of plainclothes. To overcome this shortage of qualified personnel and to promote honest and ethical conduct, the department reasoned that a fundamental change in incentives was needed to attract capable individuals to plainclothes. Thus the Gambling Enforcement Inspection and Review Board developed the "detective incentive."

Although the origin of the detective incentive is obscure, the concept appears to have been stated publicly first by the police commissioner in 1955, when he sought to "keep out of plainclothes duty potentially crooked policemen who now seek such assignments. . . . Possibly service in the plainclothes division might be made a prerequisite for advancement into the Detective Division, far and away the most attractive assignment in the department."[46] The detective incentive involved the use of a simple prerequisite: Patrolmen had to serve in the plainclothes force before they could become detectives. The policy was designed to compel honest individuals who would otherwise avoid plainclothes to accept assignment if it were the only way to become detectives (see Exhibit Q in the appendix). Administrators envisioned a revitalized program of gambling enforcement executed by honest, career-minded policemen who would improve the performance and reputation of the plainclothes force. Furthermore, officials expected that because of investigative experience in enforcement of gambling laws, this new breed of plainclothesmen ultimately would improve the Detective Division as well.[47]

In spite of the hopes of its proponents, the detective incentive failed to promote honesty for three main reasons. First, periodic scandals throughout the 1960s in which many plainclothesmen were convicted and dismissed perpetuated the undesirability of plainclothes work. Second, many plainclothesmen never became serious candidates for detective because they were transferred or "flopped" back to the uniformed force to jobs no better (and in some cases worse) than those they had relinquished to enter plainclothes. Third, individuals who survived the gauntlet of plainclothes still faced screening by the Detective Selection Board. Although recommended by their plainclothes commanders, some were denied promotion by the board. Thus the policy lacked credibility because most plainclothesmen simply did not achieve assignment to the detective division.[48] To most policemen, the opportunity for advancement through plainclothes was dubious at best.

Hoping to rectify the situation, officials published statistics (an unusual action) in 1964 to stimulate recruitment by showing that in the two years previous, 156 plainclothesmen had been appointed to the Detective Division. Most patrolmen knew, however, that this figure accounted for less than one half the detective assignments made during that period, a clear signal that plainclothes was not the only way to become a detective.[49] Recurrent scandals and mass transfers in the plainclothes force, coupled with the routine "flopping" of many individuals, perpetuated distrust of the detective incentive.

Careful selection of plainclothesmen remained an important policy during the reform era of the early 1970s. Because of the continuing shortage of personnel for plainclothes, officials continued to accept volunteers for assignment. As before, prospective candidates were recommended by commanding officers and then screened for suitability by superior officers in the Organized Crime Control Bureau. To improve the image of gambling enforcement, the OCCB changed the title of plainclothesmen to "investigators"; the term "plainclothes" and all its derivations were later deleted from the department's official lexicon.[50]

In mid-1971 the department rejuvenated the discredited detective incentive by instituting formal procedures for assignment to plainclothes and narcotics enforcement duty. Administrators put the program (known officially as the "Career Path") "out on the table," emphasizing that no one could earn the detective's shield without first being tested in the OCCB (see Exhibit R in the appendix). Having made the OCCB the exclusive training ground for detective and other desirable assignments, officials hoped, as had previous administrators, that more capable and upwardly mobile individuals by necessity would volunteer for plainclothes and narcotics enforcement.[51]

In spite of its revitalization and initial success, the Career Path program fell short of its goals. At first, some individuals did get the gold shield, but after two years the OCCB had more people eligible under the program than the detective bureau could absorb, and many plainclothesmen were returned to precincts. Moreover, under a 1973 program to retain better personnel in the patrol force, detective shields and pay (though not the title) were given to uniformed officers and investigators throughout the force, blotting the last vestige of credibility left in Career Path for the OCCB. With only a limited number of detective assignments available, the OCCB's efforts to recruit new investigators were frustrated; policemen could earn the coveted gold shield without exposing themselves to the moral risks of gambling or narcotics.[52]

A related issue of policy in the program for selection concerned the most appropriate length of prior service for plainclothes candidates. There were two schools of thought. Some members of the Gambling Enforcement Inspection and Review Board favored candidates who had fifteen or more years of experience "on the job." Such veterans, they reasoned, were not likely to be coopted and thus risk losing their pensions, and they would probably resist temptations that might overwhelm younger people. Objections to this view included the fear that patrolmen who were close to the end of their careers and anxious not to jeopardize their retirements might adopt passive, "hear no evil, see no evil" attitudes; the possibility that older patrolmen might accept opportunities to build nest eggs in preparation for retirement; and the long-honored tradition of giving "short-timers" work involving little risk or physical danger.

Other members of the board thought new patrolmen, even probationers, should be assigned to plainclothes. These people, the argument went, had not been coopted by organized gambling nor were they cynical and "street-wise," but still idealistic and thus likely to reject temptations because of plans for long careers in the department. Precedent supported this view with the Gross scandal of the 1950s, in which probationary patrolmen had been assigned directly from the police academy to investigate corrupt policemen because they were "virgins," unknown in the force. Detractors of this approach pointed out that because inexperienced plainclothesmen would be less effective investigators, the enforcement of gambling laws would suffer.[53]

Officials compromised on the question of prior service: Most patrolmen assigned to plainclothes had moderate experience, generally three to five years on the force. Orders issued in the late 1960s directed commanders not to recommend patrolmen for plainclothes who had less than two or more than fifteen years of service.[54] Because the actual criteria for selection remained the number of arrests made, plainclothesmen in the 1950s and 1960s were "street-wise" veterans, conditioned to accept corrupt practices by their peers.

In the 1970s administrators reversed this policy. When the OCCB was being formed, most experienced plainclothesmen were screened out and numerous replacements had to be found. Officials chose inexperienced patrolmen, with only one or two years seasoning, to form the new generation of gambling and narcotics investigators. The OCCB's leaders were willing to trade some short-term losses in efficiency for potential gains in integrity.[55] When the OCCB could not attract enough new investigators in the mid-1970s, the Career Path requirement of two years of patrol experience was waived for a small number of patrolmen. These people, who had just completed their one-year probationary period, were to be tested in a controlled situation to determine if their inexperience precluded effective investigative work.[56]

The last important issue that was related to the strategy of selecting better personnel was the establishment of a specific period of tenure for gambling enforcement. One of the GEIRB's earliest considerations was to reduce exposure to corrupting influences by limiting tenure in plainclothes. Board members favored a two-year assignment because they thought that an individual should not be subjected to extreme temptations for an unreasonable time. Police executives rejected the two-year limit on grounds of efficiency. They reasoned that if it took one year for a plainclothesman to become proficient in his work, the second year's service was an insufficient return on the department's investment in the criminal investigation course and on-the-job training. Thus the department established a four-year tenure for plainclothesmen, which justified its investment and created a reasonable testing period for promotion if the person performed successfully. But the policy was never fully implemented because the unavailability of replacements required that many people with more than four years of service remain in plainclothes.[57]

Administrators in the 1970s strongly believed that a reversal in tenure policy was needed. Accordingly, assignments to plainclothes or narcotics squads in the OCCB were limited to two years, and "successful completion" of this term was required for advancement to the Detective Bureau or other choice detail. Because of renewed concerns for efficiency in these vital areas, however, officials later modified the two-year tenure in the OCCB. They established "a permanent cadre of experienced superiors, detectives, and patrolmen" to stay on in gambling and narcotics enforcement after careful screening for ability and integrity. Significantly, the OCCB's permanent administrators and investigators were to be eligible for the detective's higher salary and gold shield. In effect the detective incentive had come full circle, with service in gambling and narcotic squads elevated to the level of a detective assignment.[58]

After a few years, however, the department again felt the need for greater productivity in these areas of enforcement. Although the two-year tenure was maintained as official policy, it gradually fell into disuse. The OCCB's investigators who were considered qualified and trustworthy were allowed to remain in gambling and narcotics squads with their commanders' sanction. The tenure policy weakened because of the same reasons as before: insufficient return of the department's investment, lost expertise, constant retraining, and the natural preference of commanders and investigators to continue to work with people they had come to know and trust.

The Training of Plainclothesmen

Whereas training was an important tool for enforcing gambling laws, the department's emphasis lay more with improving efficiency of operations than with promoting honesty and rectitude. An early attempt at department-wide instruction for gambling enforcement was made in 1960 through a concise, pocket-sized manual called *A Legal Guide for the Enforcement of Laws Pertaining to Gambling, Prostitution, and Liquor Violations*. Intended as a comprehensive aid and convenient reference, the booklet offered brief summaries of statutes and factual illustrations of various violations in gambling and public morals. All policemen were expected to know the contents.

The concept of broad training was championed by the Gambling Enforcement Inspection and Review Board. Its first recommendation, made shortly after its inauguration, was that all members of the force received an intensive, two-day course in gambling enforcement. The board's objective was to inform all policemen of their responsibilities in this area and to give them specialized knowledge to do their jobs. But nowhere in the proposed syllabus was any material relating to the hazards of corruption inherent in enforcement of gambling statutes.[59]

From 1950 throughout the 1960s, patrolmen selected for plainclothes attended the police academy's criminal investigation course to prepare for enforcing gambling and public morals laws. Occasionally, patrolmen entered plainclothes without that training because attendance was not mandatory until the late 1950s. Originally involving forty hours of instruction in one week, the course expanded gradually until it lasted six weeks by the early 1960s. Plainclothes and detective candidates matriculated together, which was appropriate when the detective incentive was implemented. In 1965 the course was reduced to four weeks for plainclothesmen, with the two extra weeks only for detective candidates. Officials wanted to save specialized material until successful plainclothesmen were promoted to the Detective Division. Condensation of the course also released plainclothesmen for field assignment two weeks earlier.

The course involved lectures, demonstrations, and a few field trips, all having a practical emphasis on violations of gambling and public morals statutes. Lectures were given by members of the academy's staff, plainclothes commanders, technical experts, and guest instructors. Periodic quizzes and a comprehensive final examination determined each student's academic rank, which was used, in turn, as the criterion for assignment. Highest-ranked students were assigned first while the others returned to the uniformed force to await vacancies.[60]

Training for plainclothes was more notable for what was omitted than what was included. Plainclothesmen were not prepared for practical problems such as systematic competition and secrecy within the force, or for ethical dilemmas involving productivity and perjury. They were never exposed to lessons learned from the department's history of scandals in gambling law enforcement, and they were not conditioned for organized gambling's need to coopt the police, for the temptations of corruption, or for the work-group norms of the plainclothes force.

Although corruption was on everyone's mind, it was never a subject of discussion during training. The course made no attempt to mold attitudes that could counter hazards of corruption; it concentrated instead on procedures and law. The only mention of honesty and ethical behavior came at the conclusion of the course when the first deputy commissioner—or a high-ranking official from the police commissioner's office or a chaplain—delivered a brief lecture. But these were paternalistic sermons that referred to moral temptations and not to realistic problems of cooptation and unethical behavior. Plainclothesmen learned the realities of their work during "bull sessions" between classes.[61]

Supervisors were often assigned to plainclothes squads without receiving training in enforcement of gambling laws, and it was not until 1964 that they were required to attend the academy. By late 1969, their schooling had been expanded to forty-eight hours spread over a twelve-week period. The syllabus covered several areas, including administrative duties, supervisory techniques, and responsibilities of leadership, all of which were supposed to help officers control their subordinates and encourage productivity. Again, there were obvious gaps in training the supervisors to promote honesty and ethical behavior. Having little or no instruction in recognizing or preventing malfeasance, supervisors in plainclothes were expected to rely on instinct and past experience in matters of corruption.[62]

To supplement the academy's training program, the GEIRB invited plainclothes supervisors to its meetings to discuss problems related to gambling law enforcement. In addition, board members and public morals inspectors and deputy inspectors held "across-the-table" conferences. All these meetings were informal, and most discussions centered around problems of administration and enforcement, with little or no attention given to corrupt practices in the plainclothes force. In the mid-1960s these training seminars were expanded with a series of Command Training Conferences. The atmosphere and agenda were formal, with board members and departmental experts making presentations on timely issues to plainclothes supervisors. Because participation was generally limited and restrained, the gut issues of corruption and unethical conduct were never aired.[63]

In the early 1970s training became a prominent part of the administration's efforts "to develop and reinforce integrity as a norm." The police academy's curriculum was revised "to deal with corruption as it related to all aspects of police work rather than as a subject by itself." Recruits were given a new "integrity development course"; twenty hours of the course involved role playing in small workshops whose contents were "geared toward fostering ethical attitudes consistent with maintaining a high level of integrity." Similar training was adopted for all other members of the force.[64]

An experimental Anti-Corruption Workshop was begun in one precinct. A voluntary program, it involved a series of directed but informal group discussions about all forms of dishonesty and unethical police practices. Officials were pleased with results reflected in questionnaires that had been administered before and after the sessions because some attitudes had apparently been modified positively. As a result, the department adopted the Ethical Awareness Workshop program to modify personal attitudes and to create "a healthy anti-corruption climate."[65]

Superior officers were also indoctrinated. New supervisors and commanders spent two weeks of their orientation with the department's corruption control units to obtain "first-hand knowledge of this aspect of the problems of supervisions." Commanders were further instructed to break the barrier of silence by discussing the issue of corruption with their subordinates.[66]

The OCCB was the next to focus on educational pursuits, and in mid-1972 it created its own specialized training course "to develop and nurture a high degree of moral integrity . . . in the areas of corruption and bribery, honesty in the processing of arrests and evidence, and the preparation and presentation of testimony in court." Each of the OCCB's divisions appointed a training coordinator to research, plan, and implement instruction.[67]

Corruption Consciousness

Apathy and a dim perception of corruption within the department were continuing obstacles to reform. For decades administrators proclaimed publicly that the vast majority of policemen was honest, dedicated, and self-sacrificing in comparison to a mere handful of dishonest "rogue cops." Throughout the 1950s and 1960s most administrations held to this official view of corruption, but in the early 1970s this position was abandoned as administrators, particularly in the OCCB, spoke about dishonesty frankly and frequently. More than simply condemning malfeasance in the abstract, police executives acknowledged that corruption was widespread and was the department's "number one problem." Arousing "corruption consciousness" was one of the police commissioner's major strategies to eliminate unethical conduct.[68]

When the commander of the OCCB asked his people to estimate the extent of corruption within their ranks, the overwhelming response was 5 to 15 percent, the lowest choice on the questionnaire. His estimate, over 50 percent, created much resentment and reinforced the case for corruption consciousness.[69] After an almost entire plainclothes squad in Brooklyn was discovered to have been in collusion with gamblers, the OCCB issued a memorandum that condemned the guilty and urged other plainclothesmen to "consider the shame and disgrace they [the corrupt] visit on their families or the stigma they visit on you and me." Such efforts to realign the force's sympathies and sway loyalties exposed the issue of corruption to a new treatment from the administration, as officials sought to change the rank and file's passive acceptance of corruption to hostility.[70]

Administrators reinforced corruption consciousness through their campaign against "corruption hazards," those sociolegal institutions that created conditions conducive to police malpractice. Usually, "corruption hazards" resulted from statutes that gave the police regulatory powers over private enterprises, particularly the "Sabbath laws" prohibiting commercial activity on Sunday, the ordinances regulating taxicabs and building construction, and the laws governing the sale of alcoholic beverages (ABC laws). The businesses that were affected regarded prohibitions and regulatory codes as nuisances, whereas the public was either oblivious to or participated in violations. By tradition, businessmen who were vulnerable to the regulations were amenable to paying for nonenforcement. Policemen could adopt, as many had, widespread practices to forego enforcing these statutes for fees or other gratuities.[71]

The program against corruption hazards had two objectives: to eliminate individual dishonesty, and to eliminate the ethos that was conducive to more serious malpractice in the enforcement of gambling and narcotics laws. Officials reasoned that because a majority of policemen were involved in some form of lesser malfeasance, there was a general unethical climate that nurtured the rank and file's tolerance of criminal offenses. Senior administrators visualized department-wide corruption as being distributed along a continuum. At one of two extremes was a small number of "saints," and at the other, a small number of so-called "meat-eaters" who aggressively sought opportunities to make an illegal dollar. Between them was the preponderance of the force, who were caught up in minor malfeasance generated by various corruption hazards.[72] Because most people on the force were too compromised to be indignant at cooptation in gambling or narcotics enforcement, they were reluctantly tolerant of "meat-eaters." By eliminating corruption hazards, officials sought to isolate the most serious wrongdoers from the majority, increasing opportunities to attack conspiracies in gambling and narcotics enforcement.[73] Thus the program against corruption hazards was designed to identify and eradicate sources of illegal practices. After a few months in office, the administration abrogated the force's discretion to enforce the Sabbath laws. Under new guidelines, a patrolman could issue a "Sabbath summons" only after receiving a specific complaint from the public about a violation and only after his superior had approved enforcement. For obvious reasons the police commissioner could not formally order nonenforcement of any statute; thus the restrictions on Sabbath law enforcement were promulgated informally—orally—down through the hierarchy.[74]

Similar controls were initiated by the administration. The police commissioner urged the creation of an independent commission to regulate the taxicab industry. Officials hoped to stop illegal payoffs by ending police responsibility to test the condition of taxicabs and the qualifications of licensed drivers. The department discontinued its practice of serving "liability notices" to landlords on whose property gamblers and prostitutes had been arrested. Enforcement of liability notices at times generated illegal payoffs from landlords and owners of licensed premises who wanted to avoid wasting time and money by having to appear in court. Subsequently the department eliminated another cause of malfeasance by initiating city-wide contracts to pay for commercial washing of the department's vehicles. Prior to that time, patrolmen usually had "chiseled" free washes, a compromise that obligated them not to enforce Sabbath laws.[75]

Routine inspections of bars and cabarets, carried out under the auspices of laws regulating the sale of alcoholic beverages, were drastically curtailed. Members of the uniformed force were prohibited from entering licensed premises, except in the course of an investigation or in response to a complaint or call for service. Thus inspections were to be conducted only by plainclothesmen and Youth Patrol units and were limited to premises with "high hazard" ratings.[76]

Administrators expanded programs against corruption hazards by changing an adversary relationship to one of participatory management. The commissioner directed his highest-ranking officers to submit detailed reports of their efforts against malfeasance in their commands. Borough and other superior commanders were to identify, in rank order, corruption hazards in their commands and then to develop programs to eliminate hazards. Involvement was the keynote. Commanders were forced to commit themselves periodically in written self-assessments, realizing that failure to recognize hazards would be as professionally damaging as failure to eradicate corruption (see Exhibit S in the appendix).[77]

None of these efforts was lost on the department's rank and file. It was the police commissioner's intention, through his public statements and through pressures created by the coordinated and cumulative impact of his programs, to sustain a broad consciousness of corruption and general feeling of apprehension that might best be described as "functional anxiety." Functional anxiety was a positive fear intended to produce an ethos sufficient to overcome all pressures and incentives toward cooptation. It was viewed as a deterrent against and a brake on individual misconduct because it created fears of discovery and punishment. Functional anxiety could achieve what was beyond the scope of any single policy or procedure. It was perceived as being particularly insidious because it generated fear of discovery by a superior as well as betrayal by one's peers. Not only did it threaten corruption in gambling enforcement, it also restrained many policemen who were forced to quit accepting free meals, soliciting payoffs from merchants, and "cooping." Its moral desirability aside, functional anxiety was indisputably a powerful and effective tool that remained in use throughout the administration's term.

But functional anxiety had substantial costs. First, it created outspoken antagonism against the commissioner. Most officers, including many not involved in illegal activities, resented attacks on the department's integrity and the resultant embarrassment suffered by their families. Even younger members of the force, who agreed with the commissioner's aims, repeatedly avowed that "they would never forgive him for tarnishing their image." Many complained that the administration had gone too far on the corruption issue, that it was time to get back to fighting crime, asking, "Who's going to help us if they believe we're all dishonest?"[78] Second, hostility generated another cost for the administration, a general resistance to programs unrelated to integrity. Resentment added to the usual bureaucratic tendency to resist change. The commissioner's efforts against corruption threatened everything he sought to do.

Moreover, his strict moral tone had to apply to everyone in the department, high and low. Thus the suspension of the chief of detectives, a trusted friend, was necessary after the discovery that he had accepted an expensive free meal. In spite of "official" exoneration of malfeasance, his reinstatement was seen by the rank and file as the administration's application of a double standard, and it weakened the commissioner's most important asset—his credibility.[79]

Career Incentives

Promotion and demotion have always been powerful levers for police administrators. Except for the detective incentive used to attract better candidates for plainclothes, however, this management tool was not used to promote honesty in gambling enforcement during the 1950s and 1960s. In spite of official commitment to the policy of accountability, few commanders suffered because of their subordinates' malfeasance unless the supervisors were personally "on the take." Nor was promotion offered as an inducement or reward for the discovery or thwarting of corrupt practices. A powerful incentive lay idle.

Administrators in the early 1970s relied on career motivation as a useful strategy to promote honesty and ethical behavior. Indeed, there were few more significant incentives than to protect one's high-level post that had been earned over a lifetime in the department. In his initial remarks to his executive corps, the police commissioner identified the touchstone of his strategy for management of personnel–accountability of leaders for the malfeasance of their subordinates. He reemphasized his early admonition with a formal warning to his senior commanders:

> I am dissatisfied with our progress in reducing corruption. I am concerned that too many of you have failed to believe what I have said or to follow my direction. What I said in October was not rhetoric or just for the record! I am determined to make basic changes concerning corruption. If you fail to believe that or act aggressively against corruption, you do so at your peril. . . . It has been said that the Police Commissioner must bite the bullet, regardless of how much it hurts. I intend to do just that, even taking the most personally painful step when necessary of removing any executive who fails to identify and correct his problems.[80]

Although accountability was "old hat" to the department, this administration gave it a new fillip, a commitment that went beyond rhetoric to actual implementation. Because careers were at stake, the commissioner rejected a standard of absolute liability, and determined instead "whether the deficiencies were so serious, repeated or widespread that he [the commander] either knew or by reasonable diligence should have known of them, or that the conditions would not have developed or persisted if he had demonstrated" proper leadership.[81] Later, the range of accountability was expanded from punishment for misdeeds of subordinates to liability for unwillingness to prevent wrongdoing.

During its two and one-half years of tenure, the administration enforced its policy of accountability. Commanders who, in the judgment of the police commissioner, failed to demonstrate initiative or leadership against corruption were forced to retire or accept demotion. Turnover in the executive corps was extremely high. Officials sought to strengthen the corps of senior officers by phasing out those who were found unable or unwilling to prevent corrupt practices.[82]

Subsequently, the concept of accountability was extended to the departmental processes for selection and evaluation. Officers recommending members of the force for "advancement, assignment to specialized units, or to positions of special trust" were to be held accountable for the "soundness of appropriateness of their recommendations." A special committee was created "to examine cases of members assigned to specialized units such as the OCCB who . . . failed to perform as expected" when later they were discovered to be corrupt. Committee members were instructed to review the recommendation that led to the individual's appointment, and a copy of their findings was to be placed in the evaluation folder of the superior officer(s) concerned. Gone were the days of casual recommendations and the "hook," when an individual's connections were all that mattered. Commanders were now compelled to be circumspect because their own advancement would depend in part on the success of their protegés in plainclothes or narcotics.[83]

If career incentives could stimulate high-ranking commanders to exert greater efforts against corrupt practices, administrators reasoned that they also might work with other upwardly mobile individuals. Accordingly, the police commissioner's directive that members of the force arrest any and all who offered bribes was augmented with a program for promotion similar to the detective incentive. Several patrolmen who made notable arrests for bribery were rewarded with immediate promotion to detective, a policy somewhat inconsistent with the Career Path effort. The incentive of a preferred assignment or some other career opportunity produced so many arrests for bribery that officials had to establish a Bribery Arrest Evaluation Board to identify and reward the most deserving people.[84]

By the end of 1973 this scheme for motivation was expanded in scope and scale "to establish a self-perpetuating climate of service and integrity within the department." The basis for recognition was extended beyond resisting the offer of a bribe and arresting the would-be corrupter, to include all acts demonstrating integrity, particularly furnishing information about corrupt practices of other members of the force. Thus the Bribery Arrest Evaluation Board was redesignated the Integrity Review Board. Promotions to detective continued and new rewards were added, including transfer to a desired precinct, waiver of required experience for certain assignments, and the award of the department's medal for "Excellent Police Duty."[85]

Strategies to change individual attitudes and incentives that were applied during the 1950s and 1960s appear to have had practical rather than intellectual limitations. Although the detective incentive and accountability of commanders were established policies, weak implementation undermined their credibility as incentives to promote honesty. Officials made no attempt to change individual attitudes through training or to prepare plainclothesmen for the moral hazards awaiting them. Informal socialization filled the administrative vacuums instead, perpetuating attitudes conducive to continued malfeasance. The use of functional anxiety as a managerial strategy in the early 1970s contrasts sharply with previous efforts to make honesty the norm. It represents a new and perhaps frightening approach to public administration whose implications will be explored in Chapter 5.

Productivity

Quotas of arrests for violations of gambling statutes dominated plainclothesmen's lives. Instead of promoting honest and diligent enforcement, (their ostensible objectives), quotas created myriad forms of corrupt practices. Procedures for evaluating performance, for reimbursement of investigative expenses, and for awarding extra compensation reinforced malfeasance. In the early 1970s reformers sought to eliminate the department's administrative incentives to corruption.

The Need to Produce

For generations, police administrations had been concerned about the volume of arrests produced by the force, especially in enforcement of gambling and public morals laws. Sensitive to the public's charges of inefficiency and corruption, officials believed that perpetual violations in gambling and public morals reflected on the department's credibility and on them personally. Whereas the department never formally established a minimum number of arrests for each plainclothesman, for many years it was an open secret that there were indeed unofficial production norms.

The existence of unofficial quotas for arrest activity was neither haphazard nor accidental; it appears to have been a rational, conscious, and understandable bureaucratic policy. Its rationale was that many arrests of gamblers provided police executives with objective evidence of their good-faith efforts to enforce gambling laws honestly. Administrators also assumed that if plainclothesmen were compelled to arrest gamblers, they would be unable to enter into conspiracies with them and form "pads."

Officials underestimated their adversaries. Gamblers obliged the hierarchy by providing coopted plainclothesmen with stand-ins as well as with "old work" (outdated betting records), so that plainclothesmen still met arrest quotas and appeared to be effective investigators. When departmental pressures compelled quality cases, high-ranking gamblers submitted to prearranged "courtesy arrests" to accommodate plainclothesmen, knowing that the charges would be minor or that a legal "hole" allowing for acquittal would be left in police testimony.

To promote honest enforcement, in fact and appearance, high-ranking administrators often relied on timely campaigns against gambling. Concern at higher levels spread through the department, especially the plainclothes force, like ripples in a pond. When headquarters' squads made arrests for violations of gambling laws, or if statistics of arrests were low, officials assumed immediately that the plainclothes force or individual units were lax or had been compromised. In these circumstances, administrators only had to remind borough commanders that arrest activity in their jurisdictions would be the basis of their own assignments and promotions, and this "understanding" flashed down the chain of command from borough and division commanders to all plainclothesmen.

Statistics of arrest and convictions for the plainclothes force underwent regular scrutiny, usually in comparison with the previous year's results. Underachieving squads and individuals had to increase production "to a figure comparable to that of other units." Each plainclothesman was evaluated by his commander for his "contribution" to the unit's total performance. Thus productivity, a questionable guide to a plainclothesman's dedication, was an ubiquitous tool for the promotion of ethical behavior in gambling enforcement.[86]

"The Sheet"

Although the Gambling Enforcement Inspection and Review Board touched on the idea of establishing minimums for production to foster efficiency and to define reasonable amounts of work for plainclothesmen, board members never considered the subject seriously. Nevertheless, unofficial but real quotas for production were perpetuated by the department's procedures for reporting. Throughout the 1950s and early 1960s (and indeed for many years earlier), each plainclothes squad's daily arrest and summons activity was reported by telephone to the borough office every morning. After being collated, statistics were forwarded to police headquarters, where they were consolidated into a daily, city-wide summary on gambling enforcement. Because of its single-page format, the report was known throughout the department as "the sheet" (see Exhibit T in the appendix). In addition to the daily report, each command forwarded to police headquarters a monthly summary of statistics. Although prepared for the chief inspector and the police commissioner, more likely than not the sheet was infrequently seen, though well known to them.[87]

In 1962 the sheet was officially designated the "Daily Report for Public Morals Enforcement Activity." Still consolidated at headquarters, the sheet was expanded to include more information about defendants, their position in the gambling hierarchy, details of the arrest, and descriptions of evidence seized. Probably a more significant change was that squads had to file "negative reports" reflecting the absence of arrest or summons activity, a requirement that called unwanted attention to commands where there was little activity for several days.[88] Except for these modifications, basic procedures for reporting remained unchanged in spite of updating in the mid-1960s and in 1970.

As one might expect, every squad felt compelled to justify its existence by "covering the sheet." Consciousness of the need to produce is well illustrated in the following anecdote, recounted by a now high-ranking officer who vividly remembered his introduction to the sheet.

I was a division lieutenant. I walked in, it was my first or second night, I think. I went to the men's room and while I was urinating, another man came in. He was the deputy or the inspector. After we introduced ourselves, he said, "Are we on the sheet?" That's what happened—we were still standing at the urinals. When I answered, "What's the sheet?" he added, "Are we on—are we making collars?" Well, that was my first experience with the sheet. At first I didn't know what it was and then, in six months' time, I would come in and the first words out of my mouth were, "Are we on the sheet?" I used to yell that down the hall. Of course, the word was that you didn't have to cover the sheet, but when you didn't, some higher-up would call to ask "How come there's nothing on the sheet?" So, in other words, you had to be on the sheet, that was manifest from the top all the way down to the bottom. That sheet had to be covered even with an ABC or some drunken bum in the Bowery. That's how bad it was.[89]

Some squad commanders further institutionalized pressures for arrests by posting statistical charts that compared each plainclothesman's activity for the current year with his results in corresponding months of the previous year. To many plainclothesmen, this was the real sheet.

Results of the Sheet

Ubiquitous pressures to produce or "get on the sheet" generated two significant results in gambling enforcement: gross inefficiencies and a variety of unethical practices.

Inefficiency in the plainclothes force stemmed from competition for arrests, which precluded teamwork within squads because each individual had to accumulate his own statistics. Plainclothesmen were discouraged from conducting prolonged investigations that might have produced quality arrests of high-echelon gamblers because of the need to maintain competitive "batting averages" through quick arrests—hence quality was sacrificed for quantity. Coordinated investigations based on long surveillances were bypassed for "jump collars," in which plainclothesmen simply confronted gamblers in the street, searched them, and subsequently arrested them if they had incriminating betting records. The effectiveness of wiretaps was similarly weakened because plainclothesmen made arrests after overhearing minimally incriminating conversations instead of waiting to develop evidence inculpating other people in the gambling enterprise.

To keep up appearances for themselves and their squads, plainclothesmen made numerous "garbage arrests," apprehending many unimportant members of gambling hierarchies. Even borough and division members, supposedly the experienced core of the plainclothes force, were guilty of making low-level arrests (including players in dice games on the street) to cover the sheet. Practices of splitting arrests among teams of plainclothesmen and sharing multiple arrests to maintain equity in statistics wasted thousands of man-hours that could have been used in quality investigations had only one plainclothesman been required to appear in court. All these inefficiencies resulted from the need to cover the sheet so that plainclothesmen and their commanders would not be put on the defensive, or even worse, arouse headquarters' suspicions.[90]

What were the unethical practices generated by the need to cover the sheet? The following anecdote reflects behaviors typical of plainclothes squads.

> The unfortunate part of our need to cover the sheet was that we made low-quality arrests. So, at 8 A.M. when the tour began, the squad supervisor would say, "All right, fellows, go out and let's see if we can cover the sheet." If someone was fortunate enough to make a bookmaking arrest in the morning or a policy arrest after noon, the sheet would be covered, which eased the pressure on the rest of the squad to make an arrest that day. Then, the men could spend time amassing evidence or getting a search warrant or wiretap, or they could conduct surveillances in connection with communications they had been assigned. At the end of the day, 5 or 6 o'clock, the lieutenant would notify the night team if there weren't any arrests made yet. Then it would be incumbent on these men to cover the sheet with some violation. They would go out to look for a homosexual or a prostitute to arrest. If at 12 o'clock nothing much had happened, they would run into some social club and arrest men for gambling or for disorderly conduct when, in fact, the men weren't really doing anything but playing cards.[91]

Making expedient arrests was widespread, but not the least of the unethical procedures used by plainclothesmen. Another illegal practice, probably the most commonplace, involved false reporting. Because plainclothesmen lacked time to conduct investigations of assigned known gamblers (KGs) and still remain competitive for promotion, they sacrificed activities that produced few arrests to concentrate on productivity. They "covered" all nonfeasance by reporting, for example, that surveillance of the KG or suspected premises had been conducted but that no violation had been observed ("NVO"). Plainclothesmen occasionally juggled the numbers of their arrests by padding totals on monthly activity reports, a dangerous practice should they have been called to account. They risked the consequences nevertheless, believing that their superiors, interested only in numbers, accepted them at face value. To make it appear that they were producing quality cases, plainclothesmen also distorted records of arrests, misrepresenting low-level gamblers as higher-echelon figures. Occasionally, facts were exaggerated so that misdemeanors became felonies. The crime charged at the time of arrest was the determinative fact statistically, not the ultimate disposition in court.[92]

Unethical behavior generated by the sheet had its lighter moments, too. When an ABC summons was needed to meet the month's quota, a plainclothesman might steal the soap from a tavern's restroom. Minutes later, his partner would issue a summons for "no soap in the washroom." No doubt patrons were puzzled later when they found a bar of soap nailed to the washroom wall.

On the whole, the plainclothesman's lot was not happy, considering pressures generated by the sheet and resulting personal tension and frustrations. Because of their conflicts, many of them felt compelled to compromise themselves, even to commit courtroom perjury. To some extent, the problem of police perjury was a response to the Supreme Court's decision of 1961 (*Mapp v. Ohio*) that prohibited use of illegally seized evidence in state courts. Prior to the decision, plainclothesmen usually relied on "jump collars"–informal confrontations in the street–to maintain arrest quotas. They sometimes engaged in a more unscrupulous practice, "flaking," in which they planted evidence on suspects and justified the action to themselves by rationalizing that the people were guilty anyway. The Supreme Court's ruling posed a serious dilemma because whereas plainclothesmen could no longer introduce betting records seized illegally during an arrest, they still faced the same norms of production. Although police executives condemned the ruling because of its implications, they did not reduce pressures to produce.[93]

To resolve their dilemma, plainclothesmen at times resorted to perjury. Instead of testifying truthfully that they found betting records in the suspect's pocket, they swore under oath in the arrest affidavit that as they approached the gambler, he either dropped the work, tried to hide it somewhere, or that he was observed accepting bets. Having made such allegations, plainclothesmen hoped that the gambler would accept arrest stoically and pay his fine, regarding it as a necessary business expense, and not waste his time in court. But if the gambler pleaded "not guilty," requiring the officer to testify at a trial, the plainclothesman, having committed himself in the arrest affidavit, was forced to repeat his lie under oath.

As alternatives to perjury some plainclothesmen failed to appear in court, allowing charges to be dismissed, whereas others chose to leave a legal loophole in their affidavit through which the gambler could win acquittal. Still others weakened their testimony, "conceding" under cross-examination that their observations were obscured or that they failed to have the defendant under continuous surveillance. Adulterations of testimony precluded convictions that gamblers might appeal. A coopted plainclothesman sometimes used the same tactic if there were no stand-in provided for a gambler he had to arrest, or if he had been "reached" after making a legitimate arrest.[94]

As more plainclothesmen repeated almost identical accounts of how the gambler dropped the evidence to the ground at the moment of arrest, these so-called "dropsy" cases further eroded the plainclothes force's credibility. After the administrative judge of the city magistrates' court alerted police officials to these delinquent practices, the Gambling Enforcement Inspection and Review Board developed a series of supervisory measures to control the problem. At the same time, the courts began scrutinizing all affidavits for arrests and search warrants.

Denied the expedient "dropsy" ruse, plainclothesmen began to rely more heavily on informants to substantiate applications for arrest and search warrants. Due process required police to submit affidavits stating specifically their probable cause to believe that a particular person or premises was involved in illegal gambling. To prevent new abuses, the courts demanded that an informant be "of proven reliability," meaning that he should have furnished accurate information on previous occasions. To establish such reliability, plainclothesmen would attribute past jump collars and convictions to their tipsters (see Exhibit U in the appendix). Having thus proved "reliability," plainclothesmen could substantiate future requests for warrants on information falsely imputed to the informant. Misuse of the system took other forms, including preparation of affidavits based on allegations ascribed to fictitious sources. These unethical practices were no secret in the department.[95]

In 1970, after years of indecision, the department implemented controls that swung the pendulum to the opposite extreme—members of the force were required to fingerprint and register all informants. By imposing stringent requirements, the department apparently intended to squelch the use of informants altogether. Officials succeeded; no informants were registered.[96] The policy served only to drive the use of informants underground and undoubtedly created new abuses because plainclothesmen then needed personal funds to pay unregistered sources.

More realistic controls for the use of informants were subsequently adopted by the OCCB, although they were intended primarily for narcotics enforcement rather than for gambling. Rarely could the Public Morals Division develop informers in organized gambling because police had nothing to offer; fines were so small and jail sentences so infrequent that gamblers had little inducement to cooperate. In narcotics enforcement, however, informants were needed and could be cultivated. Because the stringent regulations calling for registration of all informants were self-defeating, the OCCB liberalized them in 1973. Rules still required the central registration of informants, along with controls for using them and safeguarding their anonymity, but they eliminated unduly restrictive requirements.[97]

Of all the reforms adopted by the administrations of the early 1970s to modify attitudes and incentives, none had a more dramatic impact on honest and ethical enforcement of the gambling laws than those related to productivity. Officials disavowed publicly the department's past incentives to corruption and undertook to correct them. Reorganization of the enforcement program in public morals was predicated on a renewed emphasis on quality enforcement. Commanders of gambling (and narcotics) units were directed "to preclude any type of 'quota' system which might have encouraged such past practices as 'flaking,' false testimony, and 'stand-in' arrests." Officially, the department had always emphasized high-echelon arrests in gambling enforcement; this blunt reiteration was intended to convince the force that the administration meant what it said.[98]

The OCCB commander's first policy memo broached these subjects with a frankness unknown in communications to the force. He did not mince words when he announced, early in 1972, "One of the main objectives of my administration has been to eliminate any administrative incentives to corruption. . . . No officer of this command will be required to do anything which is not honest and/or not legal. . . . It is the policy of this command: To eliminate the 'sheet' and any implications to be drawn from the maintenance of the 'sheet.' "[99] This theme became the OCCB's cornerstone—illegal enforcement would be neither encouraged nor tolerated. Of course plainclothesmen were wary of the new deputy commissioner, but he felt that they would welcome this innovation; no longer would they have to commit unethical or criminal acts to survive. He had to convince the plainclothes force that the administration was sincere. To implement his policy, he made drastic changes in the OCCB's procedures for gambling enforcement, particularly in reporting and supervisory practices, which we will survey in the following chapter.

Evaluation

Pressures for productivity generated by the sheet were reinforced by other administrative policies. As a result of a recommendation by the GEIRB in 1962, the department adopted a program for evaluating plainclothesmen. Semiannual evaluations in March and September afforded commanding officers "the opportunity to appraise objectively the value of each man's contribution to the team effort." Besides having to check off appropriate comments on individual traits, commanders had to appraise and rank the plainclothesmen in numerical order beginning with the best. Advancement to the Detective Division hinged on being rated first or second in the squad. It was common for plainclothesmen to rise in ranking suddenly as their four-year tenure ended and they were being considered for promotion. But commanders unwilling to lose their best people frequently listed their most effective investigators third and fourth in the squad. Although their recommendation for detective was delayed, these plainclothesmen enjoyed the esteem of their peers and were later rewarded with choice assignments or more rapid advancement within the Detective Division.[100]

The most insidious element in the program was the evaluation report itself, because most of the form called for a statistical summary of the individual's arrests in each category of gambling and public morals offenses (see Exhibit V in the appendix). It was no surprise, then, that the number of arrests became the sole basis of all evaluations and rankings. Commanders relied entirely on raw figures and evaluative impressions of the quality of arrests. Use of statistics was acceptable to the plainclothes force as a more equitable means of evaluation than a commander's subjective opinions and personal relationships. Statistics allowed equal opportunity for high ranking. And semiofficial arrest quotas also served as useful parameters to check unbridled competition, preventing the eager from establishing records that could not be matched the following year. Of course, plainclothesmen tried to stay near the upper limits of the quota to achieve higher ratings.

The form did not convey any realistic estimate of the individual's effectiveness as an investigator. The space provided for narrative evaluations was generally filled with vague and stereotyped comments patterned to fit the person's numerical ranking. Commanders disliked having to express critical or negative views lest they offend subordinates and reduce efficiency, so they too were receptive to using statistics as the determining criterion. Thus the system of evaluation intensified pressure for quantity instead of quality in gambling enforcement, placing the highest premium on quick results rather than on diligent and ethical investigative procedures.[101]

In the OCCB during the early 1970s, procedures for evaluating performance were revised to eliminate the "productivity mentality."[102] Gone were "score sheet" forms on which commanders listed each plainclothesman's arrests and ranked him accordingly. Statistics of arrest were out. Instead, commanders were to evaluate plainclothesmen on integrity and performance as measured by prescribed criteria, including:

1. the number of cases in which they developed significant information for their investigative team
2. the number of "quality arrests" made by their team
3. the number of "incomplete, erroneous" investigations they made
4. the amount of money, guns, drugs, or gambling equipment they seized
5. the interrogation skills they demonstrated by the contribution of significant information received from suspects and witnesses
6. their preparation of reports and handling of evidence
7. their testimony in court and conviction rate
8. a plethora of personal qualities such as intelligence, education, and ability to work with fellow officers[103]

Supervisors were directed to keep records on each person they rated in preparation for defending their judgments with concrete evidence, not statistics of arrests. Efforts such as these were intended to eliminate the sheet as the primary motivation in gambling law enforcement.

Investigator's Compensation and Expenses

Reinforcing norms of production throughout the 1950s and 1960s was a program that offered rewards to plainclothesmen (and other patrolmen) for outstanding work. Those selected were awarded $389 per year as "extra compensation" for their efforts. In the mid-1960s, thirty-five of the department's seventy-one available designations for extra compensation were held by members of the 579 plainclothes force. Whereas the award added only one dollar per day to income, these stipends were actively sought and created more competition in the squads. Because the allowance was usually given to the highest-ranked plainclothesman, the policy helped sustain the emphasis on arrest activity.

In 1965 the Gambling Enforcement Inspection and Review Board recommended that eighty-five new designations be awarded to the plainclothes force. The board was hoping to establish greater parity with detectives who received additional pay ranging from $700 to several thousand dollars. An increase was justified, according to the board, because plainclothes work demanded "a high sense of integrity and unquestioned loyalty to the department." Pressures to retain their extra compensation from other specialized units, such as the Aviation and Communications Bureaus and the Emergency Service Division, prevailed and precluded increases for the plainclothes force.[104]

In a related area of policy, administrators realized that to associate with gamblers and other violators of public morals statutes, plainclothesmen had to spend money to place bets, to buy alcoholic beverages, to engage a prostitute, and, most important, to pay informants. Officials feared that unless these funds were provided, the plainclothesmen would find other sources, not necessarily legal ones, to cover expenses. Plainclothesmen were thus authorized to claim monthly reimbursement for personal funds used in the course of each investigation. Expenditures were itemized on an expense voucher, approved by the commanding officer, and submitted to police headquarters for payment. There were few restrictions on how the money could be spent—the only official one was that no one could exceed $100 in a month's time without specific approval from the commissioner. As one might expect, the inadequacy of this system generated a unique array of unethical procedures and practices that were common knowledge in the plainclothes force.

Underlying inequities were, first, that plainclothesmen had to spend personal funds instead of receiving advances from the department. Second, the $100 monthly limitation was illusory because plainclothesmen could not hope to cover daily costs, including maintenance for their personal automobiles, with that sum. In many cases they actually spent more than they could recover legitimately, a hardship for their families on a plainclothesman's salary. The department's insincerity toward expenses was evidenced in its secretive attitude toward payments to informants and its failure to provide the force with automobiles, a necessary tool for gambling enforcement. These unrealistic, even hypocritical, policies bred new forms of systematic false reporting.

Because unwritten policy required that claimed expenditures be justified by production, plainclothesmen could not submit vouchers listing large payments to informants or expenses for vehicle maintenance. Monetary quotas were tied to arrests; unofficial norms allowed reimbursement of a prescribed amount of money for a particular type of arrest. A bookmaker or controller, for example, was worth $25 to $50; a policy runner was worth $15 to $25; and lesser amounts were claimed for prostitutes or ABC summonses. Ironically, quality cases were sometimes made without spending any money, yet substantial amounts were spent without contributing to any significant arrests. The procedure evolved to the point where expense vouchers bore little or no relation to legitimate investigative expenditures. Even so, plainclothesmen submitted vouchers with no sense of guilt because they had in fact spent the money, not necessarily in the manner stated.

Misuse of expense vouchers had less discernible but more ominous ramifications. Plainclothesmen who could not manipulate their accounts "correctly" relied on the squad's clerical staff to help them complete vouchers with acceptable fabrications to reclaim expenses. This unhealthy dependence strengthened the clerical staff's monopoly of expertise. More importantly, plainclothesmen believed officials knew how the system actually worked and were content to have it continue in that manner.[105]

Although designed to answer specific needs, the system of expense vouchers compromised plainclothesmen, reinforcing their cynicism and leaving them disposed towards unethical practices as a means of coping with the pressure of the sheet.

Shortly after its inception, the OCCB revised these practices, committing the department to reimburse all plainclothesmen for legitimate investigative expenses, including those resulting from use of personal automobiles. Officials first created allowances for disbursements with stringent requirements for reporting. After almost one year's experience, the OCCB improved procedures further by providing investigators with an advance allowance of funds, discarding the traditional policy of reimbursement. Investigators had to account daily for their expenditures out of a $200 monthly advance. For the first time, they could officially pay their confidential informants if they were registered, and guidelines were established to request large payments when justified. Thus they were no longer induced to lie or to compromise themselves because of hypocritical administrative procedures that prompted corrupt practices.[106]

In summary, compelling productivity as a means of limiting collusive resistance between plainclothesmen and gamblers was counterproductive. Although officials succeeded in influencing individual behavior, they failed to cope with the strategies' malfunctional consequences. Indeed, much of the reform effort of the early 1970s was directed at eliminating the department's administrative incentives to corruption, diverting substantial energy from the external threat of organized gamblers.

4 The Control Strategies: 1950-1975

Where directive strategies failed to achieve honesty, the department invoked other mechanisms to contain malpractice. Control strategies had straightforward objectives: to limit opportunities for corrupt practice, to discover collusion of police with gamblers, and to punish offenders. To secure these goals officials relied on a mix of procedures, principally:

1. reporting misconduct and investigative activities
2. supervising personnel
3. discovering cooptation
4. imposing sanctions

Control strategies followed one theme to influence organizational behavior: "detecting and discouraging deviations" from official policies.[1] They came into play to close the "performance gaps" between prescribed and actual enforcement of gambling laws.

Reporting

Misconduct of Peers

Control strategies were based on a painful assessment of police behavior because experience compelled administrators to assume that corruption did exist. The earliest control strategy, dating back over 100 years, required all members of the force to report their colleagues' misconduct—corrupt acts, abuses of authority, even errors in judgment. This policy was based on the assumptions that policemen frequently observed misconduct of fellow officers and that mandatory reporting made it easier for members of the force to come forward rather than to risk punishment by remaining silent. Thus every policeman was supposed to be a potential source of information.[2]

The vast majority of policemen, not only plainclothesmen, were traditionally reluctant to comply with the regulation. Aversion to reporting misconduct had many explanations, including fears of discrediting the department itself and intense loyalty to coworkers, a camaraderie bred from a shared defensive attitude vis-à-vis the public. Most policemen held "live and let live" attitudes, recognizing that they too had committed professional peccadilloes. Few were willing to jeopardize their own careers by reporting others' mistakes. Common to all was the fear of being branded an informer—in police jargon, being "marked lousy"—and ostracized by fellow officers, for peer pressure was a formidable influence. Officials never forced the issue, however, fearing that policies severe enough to overcome the norm of silence would create a debilitating atmosphere of suspicion and mistrust. Throughout the 1950s and 1960s there was virtually no reporting of malpractice by policemen themselves.[3]

After the press reported widespread and institutionalized corruption among plainclothesmen in mid-1970, the police commissioner reminded all members of the force of their obligation to report violations of the *Rules and Procedures.* He gave police unprecedented permission to furnish information directly to the city's district attorneys or Department of Investigation (DOI) without notifying the department beforehand. The policemen were assured that "no reprisals of any kind will be permitted against a member of this department who comes forward with such information." Ordered not to investigate cases forwarded to the Department of Investigation, commanders soon flooded them with allegations of malfeasance to the point that the DOI could not manage the workload.[4]

Shortly after its installation, the new administration sought a firm hold on the department's activities against corruption. Recognizing that information was the key to eliminating corrupt practices, officials centralized input and processing of all intelligence related to unethical behavior. Notification to the Department of Investigation was discontinued and members of the force were instructed to report indications of possible corruption to the Internal Affairs Division (IAD), which was directed by the first deputy commissioner. The IAD's telephone number was published in newspapers to encourage the public to come forward, too.[5]

Information received by Internal Affairs was assessed, indexed, and disseminated. Material of a purely intelligence nature (that is, not useful for prosecution) was filed for future use. Allegations of wrongdoing were sent to appropriate field commanders for investigation. In an important change of policy, complaints of gambling were withheld from the OCCB's public morals squads until the IAD verified or disproved allegations of malpractice so that bookmaking and numbers investigations would not hinder discovery of corruption.[6]

In keeping with renewed emphasis on reporting malfeasance, the OCCB's investigators were directed "to report any matter which they had seen, any conversation which they had heard, or any matter of which they had knowledge from which one might reasonably infer that corrupt practices might be engaged in by personnel of this Department."[7] The OCCB's officials hoped that reaffirmation of policy, supported by improved procedures in enforcement and supervision, would overcome the traditional reluctance to reveal wrongdoing. In general the policy did not succeed; policemen remained hesitant to act or to become involved in anticorruption efforts. Indeed, in the mid-1970s administrators reprimanded the OCCB force for "not reporting and processing allegations of corruption or serious misconduct" that it had received.[8] Few policemen came forward to report their peers' misconduct, although in one instance investigators in the OCCB exposed their district commander for bending procedural rules—cutting the corners that lead to corrupt practices. He was relieved of command.

Personal Activities

While administrators were not able to induce policemen to report on their peers, officials required each person to account for his own activities. Beginning in 1954, plainclothesmen were required to maintain personal memorandum books to keep a daily chronological record of work performed and to make contemporaneous entries of all events. The memo book was to serve as a diary of investigative action, of details about arrests, patrols, inspections, and court appearances. Official entries were also admissable in evidence to support policemen's testimony at trials. Plainclothesmen also had to keep their superiors continually informed of their whereabouts by calling the squad office at a given time each hour. (Such calls were known as "rings.") Officials sought to limit opportunities for collusion by this constant accounting for on-duty activities, when police were most likely to contact gamblers. Plainclothesmen rarely obeyed the rules, however. Accustomed to considerable freedom in their investigative work, both supervisors and plainclothesmen viewed the regulation as administrative nonsense.

Police officials asserted that memo books were useful adjuncts for preparing reports, refreshing memories for court testimony, and avoiding duplication of investigative efforts in case of transfer or illness. And books could be used to help refute civilian complaints alleging misconduct. Whereas these justifications were valid, the department intended memo books to promote honesty and ethical behavior as well. If required to account for their time, plainclothesmen who were engaged in nefarious dealings would be forced to fabricate a complete pattern of activity, which would be vulnerable to refutation.

Members of the force believed that the use of memo books was a sham, especially because even diligent officers could not keep the book up-to-date because of the pace of investigative work. Thus record keeping became part of the administrative charade the force was compelled to play. Plainclothesmen regarded memo books as weapons to be used against them; whenever there was an allegation of corruption, the department's investigating unit first reviewed the suspected officer's memo books. Caught in such an emergency, the dishonest officer would either hastily update the book or substitute a nonincriminating duplicate.

Because the plainclothesmen found ways to defeat the intended control of the memo book, officials imposed restrictions regarding its use and maintenance.

To eliminate false and postdated entries, officials prohibited plainclothesmen from leaving blank spaces on any page, skipping pages, or tearing out or inserting pages. As a further check, squad commanders were supposed to review and initial memo books every day. More stringent rules, applied later, required that books be registered and numbered serially, so that rewritten books could not be substituted during subsequent investigations. To prevent plainclothesmen from keeping dual sets of books, supervisors had to authorize the opening and closing of books with their signatures. Completed books were held by the department for five years beyond the plainclothesman's tenure, a strategy designed to prevent "convenient losses." After five years books were returned to their owners.[9]

Understandably, all plainclothesmen were circumspect about their entries. Because of their fears, the majority practiced certain deceptions, protecting themselves by minimizing potentially damaging information in their books. The most commonly used ploy was vagueness and imprecision. For example, they would cite a case and indicate that observations at the suspect location were unproductive: "NVO"–no violation observed (see Exhibit W in the appendix). Also, plainclothesmen kept their books "open," meaning they did not make entries until their investigations had reached some conclusive development. Partners waited several days or even a few weeks before jointly updating their books, carefully dovetailing information to avoid discrepancies. Obviously, investigating officials were suspicious when two plainclothesmen differed in their accounts of the same event.

Delay also allowed plainclothesmen an opportunity to cover themselves by adding self-serving material in case there were unforeseen circumstances, legitimate or otherwise. An individual might embellish his narrative of an arrest or search, for example, to show that he had followed departmental rules and procedures in processing the case, a useful history when defendants alleged some infringement of due process. After making an arrest, plainclothesmen could insert fictitious "prior observations" to show probable cause to support the arrest. They used the same technique to secure search warrants.

In spite of the rule that supervisors were to read and initial memo books each day, plainclothesmen had a variety of legitimate excuses for postponing entries. Supervisors were not always in the office at the end of their subordinates' tours, and sometimes they were absent because of official business or vacations. Distracted by other concerns, they knowingly neglected their responsibility to review and sign books. These well-known shortcomings notwithstanding, the Gambling Enforcement Inspection and Review Board recommended that plainclothes supervisors below the rank of captain keep their own memo books "to increase the quality of supervision and to provide a permanent record of duty performed." Rather than improve the quality of supervision, however, the requirement drew supervisors further into the system of fraudulent reporting.[10]

Reporting was continued by the new administrations into the 1970s. As before, plainclothesmen had to submit detailed reports on their activities each day. The Public Morals Division (PMD) required commanders to establish daily "ring" schedules that kept their people in telephone contact with district supervisors. When district offices were closed, plainclothesmen had to call the OCCB's Administrative Division, which was open around the clock.

In a significant break with the past, however, the traditional memorandum book was discarded in 1971 and replaced in 1972 by a new investigator's Daily Activity Report (DAR). All plainclothesmen and their superiors were required to complete DARs, which were almost identical to memo books in substance, if not in form, and served the same purposes. In addition to the usual minute-by-minute account of activities, DARs also required plainclothesmen to list daily investigative disbursements. Mandatory accounting eliminated end-of-the-month scrambles to balance necessary expenditures with arrests, and it brought a semblance of honesty to the system of reclaiming expenses.

In spite of surface similarities between memo books and DARs, there were some genuine improvements in reporting to make DARs a more reliable control mechanism. Plainclothesmen were allowed to complete DARs at the end of their tours, not immediately after each activity. This accommodation was realistic because it did not cause noncompliance at the outset. In a significant yet simple change, DARs had to be forwarded to the OCCB's Administrative Division at the end of the tour of duty or the next day at the latest. Investigators could no longer keep records "open" to modify narratives days or weeks later in light of subsequent developments. They had to commit themselves to the facts promptly.[11]

Even with improvements, the DAR was no panacea. Imprecise reporting still haunted the system. Whereas previous administrations had tolerated the problem, officials in the OCCB drummed out one message to their people—to be specific. And after less than one year in use, the DAR was revised to solicit more investigative detail for supervisory purposes. Plainclothesmen had to explain why they visited the district attorney's office, the property clerk, the police laboratory, or criminal court. They had to list each other's names in their DARs and had to give descriptions of their private automobiles used on official business—information needed for surveillance by the OCCB's Field Control Division. Officials made it unmistakably clear that DARs would be verified.[12]

Investigative Activities

Throughout the 1950s and 1960s, officials imposed strict procedures for reporting investigative activities as well. Promptness in reporting was intended to eliminate opportunities to falsify or subsequently weaken incriminating evidence. Forcing plainclothesmen to commit themselves in writing without delay was supposed to discourage them from engaging in corrupt practices, including extortion (offers to "forget" arrests) and the selling of "work" back to gamblers. Requirements for specific accountings were to prevent subsequent embellishments or deletions.

Administrators in the mid-1950s instituted stringent procedures to control processing of known gamblers, beginning with the immediate reporting of arrests of KGs. General investigative activities relating to KGs, hard-core locations, and communications had to be fully described on report forms that supplemented personal memo books.[13] It was no accident that the printed forms had a unique proviso, warning plainclothesmen that "falsification of any statement made herein is an offense, punishable by a fine or imprisonment or both" (see Exhibits L and M in the appendix).

As further safeguards, plainclothesmen had to submit detailed affidavits describing each arrest of a gambler, one copy of which was given to their commanding officer, who reviewed entries for accuracy. Desk officers in the precincts of the arrest were required to forward a copy of blotter entries to plainclothes commanders, a procedure intended to ensure that neither gamblers nor evidence was released. Commanders were supposed to verify that testimony in subsequent prosecution coincided with details in affidavits to prevent plainclothesmen from cooperating with gamblers.[14]

Over the years, officials were forced to develop new procedures to control wiretapping, a vulnerable tool subject to abuses such as extortion. Plainclothesmen first needed their superiors' permission to apply for court authorization to tap a telephone line. After obtaining a wiretapping warrant, they were required, when monitoring the tap, to record all intercepted communications, to safeguard recordings, and to report their contents. Commanders were obligated to file monthly accounts of the number of orders for wiretaps, dates of their use, and results achieved in terms of arrests.[15]

Systems of investigative reporting were often easily thwarted, as was the memo book, as administrative controls. To protect themselves, plainclothesmen used a vague, stereotyped format in their narratives. In a typical account, consisting of a few paragraphs, the officer described the suspect premises and presented a history of past arrests made in that location. He then listed new observations, with dates and times, and concluded with the standard "NVO" (no violations observed), after which he recommended that the matter be filed. Supervisors usually accepted these "formula" statements at face value.[16]

Plainclothesmen wrote memoranda on KGs in similar noncommittal style, claiming that when they located the individual (although they often did not), they observed no violation. Many of these accounts were blatantly fictitious, a result of plainclothesmen's burdensome responsibilities and the department's unrealistic standards. Frequently, two plainclothesmen would sign forms jointly, making it difficult for supervisors to determine who had done the investigation. To meet demands for "quality arrests," they sometimes characterized low-level gamblers as important figures. They justified perfunctory narratives as their only means of meeting the department's "volume" requirements. Underlying such rationalizations was the widespread belief that records were used only as sources for statistics, that numbers were all that mattered.[17] The plainclothesmen thought they had little to fear from false submissions because their superiors were not concerned with truthful details. Procedures for reporting thus imposed no controls and were ineffective tools against corruption.

In the early 1970s officials made a strong bid to rejuvenate investigative accounting. They replaced the traditional "Public Morals Investigation Report" with a revised form on which plainclothesmen were to submit separate statements on each case or communication they investigated. As before, forms called for detailed information. Two or more people covering the same case were required to file individual accounts. More important, they had to submit these forms immediately after each tour of duty, not at the conclusion of the case, to prevent subsequent additions or deletions. Administrators relied on improved supervisory procedures to support their new system for reporting.[18]

Individual memos were supplemented by squad reports. Early in 1972, the Public Morals Division directed that there be more reporting to it. Public morals district offices had to call PMD headquarters by 10 a.m., Monday through Saturday, to submit oral accounts of each arrest made. "Negative reports" were filed, too. In appearance, this procedure resembled the sheet. OCCB officials were quick to assert, however, that there was no substantive pressure for investigators to make arrests. Instead, the Organized Crime Control Bureau's leaders held monthly meetings with commanders to review progress on active cases. Daily telephone calls were intended only to inform the OCCB's officials of progress made in these cases. Thus any pressures on commanders to make arrests were not ostensibly generated by the system of reporting, as officials claimed to have eliminated the mentality of the sheet.[19]

Administrators also tried to strengthen controls related to search warrants. Under modified procedures, supervisors in the OCCB had to approve a comprehensive Search Warrant Investigation Report and verify sufficient probable cause to prevent perjury and subsequent invalidation by the courts.[20] This new requirement, as well as those for DARs and investigative reports, were probably less important than related changes in the strategy of supervision that underlay all reporting.

Financial Questionnaires

Questionnaires requiring listings of all personal assets were widely used by the Brooklyn grand jury that investigated police cooptation in the Gross case in the early 1950s. Subpoenaed witnesses had to complete twenty-three pages with information about savings, personal property, and real estate holdings. In the early 1960s the Gambling Enforcement Inspection and Review Board adopted a similar questionnaire, called the "Plainclothes Survey Form," and directed all plainclothesmen to disclose their assets. But the board did not verify completed forms. Subsequently, it established a continuing program involving financial questionnaires for the plainclothes force, asking for updated information to determine "whether a man had incurred liabilities that were not consistent with his income." Discrepancies were supposed to have been investigated by the plainclothesman's commanding officer, but as before, no information was verified.[21]

In spite of officials' neglect, the use of this control came under attack when members of the force challenged the legality of questionnaires. In a formal brief, the director of the department's legal bureau advised the GEIRB that according to legal precedents, financial questionnaires could not be used for nonspecific purposes or "fishing expeditions," nor could officials demand unreasonable amounts of detail and general information. The director further maintained that without probable cause the police commissioner lacked authority to require the entire department to complete the questionnaire. He concluded that the existing twenty-six page survey form was "oppressive, too long, too detailed, and unreasonable in fact and law."[22] This counsel notwithstanding, the board periodically reissued survey forms to the plainclothes force.

In 1967, use of the questionnaire was expanded as members of the Police Commissioner's Confidential Investigating Unit and the Chief Inspector's Investigating Unit were required to answer the survey, too. The board was also challenged by the Captains' Endowment Association on this policy of requiring superior officers to complete the questionnaire. Although concerned about creating a double standard within the plainclothes force, the board compromised, allowing captains and those of higher rank to "decline to answer questions at their option as they had in the past."[23]

Obviously, the questionnaire offered only a limited means of control. The GEIRB realized that coopted plainclothesmen would never list assets acquired illegally—people willing to risk their careers would not hesitate to submit false information. But the survey did have some genuine objectives: It established a financial base for any investigation of a plainclothesman's assets, and it provided grounds for dismissal when unexplainable wealth was discovered during investigations of corruption. The department's inaction, however, undermined these objectives because the reports were never verified, just filed. Coopted policemen thus remained free to lie and conceal illegal assets.[24]

Administrators continued to use financial surveys into the 1970s. The commissioner demanded questionnaires from all superior officers in appointed ranks above captain (deputy inspector, inspector, deputy chief inspector, and assistant chief inspector) to assure their "past integrity" and to aid in making promotions and assignments. New plainclothesmen and supervisors in the OCCB had to complete an "Original Personnel Survey," a financial statement. Thereafter, each investigator completed a "Semi-Annual Personnel Survey" in April and October. As in the past, however, disclosures were not verified or checked routinely. Filed at the OCCB's Administrative Division, the forms were available for review during investigations of corruption.[25]

Overall, reporting was a nominal strategy for controlling plainclothesmen's behavior. Officials tolerated the rank and file's code of silence regarding corrupt practices. Requirements for immediate, detailed accounts were thwarted by the use of stereotyped narratives, and only a weak gesture was made in demanding financial disclosure. Reformers in the early 1970s adopted simple yet effective improvements in self-reporting, but they made their most dramatic thrust in developing peer reporting of malfeasance, which is covered in following sections. In addition to these shortcomings, the underlying weakness of the reporting mechanism was its dependence on the strategy of supervision, which will be considered now.

Supervision

The Supervisors

The department's primary strategy to promote honest and ethical behavior in gambling enforcement was based on control of the plainclothes force by a corps of senior officers. Indeed, all policies and procedures related to ethical conduct were in some way linked to the system of supervision. Although it underwent several changes, the supervisory structure of the plainclothes force that was established in the early 1950s endured for almost twenty years; its cornerstone was an exaggerated differential in rank. In 1951, the use of sergeants and acting lieutenants to direct plainclothesmen was discontinued because these officers were too close to patrolmen in rank and outlook. Instead, lieutenants and deputy inspectors were given control of division plainclothes squads, while captains and inspectors guided borough units.[26]

Stewardship of plainclothesmen mirrored the department's traditional thinking. For generations the department had used lieutenants and acting captains as "supervisors of patrol" to monitor the uniformed force. Assigned to headquarters staffs for borough and divisions, superior officers discreetly observed the patrol force in action, making sure that policemen performed their duties in accordance with the *Rules and Procedures.* These roving surveillants, caricatured as "shoo-flies," issued official complaints against violators of departmental regulations. Shoo-flies were feared and hated. In 1961 the Gambling Enforcement Inspection and Review Board considered using them to supplement supervision of plainclothesmen, a proposal supported by the fact that plainclothes was officially part of the patrol division. The proposal was to have staff captains patrol areas of known gambling activity, locations that could be easily selected from reports of arrest and "suspected premises," to see if plainclothesmen were suppressing gambling. Board members postulated that captains, after being "bloodied" for two or three years in the management of gambling enforcement, would be better prepared to command patrol precincts and to become public morals deputy inspectors (PMDI). The board discussed this plan until 1964 but never put it into effect.[27]

The supervisory system was based on accountability. Plainclothes commanders were reminded repeatedly that they would be held responsible for the performance of their people, especially in cases of malfeasance. But the department never publicized this standard of accountability. One extreme would have been a standard of absolute liability, which would hold commanders answerable even if they could not have known of their subordinates' misdeeds. Administrators never seriously considered such a policy, however, and held leaders accountable only when they could have reasonably known of misconduct. Few commanders were penalized for corrupt practices unless they were wrongdoers themselves.[28]

Although the GEIRB hoped that increasing the number of plainclothes supervisors at the level of deputy inspector would strengthen control through the prestige of rank, the policy was hindered by a serious shortage of qualified personnel. Indeed, finding acceptable candidates for positions of leadership was more difficult than finding volunteers for plainclothes. Most superiors who were found, though they had personal integrity, were deficient professionally. Plainclothes commanders, from public morals inspectors on down, usually had no experience in gambling enforcement prior to assignment, and until the mid-1960s they received no formal preparation to oversee plainclothesmen. Because of this weakness, supervisors usually had to accept on-the-job training from their subordinates.[29]

One of the GEIRB's first suggestions for improving management was to change incentives for leadership within the plainclothes force. Its recommendation to revive an earlier policy of assigning only people on promotion lists to supervisory positions was accepted. Beginning in the early 1960s, all lieutenants awaiting promotion to captain were "drafted" into plainclothes, as were some lieutenants commanding detective squads. The strategy was justified on several grounds. First, officials thought that lieutenants would be more effective as precinct captains because of their experience in gambling enforcement. Second, administrators hoped that in the long run, the experience would make the lieutenants better public morals deputy inspectors and inspectors. Third, because people on promotion lists were presumed to be intelligent and career-minded, they were expected to favorably influence their subordinates. Fourth, executives reasoned that because assignment was involuntary, draftees would not have base motives as did some people who sought the position. And finally, the department expected that these lieutenants would exert strict supervision over their plainclothesmen because they had a compelling incentive to prevent corruption—forthcoming promotion. Most draftees protested their selection vehemently before the screening boards, panels similar to Plainclothes Selection Boards. Ironically, reluctance only served to recommend them.[30]

By 1966, the supply of lieutenants on promotion lists had been exhausted. To attract qualified officers to plainclothes thereafter, the GEIRB sought to substitute the carrot for the stick by recommending that all commanders of detective squads (a choice assignment) be appointed from among the experienced lieutenants in plainclothes. At about the same time the board, seeking a new pool of supervisors, asked the Personnel Records Unit (PRU) to compile a list of sergeants and lieutenants who held college degrees. The list was never used, and lieutenants in plainclothes were not assigned as commanders of detective squads.[31]

Thus, during many years, plainclothes supervisors were selected from promotion lists. Although this policy was popular among officials, most lieutenants loathed it and often prevailed on their commanders to help forestall selection by requesting exemption. Widespread resistance forced administrators to strengthen their hand in mid-1968 by declaring that exemptions would be allowed only when the individual's absence from his current assignment would cause serious disruptions in efficiency. Thereafter, lieutenants tried to dodge selection by asserting that their skills were unique within their units. Neither this ploy nor others were successful in evading plainclothes assignments.[32]

Supervisory Procedures–the Formal Rules

Supervisors in plainclothes were guided even more than plainclothesmen by the *Rules and Procedures* and by a continuous flow of directives. Borough, division, and precinct commanders shouldered ultimate responsibility for enforcing gambling and public morals laws in their respective jurisdictions, and they were expected to supervise their people through staffs of superior officers. Commanders of plainclothes squads, in turn, delegated considerable authority to their supervisors in the field.[33]

The department's principal objective in supervision was to fix responsibility and thus accountability for lax and corrupt enforcement. Commanders' attempts to assign investigative responsibilities according to violations (bookmaking or prostitution, for example) failed because there was no way to hold individual supervisors liable for these continuing offenses. The Gambling Enforcement Inspection and Review Board feared that where there was "collective responsibility" there was, in fact, no one responsible. Thus it urged creation of small, manageable territories to increase accountability. In divisions, for example, each deputy inspector (there were usually two) was responsible for all gambling and public morals enforcement within two or three specific precincts.[34] Commanders and supervisors in plainclothes did essentially the same work, their differences having been in scale rather than substance. For this analysis, I have grouped their duties into three categories: administration, field work, and leadership.

Administration. Administrative duties included coordinating and directing a squad's investigative efforts. Supervisors first had to read incoming communications and complaints, which they apportioned in fair case loads. Each day, they were expected to oversee investigations, to review daily progress reports, to monitor the squad's activities by means of hourly "ring schedules," and to approve memo books. Commanders proofread investigative reports for thoroughness and accuracy and reviewed affidavits of arrest to ensure that proper procedures had been used. They also approved monthly expense vouchers as well as affidavits supporting applications for search warrants and wiretaps. These procedures were intended to keep squad leaders informed of activities, making them the primary deterrents to false or exaggerated reporting. And every month, superiors were expected to analyze all reports to discover weaknesses in enforcement, assessments that were supposed to diminish opportunities for corrupt conspiracies. The department expected these administrative controls to be effective because they forced supervisors to commit themselves in writing, which made them parties to irregularities that might be discovered later.[35]

Fieldwork. Field duties were intended to complement administrative controls so that commanders would not rely on hearsay in monitoring the squad's activities. In addition to making routine patrols with their people to become familiar with local gambling conditions, squad leaders were also expected to make independent inspections and discrete observations of their plainclothesmen in action. Such experience helped them gauge the accuracy of their subordinates' reports. Superiors were supposed to be present so they could lead all arrests, raids, and searches to prevent bribery of their people or the use of "stand-ins." Their presence was also mandated during interrogations and bookings to minimize hazards of corruption.

After a headquarters unit (the borough squad or PCCIU, for example) made an arrest in the field, supervisors were expected to study the case and determine why their own people had not discovered the violation. Field responsibilities also required superiors to visit gambler's courts to verify plainclothesmen's testimony and to make sure that the evidence presented conformed to information in arrest affidavits. When the court dismissed gambling charges, commanders had to interview the plainclothesmen involved to ascertain the cause and institute corrective action, including additional training, if necessary.[36]

Leadership. Superiors had to give practical guidance and training to each person when necessary. Commanders were supposed to encourage productivity, desirable attitudes toward plainclothes work, and "high levels of integrity" in dealing with violations of public morals.[37] To accomplish these objectives they had positive and negative disciplinary measures at their disposal—formal and informal tools such as departmental charges, efficiency reports, and recommendations for transfer back to patrol.

Like plainsclothesmen, supervisors were rated by senior commanders and ranked numerically within their commands. The main criteria in supervisors' evaluations were the absence of corruption and complaints of corruption; quantity and quality of arrests; rates of conviction; and demonstrated initiative in problem solving. Evaluations were important for making assignments because even though a lieutenant in plainclothes might be promoted to captain from a civil service list as a matter of course, the quality of his new command hinged on the rating. In mid-1965, the Gambling Enforcement Inspection and Review Board proposed that as a further check, superiors be required to maintain memo books daily to increase the quality of management. A controversial suggestion, it was not implemented until 1968, and then it was limited to officers below the rank of captain (that is, lieutenants). On the whole, supervisory procedures were intended as much to control the supervisory force as the plainclothesmen.[38]

Supervisory Practices—the Reality

Circumstances surrounding appointments of superior officers to plainclothes had a significant impact on supervisory practices. Without previous experience in enforcement of gambling or public morals laws, most plainclothes supervisors were forced to rely on their subordinates for on-the-job training. This initial dependence compromised their leadership. Commanders received no preparation for detecting and dealing with malfeasance, but relied instead on their general experience. More significant, however, was that the overwhelming majority was drafted reluctantly. Once assigned, they had to face a difficult and perhaps dangerous period in their careers. Their reactions to challenges had a far-reaching effect on honesty and ethical behavior.[39]

Most superiors accepted assignment ruefully, keeping a watchful eye on the promotion list. The department's axiom of accountability loomed large in their minds because malfeasance in their commands could cripple their careers. Newly assigned lieutenants and deputy inspectors were quickly discouraged when they learned that it was virtually impossible to perform all duties and meet all responsibilities. Thus they entered plainclothes brooding about the liabilities of their stay, determined to do whatever was necessary to get through with an unblemished record.[40]

Viewed on a continuum, service in the plainclothes force ranged from honest effort to apathy to intentional thwarting of departmental policies. Superiors were cautious, a result of a common set of attitudes based on their lack of training, involuntary assignment, unrealistic work loads, and personal trepidations. Because they were indifferent, passive, and fearful, squad leaders often ignored evils when they could, neglecting rules and procedures designed to promote honesty and integrity. Administrative duties were awesome and unrealistic and left little time for conscientious leadership. Even those who at first tried to maintain control by reading every communication, report, affidavit, and memo book realized that they lost contact with their people as they succumbed to paper work. Some supervisors used administrative details as an avenue of escape and intentionally buried themselves in mountains of paper to avoid confronting evidence of corruption.[41]

As a result of evasion and in some cases of misguided energies, management of plainclothes squads was inconsistent and widely varied. When squad leaders were busy, as they frequently were, incoming communications were screened and assigned to plainclothesmen by clerical patrolmen, a substitution of authority that reinforced the clerical staff's unfortunate monopoly of knowledge. Heavy work loads made it necessary for commanders to accept reports after investigations were completed–when falsification was easier–instead of daily. Superiors unable to keep pace with memo books allowed days or even weeks to pass before they made reviews, and some even announced forthcoming checks, which gave their people time to update their entries. By common practice, supervisors accepted reports of arrests and affidavits for search warrants at face value with little or no inquiry about how information was obtained or arrests made.[42]

While administrative procedures were often neglected, leadership in the field was almost nonexistent because few supervisors directed the actual investigative activities of their people. Typically, plainclothesmen reported to the office, checked with the clerical staff or the commander for new work and then went on their way for the remainder of the tour without any itinerary. Plainclothesmen, not superiors, determined their own investigative priorities. Far from the theoretical directive model of investigation, theirs was a scavenger model, based on the urgent need to cover the sheet and meet production quotas. A substantial number of arrests made early in the month allowed them to "coast" or to work on personal interests; slow activity in arrests caused a last-minute scramble against being "shut out," having to file a negative report. When they accompanied their people on patrol, supervisors usually did so for appearance, often after they announced their intentions beforehand. More often than not, squad leaders were absent from arrest and booking procedures. Rarely did commanders discover or report police cooptation; generally, they preferred to leave such matters for the Police Commissioner's Confidential Investigating Unit. When headquarters' squads made "overhead" arrests, most superiors reacted defensively and ordered follow-up arrests instead of thoughtful inquiries.[43]

Supervisors were not unaware of cooptation or unethical behavior; indeed, many illicit practices were conducted with their knowledge and forbearance. They realized the extent of their dependence on clerical staffs; they knew entries had been "past posted" in memo books; they surmised that some "reliable informants" were actually fictitious; and they recognized that plainclothesmen were making jump collars and later perjuring themselves in testimony as well as in affidavits. In spite of all this, the leaders did not, indeed could not, make any changes. "The ability of one man to direct, coordinate, and control immediate subordinates—has physical limits, because he can only be in one place at one time, and he cannot work 24 hours a day." The supervisors' wide span of control—one lieutenant over ten to fifteen plainclothesmen, for example—was a major factor in the breakdown of supervision. At best the supervisors could direct only a few people at critical times when gamblers were arrested and evidence seized. Even armed with evidence of malfeasance, superiors were discouraged by the system itself from fighting corruption—they would jeopardize their own careers by airing "dirty linen." Squad leaders, perhaps more than plainclothesmen, yielded to the pressures of the sheet and to an impossible work load and were forced into a mutual accommodation of daily compromise with their people. In constant dread of scandal and the inevitable question, "Why didn't you know about this?" supervisors kept production high.[44]

Fortunately, the breakdown in leadership was not universal, so that departmental strategies against corruption were implemented by some diligent commanders who met the spirit if not the letter of their responsibilities. Such commanders spent many overtime hours reading investigative reports, observing their squads on patrol, and analyzing arrest records to find evidence of unethical practices, such as the use of stand-ins. Although the Gambling Enforcement Inspection and Review Board might have strengthened methods of inspection for the entire plainclothes force, only a few supervisors showed any initiative in seeking out corrupt practices (see Exhibit X in the appendix). Moreover, chances for reform were undermined by a constant turnover of policy makers and commanders in the plainclothes force. By the time officials grasped the issues and devised counterstrategies, these people usually were transferred to other duties or retired from the department, leaving problems as they found them for their successors.[45]

A Directed Model of Investigation

From the time they took office, administrators in the early 1970s emphasized new leadership procedures as a central theme of their reforms. Many innovations were adopted and old procedures were revised in the Organized Crime Control Bureau, as officials dramatically increased the number of supervisors in gambling enforcement. A reduced span of superintendence was intended to give administrators "greater control over all phases of an investigation and reduce the opportunities for [plainclothesmen] to become involved in acts of corruption and misconduct." In his first formal order, the commander of the Public Morals Division subdivided all gambling units into investigative teams called "modules," which consisted of a sergeant and six plainclothesmen. This supervisory ratio was based on the PCCIU's experience where the span had proved effective in preventing corruption. Sergeants were directed by public morals district commanders, usually captains, plus a staff of other superior officers. Commanders assigned work to each investigative module and to clerical staffs working at district headquarters. In a significant change, supervisors were no longer drafted; instead, they volunteered for the OCCB under the Career Path program.[46]

Administrators wanted more than structural changes in supervision; they sought to shift gambling and narcotics enforcement from the scavenger model to a directed model of investigation. In a series of policy directives, the OCCB's Commander told his people:

> We cannot allow our investigative resources to be dissipated on minor, non-productive investigations. The activities of all our investigators will be planned and directed by a superior.[47]
>
> This "case-by-case" approach to the gambler or the narcotics violator, similar in essence to a series of contests between the individual policeman and an individual criminal about an individual crime is fatally defective. . . . Arrests shall be made in a way that best attains our objective, diminishing the scope, the power, and activities of organized crime. . . . We must reorient the department's efforts toward a new strategy—to attack this 'big business' in such a way that our own efforts are not diffused.[48]

To implement this policy, the OCCB promulgated a new set of investigative and supervisory guidelines. It revised "target" programs to help concentrate efforts on only "quality" investigations. Plainclothesmen were no longer assigned to investigate individual known gamblers. Instead, officials regrouped KGs into new "combines" according to organized gambling's most recent hierarchy. Combines were then assigned to sergeants, who supervised six-person modules of investigators. These sergeants shouldered full responsibility for investigating and reporting, using assigned plainclothesmen as their eyes and ears.[49]

In accordance with the directed model, plainclothesmen were no longer free to determine their own investigative priorities; their supervisors gave them explicit assignments for their tours of duty. Using a Daily Assignment Sheet, sergeants specified all investigative activities; they told investigators which cases to work on, what individuals or locations to keep under surveillance, and when to perform each duty during the tour (see Exhibit Y in the appendix). Supervisory effectiveness may have suffered, however, because inexperienced sergeants were rotated regularly. Although rotation reduced their exposure to corruption hazards, they were often not so "street-wise" as their subordinates.

Significantly, plainclothesmen's discretion to make arrests was eliminated. They were expressly prohibited from making jump collars or pickup arrests; in fact, they were forbidden to make any arrests unless their sergeant or another superior approved and was present, a condition that was a dramatic break with traditional practice. Similar limitations were imposed for the execution of search warrants; the OCCB's guidelines provided that "as many supervisors as are available shall be assigned to the search party." Thus leaders had to be present at all "critical moments" when plainclothesmen were in contact with members of organized crime and when they were likely to be exposed to hazards of corruption. Arrests and searches were "scheduled" only after supervising officers determined that investigation would yield no more information regarding higher echelons in the gambling enterprise. Some investigations were continued for more than a year before arrests were made.[50]

Sergeants of modules had complete responsibility for field work, being required to spend almost all their time directing two-man teams and participating in "key observations." Increased participation was intended to prevent unethical conduct and at the same time to keep supervisors abreast of investigative activities. Pushing paper was subordinated to street work, and rotation of sergeants compensated for their proximity in rank to investigators.[51]

Some Public Morals Division commands established their own guidelines to control plainclothesmen's behavior during unanticipated "critical moments" when supervisors were absent. A plainclothesman confronted unexpectedly by a gambler during a surveillance, for example, had to call his district office immediately to report the conversation and have it entered in the office's blotter. This action protected the plainclothesman (as well as the absent superior) if the contact had been observed by an investigating unit. Similarly, if approached by a defendant or his attorney while "in the environs of the court," all the OCCB's personnel were instructed to reply, "I don't want to talk to you," and then walk away. A plainclothesman was not allowed to speak with defense counsel except in the presence of a district attorney. There was to be no legitimate intercourse between plainclothesmen and gamblers.[52]

In the mid-1970s administrators continued the momentum for integrity through the directed model of investigation and sought to check any return to initiative by plainclothesmen. Officials reminded investigators in the OCCB that only commanders could select targets for investigation, that any bribe offers or contact with gamblers was to be reported immediately, and that investigators were never to associate with known criminals. Superiors were reminded that they were to "direct and control activities of their investigators on a daily and continuous basis."[53] These new and revised supervisory policies, implemented with commander-accountability, were intended to give supervisors in the Public Morals Division a set of realistic incentives and tools for maintaining honest, ethical behavior in gambling enforcement.

Throughout the 1950s and 1960s failures in leadership were attributable to weaknesses in the structure and dynamics of the supervisory strategy. Supervision was limited to on-duty hours while corrupt schemes could flourish at times and places outside a commander's jurisdiction. A burdensome workload and an unmanageable span of control crippled the framework for leadership.

More important, the fear-laden and passive attitude of superiors undermined the very fabric of supervision. Not until the adoption of a directed model of investigation in the early 1970s was the strategy of close supervision to control malfeasance fulfilled in any meaningful way.

Discovering Deviation

The department had few independent means for maintaining integrity in the plainclothes force, as allegations of corruption were routinely sent to plainclothes commanders for investigation. Administrators depended on a few elite units who worked under the direct supervision of the highest officials to discover corrupt practices. Efforts to eliminate malfeasance were later restructured and reoriented as more radical strategies for discovery were inaugurated.

Inspections

Traditionally, the department used continuous inspections in the field to detect deviations from the *Rules and Procedures.* Discovery was intended not only to identify malefactors and patterns of irregularity but also to encourage compliance with directives through fear of detection. In the nineteenth and early twentieth centuries, police "roundsmen" (officers comparable to sergeants) surveilled patrolmen to verify that the uniformed force performed its duties. Some time after roundsmen were abolished, officials adopted the shoo-fly system, in which superior officers were assigned to supervise the patrol force. Because plainclothesmen were not easily observed, the shoo-fly approach was not suited to discovering corruption in gambling enforcement.

Although a paramilitary organization, the department lacked a systematic program of inspection to encourage compliance with its regulations. Throughout the 1950s and 1960s responsibility for inspection was lodged with borough, division, and precinct commanders rather than with any centralized or specialized unit. Inspections were considered a tool of command to give commanders authority commensurate with responsibility. The department relied on its program of close personal supervision to control the plainclothes force. No one in the department welcomed an inspection; intervention was interpreted as interference devoid of corrective value.

One of the Gambling Enforcement Inspection and Review Board's primary assignments was to "inspect and report on the effectiveness or lack thereof" in the plainclothes force and in the uniformed force involved in gambling enforcement. In 1961 and 1962, the board considered the possibility of creating an inspector general with an appropriate staff to oversee plainclothes units, but the idea was never developed. Although the board did undertake limited checks (visits to gamblers court, for example), there was no meaningful follow-up. The sketchy program was formalized in the mid-1960s when captains who had legal training were assigned to gamblers courts to observe plainclothesmen testify and to squelch abuses such as perjury. A valuable tool, the policy received conscientious but limited application. Because of inadequate staffing and follow-up this program never achieved its potential and eventually fell into disuse.[54]

The department's only productive auditor, an ad hoc unit, was formally organized in 1961 as the Police Commissioner's Inspection Squad (PCIS). The PCIS had four objectives: to determine the effectiveness of field units through on-site inspections; to discover and correct operational weaknesses; to improve managerial practices at the precinct level; and to communicate the police commissioner's policies to the force. Whereas misfeasance in gambling enforcement was one of its concerns, the PCIS focused primarily on the patrol precinct and the uniformed force.

In the mid-1960s, the PCIS conducted seventeen in-depth inspections of patrol precincts, and its findings served as the agenda for a series of round-table command conferences held with ninety precinct captains at the police academy. Through discussion, commanders were supposed to gain a better understanding of the inspectional process and thus a more cooperative attitude toward the PCIS. According to the surveys, "the largest number of deficiencies was found in matters relating to gambling enforcement," with weaknesses such as the poor maintenance of records and files, the uniformed force's limited knowledge of gambling conditions, the inadequate reporting of observations involving gambling, and the lack of harassment of known gamblers who continued operations in the same locations. While gambling headed the list of "corruption hazards," the PCIS reported other sensitive areas such as Sabbath laws, traffic violations, and ordinances governing construction sites, tow trucks, and licensed premises.[55]

In 1966, the PCIS broke new ground by surveying a division plainclothes squad, focusing on record keeping and the assignment of communications. Pleased with the PCIS's profile report, the GEIRB again discussed the possibility of creating its own inspectional squad or expanding the PCIS. Some board members felt that the PCIS might be received more kindly if it were not part of the Police Commissioner's Confidential Investigating Unit, a dreaded interloper throughout the department. None of the board's discussions nor its infrequent checks of the plainclothes force developed into a strategy for inspection.[56]

In the early 1970s supervisory programs were established by the OCCB's Field Control Division (FCD), which monitored gambling and narcotics enforcement. A watchdog, FCD's Inspections Section conducted formal surveys looking for "deficiencies and weaknesses in record-keeping, forms control, working schedules and personnel management." Scheduled examinations and unexpected audits were carried out in much the same vein as they were by the former PCIS, with a view more toward improving compliance with anticorruption policies rather than toward punishing wrongdoers.[57]

The department also shifted its concept of the inspection strategy to one of participatory management.[58] Although the Inspections Section had significant responsibilities, public morals (and narcotics) district commanders were to be ultimately accountable for their people's performance. To assist these field commanders, and to make clear that they could not simply rely on the Field Control Division to seek out misfeasance or malfeasance, the OCCB published an *Administrative Self-Inspection Manual* and a *Corruption Control Manual.* The *Administrative Manual* gave commanders comprehensive instructions on how to review records and reports to identify and correct noncompliance with required procedures. The *Corruption Control Manual*, an adaptation of a similar department-wide handbook, was tailored to gambling and narcotics enforcement. Each corruptive hazard was described and categorized according to location, situation, administration, property, enforcement activity, and off-duty conduct. Indicators for each hazard were listed, and a range of responses was suggested. OCCB commanders appointed integrity control officers to conduct inspections and audits to detect corrupt practices before they came to the attention of the Field Control or Internal Affairs Divisions.[59]

Investigating Corruption

Because procedures for reporting and supervision were inadequate sources of information about deviant behavior, the department looked to the public for raw information about collusion in gambling enforcement. To prevent citizen complaints (and crime reports) from getting "lost" in precincts where they were often received, officials at one time had all precinct telephone numbers deleted from public directories. Complainants thus were forced to call police headquarters, a system that increased certainty of investigative action.[60]

Virtually all information from the public was sent directly to the police commissioner's office, where the staff screened it and eliminated crank letters. Complaints of serious misconduct, such as extortion and widespread corruption in gambling enforcement, were assigned to the Police Commissioner's Confidential Investigating Unit, as were sensitive or otherwise important charges. Allegations concerning the uniformed force (corruption at construction sites, for example) were forwarded to the Chief Inspector's Investigating Unit. The largest group of complaints—minor and nonspecific charges of corruption and gambling violations—were sent to the Bureau of Public Morals, a coordinating unit in the chief inspector's office, where they were indexed and forwarded to field commanders for verification. Thus the department relied largely on decentralized investigation for dealing with complaints of corruption and other misconduct.[61]

Guidelines for processing reports of corruption in the field were designed to promote uniformity and reduce individual discretion. In 1954, the *Manual of*

Procedure was amended to require that allegations concerning graft, gratuities, missing property, or other serious misconduct "be personally investigated by a superior officer above the rank of lieutenant." Superiors conducting these inquiries were authorized to make independent observations as well as to take written statements from complainants, witnesses, and suspect members of the force. Their findings led to disciplinary action when officers discovered wrongdoing.[62]

Procedures in "routine" investigations of corruption created several significant problems. Foremost, complaints were sent to those borough and division commanders under whose supervision the alleged misconduct had occurred. Obviously, their subordinates had strong incentives to minimize collusion or other misconduct lest they inculpate themselves and have to explain why they had not discovered the violations first. To ease this dilemma, officials changed the procedure in the mid-1950s to require that such investigations be conducted by "the commanding officer at least one level higher than the precinct, division, or borough in which the corruption was alleged."[63]

A second difficulty was that because captains and officers of higher rank often had no investigative experience, they lacked the skills necessary to conduct effective inquiries. Commanders obviously could not assign the work to plainclothesmen because then the plainclothesmen would be investigating friends and coworkers. Moreover, wrongdoers could have been alerted to any confidential investigation easily. Without any special staff for support, commanders usually allowed public morals inspectors and other superiors to investigate. Most borough and division commanders had confidence in their supervisors, although this was not universally true. Even so, commanders had little choice in the matter.[64]

By the mid-1960s, the Gambling Enforcement Inspection and Review Board became aware of the shortcomings in decentralized investigative procedures. The PCCIU informed the board that most allegations of corruption were quickly discredited on the grounds that no wrongdoing was found:

> Nearly all of the . . . allegations are dismissed in one paragraph. Essentially, the men state that no corruption exists. . . . Almost without exception, they never found it. . . . On the basis of these communications, I would say there is never any effective action taken.[65]

To overcome these deficiencies, the board proposed a pilot program in which certain public morals inspectors would choose their own personnel from the plainclothes force, the Detective Division, and other units to form "borough supervisory squads." These squads were supposed to concentrate on "effective enforcement by division and precinct plainclothes squads; to initiate supervisory methods; and to insure full and complete loyalty [honesty] by all plainclothes personnel." Members of such units would do supervisory work independent of the sheet; thus they would be free to cooperate with the PCCIU "on a more positive basis," which was to include sharing information. Officials hoped that because borough supervisory squads would be hand-picked, their loyalties would not be bound to precinct and division practices, inhibitions, or friendships.

The emphasis on personal selection, the cornerstone of the experiment, was the ultimate cause of the plan's downfall. Administrators feared that commanders not selected to participate would feel slighted. Also, transfers and retirements of public morals inspectors would have created personnel problems regarding reassignment of plainclothesmen who had developed strong loyalties to their commanders. The program also represented a step backward because it reversed the intent of newly developed procedures that had eliminated personal selection of investigators. No one raised this specific objection, but officials must have recognized that the subjective selection of plainclothesmen had been a contributing factor in previous cases of corruption. The proposal was summarily rejected by the administration.[66]

A few years later the concept of decentralized anticorruption squads was revived. In 1970 the outgoing commissioner directed commanders of major patrol and detective units to establish "a confidential staff who would be responsible for receiving reports of, detecting, reporting, and acting upon every evidence or allegation of corruption or misconduct within his command." Although commanders quickly assigned personnel to form the units, their staffs were small and had little impetus until the next administration took office.[67]

Field commanders' responsibility for investigations of corruption was an integral part of the new commissioner's program for decentralized authority and accountability. Because superiors were to be liable for the efficiency and integrity of their people, it was logical that they be given a primary role in the process of discovery related to these concerns. Full decentralization of investigative responsibility in matters of corruption and unethical behavior was completed early in 1972. According to the first deputy commissioner, its objective was to eliminate "the all too-prevalent notion that stopping police corruption in one's own command was the responsibility of someone else." The message was that field commanders were to become involved; they could no longer rely on units at police headquarters to do the dirty work. Integrity was no longer to be a matter of "us against them," of field against headquarters.[68]

Commanders of patrol boroughs and other major bureaus or units were directed to establish a Field Internal Affairs Unit (FIAU) headed by an internal affairs officer and staffed with an ample number of investigators. The FIAUs were to be given sufficient resources and authority to ferret out corruption. Internal affairs officers were required to initiate at least 30 percent of their own case work to prevent them from spending all their time answering communications and other referrals. Investigations were to be directed against ongoing conspiracies in gambling and other areas of enforcement, not outdated allegations. The Internal Affairs Division remained the coordinating unit over corrupt practices, referring most matters to the FIAUs. The IAD monitored the work of the FIAUs but retained high-echelon "quality cases." While the investigative structure of the 1950s and 1960s remained, administrators reallocated resources and reoriented the mechanisms for discovery. In any future revelation of widespread corruption, commanders would no longer be able to plead innocence because of ignorance or insufficient resources.[69]

The Police Commissioner's Confidential Investigating Unit

Complementing the policy of decentralized investigations of corruption was a system for discovery built around several specialized headquarters' units, principally the Police Commissioner's Confidential Investigating Unit. In addition to the PCCIU, the department had other elite supervisory squads: the First Deputy Commissioner's Confidential Investigating Unit (FDCIU) and the Chief Inspector's Investigating Unit (CIIU). These units provided the most trusted defense against widespread malfeasance, and administrators depended on them heavily. Each of these agencies pursued serious complaints of corruption, including allegations involving gambling enforcement. There were, however, no clear lines of responsibility among the squads, a deliberate overlapping intended to provide checks and balances. As a rule, each unit dealt with its cases independently and secretly, especially if it involved charges against one of the other confidential squads. Compartmentalization promoted security but also resulted in occasional duplication of effort.[70]

The PCCIU was the most active agent working against corruption throughout the 1950s and 1960s. Whereas its historical development is obscure, most police commissioners had a small squad attached to their office to conduct confidential investigations. Usually the squad was omitted from the department's organizational charts. Because the PCCIU traditionally investigated misconduct, most policemen feared it as part of a "spy" system, whereas commissioners regarded it as a necessary evil. The unit was headed by the supervising assistant chief inspector (SACI), who reported directly to the police commissioner and was a member of the Gambling Enforcement Inspection and Review Board.[71]

Fulfilling a dual role, the PCCIU attacked organized gambling at its highest levels and supervised the plainclothes force to promote honesty in gambling law enforcement. Little has been published about its organization and functioning. In 1964, the PCCIU had four main sections: a Gambling Enforcement Squad that conducted city-wide investigations of gambling and vice; three Personnel Standards Squads that investigated complaints of misconduct; an Inspection Squad (PCIS) that surveyed patrol precincts; and a Syndicated Vice and Gambling Squad that conducted extensive investigations to develop intelligence on organized gambling.[72] In 1966, the PCCIU was reorganized into two main branches, Internal Security and Public Morals Enforcement, but its responsibilities remained unchanged.

The SACI commander selected personnel for the PCCIU carefully, relying on personal recommendations from friends and trusted subordinates. No one volunteered for the unit; all who worked there were "suspect" for the rest of their careers. When a new commissioner took office, members of the PCCIU were apprehensive about possible transfer to the field. The strength of the squad varied throughout the 1950s, increasing steadily from 30 to 40 to almost 200 people by the mid-1960s, a large organization even by the department's standards. Most personnel were superior officers.[73]

The PCCIU conducted many routine investigations, such as keeping watch over departmental line organizations (for example, Patrolmen's Benevolent Association) to ensure compliance with prohibitions against soliciting advertisements from businessmen. The unit also dealt with extortion or "shakedowns" by policemen, with bribery, and with the acceptance of gratuities. Sensitive allegations of collusion with gamblers were investigated by superiors, not patrolmen or detectives. In most cases, the PCCIU used standard investigative techniques–interviews of complainants and witnesses, reviews of departmental and civilian records, confidential observations, wiretaps, and interrogations of members of the force. To facilitate the PCCIU's surveillances in cases of corruption, the Gambling Enforcement Inspection and Review Board required all plainclothesmen to submit current photographs of themselves every two years.[74]

Divided into small units with an effective span of supervisory control (one supervisor over six investigators), the PCCIU followed the directed model of investigation in which all priorities and decisions were controlled by superiors. Security was strict. Squad members were supposed to discuss their work only with colleagues participating in the same cases. Section chiefs reported directly to the SACI, who coordinated investigations and collated information. Although the PCCIU submitted statistics on its achievements in terms of arrests and other activities, it was primarily a supervisory unit over the plainclothes force, not a competitor in gambling cases. Its successes in enforcement and the discovery of corrupt practice, however, resulted from its directed activity, its prior claim to the best information, and its members' need for individual achievements. When the PCCIU was overwhelmed with work, as it often was, it diverted lesser cases of malfeasance to the CIIU, to the FDCIU, and at times to field commanders.[75]

Many investigations of collusion in gambling enforcement were predicated on those dreaded "overhead" arrests made by the PCCIU. Headquarters followed up the initial case "to ascertain whether conditions leading to the arrest of a gambler existed due to any laxity, negligence or sufferance on the part of any member of the force."[76] This typical case history of PCCIU investigation reflects the methods characteristically used by the unit:

One investigation involved different observations for a long time, but the known gambler showed up and the operation continued. The uniformed force was

> apparently aware of the situation. We have instances in which the sector car pulled up [to the suspected premise]. Motion pictures were taken. Two known gamblers were identified.... At this point a complaint was made to the precinct. The observations [by the PCCIU] were made for another period of time. The complaint was never recorded. It was just ignored. The operation continued and another complaint was made. These were anonymous telephone calls. This one was recorded but because there was one street and avenue common to two areas, the communication was forwarded to the other division where the address was located. The operation continued. Two or three days passed. Pictures continued to be taken and another anonymous complaint was forwarded to the division. Known gamblers came every night. People stood in line [to place bets]. Another telephone call was made, this time mentioning four locations, including the suspected area. Only one address was recorded. But a lieutenant and plainclothesman did observe the premises briefly while our people had it under surveillance. Their visit took five, ten minutes at the most, and they reported "no violation of law observed" ["NVO"].[77]

The use of anonymous complaints to precincts and plainclothes squads was only one of the PCCIU's characteristic ploys. Another stratagem was used in raids of gambling businesses, with the PCCIU's people posing as newly assigned plainclothesmen or supervisors from the division or borough office. By playing "dumb" and soliciting information about payoffs from those arrested, members of the PCCIU could appraise the extent of collusion in the plainclothes units responsible for that area.

Needless to say, the entire force (particularly plainclothesmen) feared, even dreaded the PCCIU, if for no other reason than for its policy of aggressive interrogation. In mid-1966, representatives of various line organizations prevailed in their long-standing objections to the PCCIU's treatment of policemen during corruption inquiries. Complaints were presented to the police commissioner through the Joint Personnel Relations Board (JPRB), created in 1961 in response to the mayor's executive order to establish grievance procedures. To resolve the matter and to sensitize the force's attitude toward constitutional rights of the citizenry, the department adopted a set of rules for interrogation, known as the Policeman's Bill of Rights. Officially titled "Guidelines for Members of the Force When Interrogated by a Superior Officer of the Department in Connection with an Official Investigation," the thrust of this document was directed at the PCCIU.[78]

Under new procedures, interrogations had to be conducted at a reasonable time of day, preferably during working hours and at the member's regular command. There were to be no more "gestapo" interrogations in the middle of the night. The policeman was to be informed of the name, rank, and command of the officer in charge of the investigation, the interrogating officer, and anyone else present. Before being questioned, the policeman was also to be told the nature of the investigation, his status (suspect or witness), and the names of any complainants. A member of the force under arrest or accused of a crime or serious violation of the *Rules and Procedures* had to be advised of his rights to remain silent, to have counsel, and to consult with a lawyer or representative of a line organization, a courtesy not required in noncriminal or minor violations of departmental rules. Furthermore, no policeman was to be subjected to offensive language, threatened with dismissal, transfer, or similar punishment. Questioning was to be limited, allowing "reasonable respites" for personal necessities. Lastly, the entire interrogation was to be recorded mechanically or by a stenographer, with no questions asked or threats made off the record.[79]

Whereas these requirements might have ended any excesses by the PCCIU and satisfied demands of line organizations, they also guaranteed that policemen would have the same minimum rights regarding counsel and silence as civilian suspects. This justification was, of course, the "official" explanation for changes in policy.[80]

In spite of the commitment of resources and its awesome reputation, the PCCIU was not an effective deterrent against conspiracies with gamblers. Its members conducted thorough investigations once they suspected the existence of collusion, but the unit had little preventive impact because there was no continuing investigative program against malfeasance. It responded to corruption on a case-by-case basis, "closing" each case upon arrest. Sometimes the PCCIU acted too quickly, moving against transgressors before developing evidence to its fullest potential. Generally, though, it was effective against flagrant cooptation.

Not only were the department's agents of discovery—PCCIU, FDCIU, CIIU—fragmented and inconsistent, they were also fallible. The CIIU reflected the problem at its worst: In 1951, the entire seventeen-man unit was "flopped" back to patrol duties after it was implicated in the corrupt scheme uncovered during the Gross scandal. A similar mass transfer occurred in 1964, this time involving nearly fifty men, and as a result the unit was temporarily disbanded until it could be restaffed under a new commander drafted from the PCCIU.[81]

When the department began to centralize the discovery function in 1967, the first deputy commissioner reemerged as the fountainhead of efforts against corruption. All investigative and inspectional services were put under his control. The PCCIU, CIIU, and other confidential squads were amalgamated, leaving an unstructured investigative force at the first deputy's disposal.[82] But for two years the combined units struggled for identity and continued to function much as they had before the merger. Because officials disagreed over responsibility for control of corruption, appropriate organizational form, and competing priorities, and because there were continuing personality clashes, the department's units of discovery remained in a state of flux and confusion. Commanders and investigators alike were given other tasks, including temporary assignments to riot control duties. A limited work force precluded continuity and investigative effectiveness for several years, until the creation of the Internal Affairs Division and the new Field Internal Affairs Units in the 1970s.

The OCCB's New Approaches

Although the OCCB's strategy to promote honesty and probity in gambling (and narcotics) enforcement reflected the traditional reliance on intelligence gathering and investigative follow-up, the bureau also introduced several new and provocative elements. One of the OCCB's four principal units, the Field Control Division (FCD), was patterned after the PCCIU. Established to detect and eradicate corrupt practices within the OCCB's Narcotics and Public Morals Division, the FCD had three subunits: an Inspections Section, a Field Internal Affairs Section, and a Special Intelligence Section. As previously noted, the Inspections Section concentrated on deficiencies in administrative matters, particularly in record keeping and office management. The Field Internal Affairs Section monitored investigators in Public Morals (and Narcotics) Squads to verify or disprove allegations of collusion, to discover corruption hazards, and to observe persons known to be "corrupters." It functioned much like its ancestor, the Police Commissioner's Confidential Investigating Unit.[83] The long-time policy of surveilling plainclothesmen, for example, was continued and strengthened. As of the mid-1970s, investigators in the OCCB were photographed by the department annually, and the pictures were filed at OCCB headquarters. Rosters were established at each unit to "ensure ease in identifying and accounting for members assigned to a command."[84]

Whereas the OCCB's organizational structure was somewhat traditional, its methods were not. The bureau was truly innovative in gathering information and pursuing investigations. Its Special Intelligence Section established covert systems to gather evidence, and to conduct comprehensive investigations, of cooptation. Court-authorized wiretaps were used against gamblers and suspect policemen to determine the existence and extent of organized corruption. Officials adopted a broad, long-term approach, hoping to identify everyone in the conspiracy. Whenever possible, numbers and bookmaking enterprises were infiltrated by police agents seeking evidence of possible collusion. The OCCB's investigators participated in several department-controlled pads, "working" with gamblers to uncover coopted policemen. Willing to go to almost any length, the department made arrangements with district attorneys and the courts to set up bogus gambling operations to attract illicit offers. Thus the OCCB conducted several "illegal" businesses, including a pornographic book store and gambling enterprises, awaiting invitations to join pads. All these efforts constituted an extensive program for testing integrity. For the future, the OCCB committed itself to greater use of infiltration techniques in gambling enforcement, with policemen posing as "cops on the take."[85]

In addition to their aggressive use of unconventional investigative techniques, officials in the early 1970s invoked other controversial programs to uncover corrupt practices. Just prior to the OCCB's creation, the police commissioner made the unusual gesture of urging members of the force who were guilty of minor malfeasance to "make a fresh start" by responding to the department's campaign against illegality. He promised the guilty "every possible consideration" to help them remain on the force. Using this policy of limited amnesty as a springboard, the OCCB developed its Corruption Intelligence program to gather information inside and outside the department. There were several innovations in the program that led to the discovery of cooptation and unethical behavior.[86]

One provocative strategy for intelligence gathering was the Field Associate Program (FAP), first conceived in 1971 and later expanded by the OCCB for gambling and narcotics enforcement. Under existing procedures for selection, officials interviewed new investigators entering the OCCB's Narcotics and Public Morals Divisions. During these routine meetings, all candidates were asked if they would cooperate with the Field Control Division covertly, without the knowledge of future commanders or peers, to report persons or circumstances that indicated individual misconduct or organized cooptation. Because the OCCB's selection procedures already included personal interviews, the FAP was implemented with little bureaucratic difficulty. More important, only a few high-ranking officials knew which plainclothesmen had agreed to become field associates. Although they were difficult to recruit, by early 1972 approximately 70 of the 925 men (7½ percent) in the OCCB were field associates.[87]

The FAP had two objectives. First, officials believed that "placement of one or more field associates in each operating division of the bureau [would] provide first-hand information about acts, practices, and patterns of corruption or conditions that [led] to corruption."[88] Second, the program reinforced the police commissioner's policy of creating functional anxiety "to destroy the confidence that corrupt policemen had in one another."[89] Fear was based on the fact that all new plainclothesmen had undergone interviews, during which they might have agreed to become field associates. Secrecy nurtured suspicion. Every new plainclothesman was a possible spy.

Another outgrowth of the police commissioner's selective amnesty was the "turn-around" strategy. Some members of the force involved in organized corruption who volunteered or were discovered were allowed to "turn around" and work for the department by continuing to participate in the conspiracy, developing evidence against other policemen and gamblers. "Turn-around" was another effort to use fear as a weapon against organized corruption.[90]

By 1972, the FAP and the turn-around program had uncovered several major cases of collusion within the OCCB, particularly in gambling enforcement; one case resulted in the dissolution of an entire plainclothes squad.[91] Occasionally, "turned" plainclothesmen were allowed to remain on the force to do clerical work in return for their cooperation in eliminating malpractice. In spite of these successes, the OCCB's commanders did not delude themselves or the public by claiming that they had eliminated corruption. The deputy commissioner for organized crime control expressed his certain belief that "the idea still, unfortunately prevails in our department that a policeman is somehow disloyal when he takes investigative action against criminals who happen to be sworn police officers." He urged that no member of the OCCB could "evade his individual responsibility to ferret out" those colleagues guilty of unethical behavior.[92]

The FAP and the turn-around program were significant elements in the police commissioner's strategy for using functional anxiety as a brake on corrupt practice. Many members of the force, not just investigators in the OCCB, deeply resented both programs, and both programs contributed substantially to the rank and file's hostility to the reform administrations. Indeed, resentment spread as field associates left the OCCB in normal career advancement, moved into other units, and continued to report their peers' corrupt practices.[93]

In summary, the discovery of corrupt practices was an important strategy in the department's arsenal of controls. Unfortunately, most cases of alleged malfeasance received inadequate investigation by field commanders who lacked sufficient resources to do the job. The PCCIU and other headquarters squads, though not effective deterrents, provided capable investigative services once alerted to organized corruption. More significant than structure and the allocation of resources, however, was the reorientation of the discovery strategy, which decentralized responsibility for detecting corrupt practices and reduced the field commanders' "them against us" attitude. The Field Associate and turn-around programs appear to have been effective strategies, but the use of functional anxiety as a policy of public administration has controversial implications that will be explored in the final chapter.

Sanctions

Wrongdoers who were discovered were subjected to administrative sanctions through the department's disciplinary process. Because work-group norms in the plainclothes force usually negated formal disciplinary procedures, mass transfer became the principal response to corruption. Sanctions were challenged through the courts and evaded through the department's retirement system.

The Roles of Sanctions

As an integral part of its quasi-military style of management, the department relied on a range of sanctions to support its other strategies for honest, ethical behavior. Disciplinary measures were frequently mixed with directive and control strategies that had different objectives. For administrators, the use of sanctions had three purposes: to deter individuals who might be inclined toward misconduct, to communicate standards of desirable behavior, and to punish individuals for malfeasance. Discipline was an adjunct strategy to promote compliance with rules and procedures.

Each new police administration promised to pursue corruption vigorously, yet the rank and file was skeptical of such pronouncements. Actions spoke louder than words. Members of the force, especially those guilty of malfeasance, looked for concrete evidence of the commissioner's intentions in the department's Special Orders, which published news of promotions and demotions and other punishments. Sanctions, not rhetoric, set the ethical tone of every police administration for the plainclothes force.

Because members of the force were traditionally aware of the rights afforded criminal defendants (especially in the 1960s, following the Supreme Court's landmark decisions), the department's disciplinary procedures were highly legalistic, forming an internal judicial system that was similar to state and federal courts. In 1974, for example, the police commissioner changed the long-time policy of suspending officers who were awaiting departmental trial; instead, he gave them "modified assignments" because they were entitled to the same presumption of innocence as anyone else accused of serious wrongdoing.[94]

The Disciplinary Process

The department's judicial machinery was set in motion when a "complaint" was filed, usually by the accused's commanding officer–or by an officer from the PCCIU in cases of corrupt practice. Like criminal charges, departmental complaints had to allege a violation of rules with specificity sufficient for the accused to prepare a defense. Because charge papers were submitted through the chain of command, division and borough commanders screened allegations as a kind of grand jury–they could order that allegations be "filed" if the complaint appeared petty or unwarranted. When charges were considered justified, the case proceeded to the next stage, departmental trial.

Conducted to determine the truth or falsity of an allegation, departmental trials met most standards of due process and followed procedures similar to those of criminal court. The defendant was represented by an attorney (his own or one provided by the department), and he had the right to cross-examine the prosecution's witnesses as well as to present witnesses in his own defense. Only the evidence presented at the trial was considered, although the rules of evidence were partially relaxed to admit some hearsay testimony. Guilt had to be established by a preponderance of the evidence, not beyond a reasonable doubt. The deputy commissioner for trials, who usually was an attorney, presided and acted as the factfinder. His recommendations and the police commissioner's final decision about sanctions ended the disciplinary process, and the results were published in the department's Special Orders. Sanctions that were used included reprimands, monetary fines, temporary suspensions, demotions, dismissals, and combinations thereof. In cases of cooptation, pensions were also at stake.[95]

Discouraged by administrative detail, the rigmarole of the formal disciplinary process, and the stigma it left on a person's reputation, most commanders were reluctant to invoke official procedures. Because the rank and file and the supervisors were united in their feeling that the formal process was onerous and harsh, certain "accommodations" developed that enabled the department to maintain effective discipline. An informal system of discipline evolved and coexisted with the official one.

Traditionally, superiors tried not to "hurt" their people. Instead, they relied on informal sanctions that allowed them to transfer an individual to a less desirable precinct, for example, or to assign him to a disagreeable post—usually a dirty, cold, and remote foot beat. If charges had to be preferred—such as when violations had been observed by a shoo-fly or PCCIU, were known to too many members in the command, were repetitive, or were simply too serious to have been lightly excused—other unofficial norms were followed. By common practice, an offender was often charged with a lesser offense, a ploy that allowed commanders to maintain a semblance of discipline and usually guaranteed that the individual would plead guilty in the Trial Room. Because filing charges often heralded serious cases, invoking the process caused the department to presume that the accused was actually guilty of a worse offense. Many reputations never recovered from the taint of a trial.

Aware of commanders' reluctance to invoke formal processes, officials struggled for many years to make discipline more palatable to the force. Beginning in 1961, the Joint Personnel Relations Board considered allowing commanders to deal with minor violations (improper uniform or equipment, absence from post, improper entries in memo books, for example) at the precinct level. For five years the department agonized over difficulties in having commanders adjudicate the guilt of their people. Complicating issues involved the possibility of plea bargaining between policemen and superiors, and the appropriate range of punishments for commanders to administer. The department ultimately favored the benefits of a decentralized disciplinary process, hoping that commanders would not overlook violations once they had a reasonable alternative to formal charges. Thus "New Procedures for Handling Certain Minor Violations of the Rules and Procedures" ("Captain's Mast") were adopted in mid-1966.[96]

The concept of decentralized administration of sanctions was expanded in the early 1970s. The Command Discipline procedure, an outgrowth of the 1966 "Captain's Mast," allowed commanders to impose punishments for minor violations of the *Rules and Procedures* without invoking the formal process of departmental trial. Although Command Discipline did not apply to serious violations of the rules or to corruption and unethical behavior, it filled a vacuum by involving middle management more directly in the disciplinary process.[97] In some cases Command Discipline was not welcomed by commanders, who preferred to leave punishment to the Trial Room at headquarters.

Discipline in the Plainclothes Force

All formal as well as informal disciplinary practices were applicable to the plainclothes force because it was part of the patrol division. Commanders in plainclothes, however, were even more reluctant to resort to formal processes than were their uniformed counterparts. Discipline was a particularly sensitive issue in plainclothes because a person brought up on charges and "flopped" not only lost all chances to make detective but also was likely to spend the rest of his career in the uniformed force. The small size of plainclothes squads helped create strong allegiances between commanders and their people, thus making superiors less inclined to invoke official procedures. The need for daily compromise and mutual accommodation created by pressures of the sheet also militated against the use of departmental sanctions because supervisors and plainclothesmen shared common concerns for surviving the assignment with their reputations intact.

In spite of the influence of mutual interests, a system of informal sanctions exerted some control and provided a semblance of discipline in the plainclothes force. Typical informal sanctions included oral reprimands, assignment of cases not likely to yield arrests, and harassment by the imposition of requirements such as having to call the squad's office hourly or having to submit a memo book for daily review. When there was serious misconduct–a gross violation of departmental rules, work-group norms, or squad mores–the transgressor was usually flopped back to the uniformed force. Either commanders requested that the individual undergo a change of assignment, or they used an indirect tactic such as filing an "unsatisfactory" evaluation, which effectively ended a person's stay on the plainclothes force.

Squad commanders lost control of the disciplinary process if a higher command like the PCCIU discovered evidence of corruption. In such cases commanders usually worried that they themselves might have been implicated or charged for negligent supervision. Plainclothesmen who were caught in collusion with gamblers were arrested and tried, often concurrently with members of organized crime. When officials lacked sufficient evidence to support a conviction in the criminal courts, they could press departmental charges. This option was advantageous because violations of the *Rules and Procedures* could be proved more easily than conspiracy or perjury, for example.[98]

Frequently, officials could fix responsibility on only a few individuals, even if there was convincing evidence of widespread if not total corruption. Discipline then became a matter of punishment for everyone or for no one, and in many instances entire units were punished indiscriminately. Administrators relied on mass transfer to shake up the plainclothes force and to generate a strong response that was visible to the public. The shortcomings of this policy as part of the mix of directive strategies have already been assessed.

The use of sanctions in the Organized Crime Control Bureau followed the pattern of the plainclothes force. Formal disciplinary procedures were rarely used. When an entire public morals squad was discovered to be in conspiracy with organized gamblers, many policemen were arrested and tried in criminal court. Policemen against whom there was insufficient evidence to support a criminal conviction faced department trials. Command Discipline was used sparingly by the OCCB's commanders, who apparently preferred to rely on informal sanctions for infractions that did not constitute corrupt practice. Indeed, disciplinary procedures were far below the range of problems that plagued the OCCB in narcotics enforcement.[99]

Challenges to Sanctions

One of the principal responsibilities of the deputy commissioner for trials was to advise the police commissioner on all matters that might have been legally contested by policemen or their representative organizations. Typically these matters involved lawsuits concerning decisions in promotion, salary, tenure, and even working hours. As one might expect, disciplinary policies and procedures were also protested in court. Members of the force had ample means to challenge findings of misconduct and the police commissioner's sanctions by appealing to state and federal courts.

A relevant example of a legal test involved Waivers of Immunity—valuable tools for discovery of corruption, especially in gambling enforcement. Because policemen were protected by the Fifth Amendment, they could not be compelled to incriminate themselves. To overcome this privilege, New York's statutes provided reluctant or deserving witnesses with guarantees of immunity from prosecution so that they could be compelled to testify about information that would have otherwise incriminated them. It was the practice in New York City, however, to deny policemen that benefit. Members of the force were asked to sign a Waiver of Immunity, in which they agreed to testify, possibly to incriminate themselves, without immunity from subsequent prosecution. The practice was justified by the presumption that honest police had no reason to fear self-incrimination, and that as holders of a public trust, they should waive their personal privilege. According to departmental policy, refusal to sign the waiver and testify was grounds for dismissal.

In 1968 the policy was challenged in the case of *Gardner v. Broderick,*[100] in which the U.S. Supreme Court held that requiring waivers of immunity was unconstitutional and that policemen could not be dismissed for refusing to waive their constitutional rights. To overcome this restriction, the mayor issued an executive order authorizing all agency heads, including the police commissioner, to adopt rules providing that an individual's refusal to testify about job performance (not refusal to sign a waiver) would constitute grounds for disciplinary action, including dismissal from city employment.[101]

The most common evasion of departmental sanctions, however, was resignation in the face of charges. In case after case, policemen accused of corruption retired from the force immediately after charges were filed against them. Retirement salvaged the member's pension rights, which might otherwise be forfeited following dismissal for misconduct. To counter this tactic, the department required that members of the force submit resignation forms at least thirty days prior to the intended date of retirement. Moreover, no resignations were considered effective until approved by the police commissioner, a policy designed to preserve the department's right to impose sanctions. In 1962, by the mayor's executive order, city employees who were under investigation by any federal, state, or local investigating body were prohibited from resigning without their agency's approval. After a test of these rules in court, the department's legal bureau advised the police commissioner that resignations tendered by members of the force were "self-executing" and did indeed terminate employment without anyone's approval, although salary and pension rights were still subject to forfeiture if there were later findings of malfeasance.[102]

Administrators sought to overcome these shortcomings by speeding up the department's formal disciplinary machinery. Legislation was proposed, first, to allow hearing officers to preside at departmental trials and thus reduce the backlog of cases awaiting determination; and, second, to extend filing time for retirement from thirty to ninety days. Resignations continued to be the most common response to charges of corrupt practice. Many policemen were able to delay their trials for more than thirty days and retire with charges against them still unresolved.[103]

To summarize this section, as a mechanism for controlling plainclothesmen, sanctions had limited value. Formal procedures were rarely used, and informal punishment consisted of shuffling minor offenders to other units or of banishing those suspected of malfeasance to the uniformed force. As already noted, mass transfer created only the illusion of vigorous anticorruption efforts. Many policemen who were discovered working in collusion with gamblers could escape departmental sanctions through immediate resignation. Only a mere handful of wrongdoers was ever prosecuted successfully.

5 Achieving Organizational Responsiveness

Having examined directive and control strategies in some detail, we can now step back and explore their implications for police and other public administrators. More specifically, we can analyze the NYCPD's efforts to achieve honest gambling enforcement and apply this insight to broader questions of responsiveness in large bureaucracies.

Facing the Past: Theory X

Strategies in Perspective

Up to this point the book has highlighted the component controls that form a system in one organization. We will now consider the impact of these mechanisms by integrating the analysis of the system's goals with the individual responses to various strategies. This chapter will broaden the perspective of the study to bureaucracies other than police and to organizational goals other than honest gambling enforcement. The police, however, remain the specific focus for generalization.

Observers of behavior in complex organizations have advanced various theories in their research, and the literature reflects an evolution of perspective from so-called scientific management to the human relations school of thought. Researchers in scientific management first sought to identify and explain basic principles of administration such as unity of command, span of control, and the need for authority that is commensurate with responsibility. Later studies focused on functions of systems in organizations, including planning, decision making, communication, control, and other dynamics of bureaucracies. More recently, social scientists of the human relations school analyzed administrative behavior through the interaction of the formal organization (structure and systems) with its human elements (informal groups, peer pressures, and individual psychology). To some extent the two approaches overlap: They both study how and why people behave as they do in the organizational social system.[1]

Among the more interesting efforts by students of behavior, and those most relevant here, are studies about leading and motivating people in organizations. These researchers classified bureaucracies according to the relationship between leaders and subordinates, identifying such styles as "exploitive," "benevolent," and "participatory" management. One of the best known and most persuasive exponents of these theories is Douglas McGregor, whose work in the late 1950s and early 1960s appears germane to my study.[2] McGregor's theories do not provide a complete framework for analysis; rather, they offer a useful perspective in which to examine managerial practices, and they provide a point of departure for considering new strategies to control police behavior. Extrapolating from McGregor's assumptions helps us to understand why police executives acted as they did and how they fared; it also enables us to deliberate the consequences of current and future efforts in police management.

McGregor's central thesis is that the whole character of an organization is determined by its leaders' theoretical assumptions about controlling behavior. That is, an administrator's style and strategies reflect his beliefs about the most effective way to direct people. Usually these assumptions are implicit in his managerial policies and actions and are rarely stated explicitly. Unsuccessful executives who wonder why they cannot implement their policies frequently overlook one basic source of failure—their inappropriate choice of controls.[3]

To illustrate his ideas, McGregor posits two sets of managerial assumptions, Theory X and Theory Y, which reflect dramatically different philosophies of human nature.[4] These assumptions are:

Theory X

1. People have an inherent dislike for work and therefore work as little as possible.
2. People lack ambition, are self-centered, indifferent to organizational goals, and therefore resistant to change.
3. People avoid responsibility and prefer to be led.
4. Therefore people must be coerced, directed, and controlled to work for organizational goals.

Theory Y

1. Work is as natural as rest or play, and people are not resistant to organizational goals by nature, but rather as a response learned from their experience in organizations.
2. Ingenuity and creativity are widespread, and people have the capacity for responsible self-direction.
3. People will accept, even seek, responsibility under proper conditions.
4. Therefore people will exercise responsible self-direction in the service of objectives to which they are committed.

The sharp contrast between these sets of ideas is that, as McGregor says, "Theory X places exclusive reliance upon external control of human behavior, while Theory Y relies heavily on self-control and self-direction."[5] McGregor presents the theories, not as extremes, but as a range of policies and practices in the "management of human resources." He postulates that assumptions of

Theory X allow organization leaders "to conceive of certain possible ways of organizing and directing human effort, *but not others*," whereas Theory Y apparently opens up unlimited opportunities.[6] Presumably, the range of options available to leaders using Theory X would be far narrower than those possible under Theory Y. Nevertheless, McGregor suggests that most bureaucracies follow Theory X, not because they espouse these assumptions, but because the assumptions are implicit in the leaders' methods of directing their agencies. In his view, Theory X explains the failures of traditional management.[7]

McGregor postulates that Theory Y more accurately reflects human nature and thus should be more helpful to executives. Under Theory Y, "the essential task of management is to arrange organizational conditions and methods of operation so that people can achieve their own goal best by directing their own efforts toward organizational objectives."[8] Theory Y obligates management to remove obstacles, to create opportunities, to encourage growth, and to nurture human development within the organization.

The cornerstone of Theory Y is the principle of integration of individual and organizational goals. In contrast, the central theme of Theory X is the scalar principle of organizational precedence over individual goals, which is based on the assumption that what is best for the organization is ultimately best for its members. Theory X promotes unilateral decisions, with little consideration for individual needs. Under Theory X, "working together" means that members must adjust to and accept the organization's requirements as determined by management, which knows best and makes decisions accordingly. Because Theory Y postulates that the organization will suffer if it ignores the individual, personal goals receive high consideration but not necessarily precedence over organizational goals.[9]

McGregor does not decry Theory X per se, only its application to all things at all times. He notes that "authority is an appropriate means for control under certain circumstances—particularly where genuine commitment to objectives cannot be achieved."[10] Overall, McGregor faults Theory X because it is "so unnecessarily limiting" and prevents management from recognizing possibilities in other strategies. He does not propose Theory Y as a panacea, as something readily adaptable to managerial practice, but as an invitation to innovation in leadership. To McGregor, it does not imply "soft management, or permissiveness"; rather, it offers the possibility of reducing emphasis on external forms of control to encourage a search for ways to achieve personal commitment. Theory X, in contrast, provides no other standard except past accomplishment. McGregor acknowledges managerial disillusionment with Theory Y policies that have failed, but he concludes that "these new approaches are no more than different tactics—programs, procedures, gadgets—within an unchanged strategy based on Theory X."[11] And this theme brings us back to the police and their struggle to eliminate corruption.

Assumptions of Police Management

McGregor offers a powerful contrast in his two models, undoubtedly a dramatic way to minimize distortion of his ideas. But to think of the X-Y theories as a dichotomy oversimplifies the situation, because in reality most organizations are highly complex. Indeed, few bureaucracies are a monolithic X or Y; some are more X-oriented and others more Y-oriented.[12]

Within the New York City Police Department, one can see a continuum of specific X-Y controls. Overall, but not exclusively, the department is a classic Theory X organization. Virtually all the assumptions of Theory X are implicit in the department's organization and policies, particularly in its system of controls. But management's strategies are diversified so that controls range along the continuum according to the task performed. At the continuum's poles are extremes of least and most regulation. Underlying the greater part of the continuum are the behavioral assumptions of Theory X that were described by McGregor; at the extreme of least control are assumptions of Theory Y.

Most of the continuum is taken up by people in the patrol force and related positions. This group is governed by basic X assumptions. Policemen are coerced, directed, and manipulated to a significant degree through directive and control strategies of preformed decisions, supervision, and sanctions. The clearest example is the patrolman who is governed by highly detailed rules and procedures, supervised regularly by his sergeant, compelled to record every activity in a memo book, required to remain in constant communication with his headquarters, and subject to informal and formal disciplinary procedures after breaking any rule.

Near the end of the continuum reflecting Theory Y assumptions, we find a small group of policemen, best exemplified by the detective division, whose members enjoy substantial discretion. Even within the detective division, however, there are varying degrees of control. For example, homicide detectives enjoy considerable freedom because police administrators assume that these detectives share the department's goal of solving murders. While achieving individual ambitions of increased status and prestige, homicide detectives also fulfill the organization's goals. In this case individual commitment may merge almost completely with organizational needs, a classic illustration of Theory Y.

Managerial strategies regulating gambling enforcement and governance of the plainclothes force appear at the opposite end of the continuum. Directive and control strategies are clearly applications of Theory X. Indeed, the strategies reflect both tenets of Theory X: distrust of subordinates' integrity and use of compulsory mechanisms. Bear in mind, however, that directive strategies such as training and changing incentives are neutral in concept, and might be used with Theory Y assumptions. But as those strategies were applied during the 1950s and 1960s, it appears that police executives subscribed wholeheartedly to Theory X, believing that plainclothesmen had to be coerced, directed, and controlled to enforce gambling laws honestly.

Directive strategies, unquestionably rife with mistrust of plainclothesmen, resulted in a system of rigorous external controls in gambling enforcement. Officials continuously changed operating policies and procedures to decrease discretion and established the GEIRB as a permanent watchdog over the plainclothes force. Cyclical shuffling of personnel and organizational hierarchy not only reflected management's insecurity, but also created internal tension through a system of checks and balances based on competition and overlapping jurisdictions. After plainclothesmen neutralized restrictions through collusive resistance, management reversed gears and centralized gambling enforcement to enhance control. The department's underlying assumption in changing individual attitudes and incentives was that good people had to be forced into gambling enforcement through the detective incentive and later, through the Career Path program. Tenure in gambling enforcement was limited to reduce exposure to temptations. Last, but certainly not least, forced productivity was used extensively on the assumption that plainclothesmen could not conspire with gamblers they were compelled to arrest.

Control strategies also reflected a managerial mentality based on Theory X. Plainclothesmen were required to report peer misconduct, and their superiors made it clear that all records would be reviewed and verified. As for the strategy of supervision, people were drafted into supervisory positions under threat of losing forthcoming promotions to captain. The assumption was that leaders in plainclothes would not work effectively unless they were under duress. Even so, supervisors had little or no discretion and were restricted either to regular work shifts or to specific geographic areas to fix responsibility for failure. Formal and informal sanctions were used regularly as intimidating tools. Plainclothesmen lived with the threat of formal charges for misfeasance as well as with the ever-present fear of being flopped to uniform duties for failing to maintain production, which was equated with honesty. A complete system for controlling behavior was built on Theory X's assumptions of distrust and coercion.

Failure of Theory X

Having examined directive and control strategies in detail, we know that they had serious limitations. To determine the impact of these weaknesses, let us briefly consider the findings of the latest assessment of administrators' efforts to achieve honest gambling enforcement. The independent Knapp Commission studied corruption in the NYCPD early in 1970, as another cycle of corruption was nearing completion. More than two years later the commission's detailed report amounted to an indictment of the department and its efforts to achieve honesty as an organizational norm. Only a few of their numerous findings are significant to this study. They fall into two general areas: conclusions about gambling enforcement and conclusions about strategies for honesty.

The Knapp Commission made no startling discoveries. It found that corruption in the NYCPD was widespread, "appearing at its most sophisticated among plainclothesmen assigned to enforcing gambling laws."[13] Moreover, those who were not directly engaged in malfeasance were found to tolerate others' misconduct and to do nothing to prevent known or suspected wrongdoing. The commission noted that systematic corruption had persisted almost unchanged for years in spite of periodic scandals and departmental efforts to eliminate it. After describing the intricate system of collusion among policemen allied with gamblers, the commission analyzed the cancerous implications of corrupt practices in gambling enforcement. "What is alarming is that plainclothes units serve as an important breeding ground for large-scale corruption in other areas of the Department."[14] Thus gambling enforcement served both to provide the expertise for sophisticated and systematic corruption as well as to create the unethical ethos in which malfeasance could flourish.

In evaluating the department's system of controls, the Knapp Commission assessed three specific strategies: discovery, supervision, and sanctions. It saw in these strategies what preceding investigating commissions had seen, and what administrators looking at the department in 1970 also could see. Indeed, officials taking office in the 1970s recognized these shortcomings and undertook drastic corrective measures. The department's investigative efforts against conspiracies were faulted for their poor organization and weak implementation. The case-by-case approach, as opposed to a broad effort to discover patterns of corruption, was cited as an administrative defect that precluded effective investigations of wrongdoing. The department was criticized for merely reacting to complaints from the public instead of initiating investigations on its own. Discovery units were censured as ineffective deterrents to malfeasance because they lacked authority, personnel, and overall coordination. The strategy of supervision failed, according to the Knapp Commission, because of the "reluctance on the part of top level police personnel" to face deep-seated problems and because superior officers were not held accountable for their people's malfeasance. As for the department's program for imposing sanctions, the commission found the system of controls to be overburdened and underused. Formal mechanisms such as procedures for trials were backlogged with delays, rendering the process ineffective. Moreover, the commission found that the sanctions available to administrators (their powers to promote, demote, and reassign) were not used adequately or effectively.[15]

In spite of the acknowledged failures of directive and control strategies, the Knapp Commission never questioned the behavioral assumptions that reflected McGregor's Theory X. On the contrary, the commission's recommendations incorporated Theory X's principal tenets—distrust and coercion. Stressing the need for "immediate action," the commission urged that a special deputy attorney general be appointed to head a new agency that would be "wholly unconnected with the police department," to investigate and prosecute corrupt practices in every part of the city's system of criminal justice. To deal with the specific problem of gambling enforcement the commission proposed that "criminal laws against gambling" be abolished, and that any regulation of legal gambling be done through "civil process," not through the police.[16]

In its recommended "Changes in Departmental Policies and Procedures Affecting Corruption Control," the Commission emphasized three approaches:

1. to improve supervision by actually implementing the doctrine of commanders' accountability for their subordinates' malfeasance
2. to strengthen discovery by establishing a separate career structure for people involved in rooting out corruption
3. to increase training for all members of the force—both recruits and commanders—to promote attitudes conducive to honesty[17]

General recommendations were also included to minimize corruption hazards, to change incentives, and to maintain the momentum for reform.

Even with the best intentions and strenuous efforts, the impact of the Knapp Commission is virtually indistinguishable from its many predecessors. Their proposals for vigorous prosecution and decriminalization of gambling notwithstanding, the commission once again left the problem of corruption to police executives by default. Interestingly, the commission expressly favored innovations undertaken by the new police administration, and emphasized that what was needed was *more* of the same initiatives. Thus as McGregor foresaw, the recommendations were no more than a series of new tactics "within an unchanged strategy based on Theory X."[18] This is in fact what followed, and we will assess the consequences and broader implications of the new strategies in a later section.

A Hostile Environment: X Applied

In this section directive and control strategies are reexamined to consider other fundamental reasons for their failure. We assess the aggregate forces—external and internal—that oppose Theory X and undermine the ability of organizational leaders to control subordinates.

The Structure of Interests

Public bureaucracies function in an external environment that influences its leaders' abilities to achieve their goals. The environment has many components, each of which exerts a different kind and degree of pressure. For public bureaucracies the principal components are usually found within a structure of interests manifested by the statutes that give the organization its mandate, the attitudes of the general public, and the influence of clients or special interest groups. The relative strength of these elements and their disposition toward organizational goals–supportive, neutral, or hostile–can have a significant impact on strategies for control.[19]

The structure of external interests changes periodically and differs from agency to agency, even varying within one bureaucracy depending on the service or function performed. One official may enjoy external support for his task, helping him obtain additional funds or other resources, while another administrator in the same organization faces antagonism from the public. The police work in such an unpredictable environment. Traditionally, they receive broad support in preventing and solving crimes related to personal safety. In a shift of emphasis in the early 1970s, for example, police expended more effort and greater sensitivity investigating sexual assaults because of public interest generated by groups concerned with rights of women, particularly victims of rape. Preserving the public morality, on the other hand, had little acceptance and resulted in a corruption more destructive than those evils the public sought to eliminate. Indeed, the injunction to prohibit gambling through sanctions of the criminal law had a significant consequence for police–a corrupting environment. Administrators have been trapped for generations by an inflexible legal mandate that obligates them to enforce unpopular statutes. Unlike other public agencies where leaders exercise some discretion in setting goals and policies–which allows them to enhance compliance with official directives–police executives could not modify the goal of honest enforcement of gambling laws to minimize resistance. In spite of the consequences, however, laws prohibiting gambling are likely to remain in New York and most other jurisdictions for the forseeable future.[20]

Because the general public was neutral if not hostile to honest enforcement, gambling enjoyed considerable social acceptance. Millions of otherwise law-abiding citizens patronized bookmaking and numbers, enhancing their status as service crimes. Citizens who did not directly support gambling generally knew little about or were totally indifferent to the question of honest enforcement.[21] Disinterest was reinforced by the low visibility of gambling enforcement. Insulated from public view and scrutiny by the press, administrators' efforts to achieve honest and ethical conduct received little or no external support. Directive and control strategies applied during the 1950s and 1960s were resented by plainclothesmen because they were based on Theory X assumptions, and thus the plainclothesmen were highly vulnerable to competing pressures in a generally hostile environment.

Organized gamblers proved a highly effective partisan group. As in other areas of public policy, whose vested interests were threatened sought to undermine agency policies.[22] Bookmaking and numbers, both durable enterprises, thrived as their operating costs remained comparatively low and as their profits mushroomed. Convictions and fines amounted to no more than licensing fees. Few organizations have worked in a more seductive environment than police do in gambling enforcement. The fact that gamblers were not a legitimate pressure group had significant consequences for police integrity, too. Public officials often negotiate openly with recognized lobbies to reduce the need of interest groups to "capture" field enforcement agents.[23] Thus in most bureaucracies there is far less pressure on subordinates to disregard their leaders' policies. Because police could not reach lawful accommodation with gamblers and thereby reduce the need for collusion, gamblers continued to coopt plainclothesmen.

Where organizations seeking influence have conflicting interests, the impact of pressure groups on individual behavior is often minimized. In this situation, one pressure group may check the ability of another to capture agency personnel and thwart organizational goals.[24] Unfortunately, such tendencies toward neutralization did not exist in the environment of public morals enforcement because organized gamblers had no competitors. Without rival interest groups to counteract gamblers' leverage, plainclothesmen faced omnipresent temptation. Also, there were no competing law enforcement agencies working against organized gambling, as there were against narcotics distribution, to compare performance or to threaten illegal conspiracies.

Of course, the presence of mutually antagonistic interest groups or competitors is no guarantee against cooptation. The possibility of redress and the nature and importance of decisions made by field personnel are significant variables. Pressure groups have more leverage to influence an organization's policies without having to coopt its agents when the leadership's decisions are incremental and continuing, when decisions do not threaten the survival of the interest group, and when local decisions can be legitimately appealed to a higher authority within the political system. But where decisions were final, essential to the existence of powerful groups, and without legitimate appeal—as in the suppression of organized gambling—pressures for corruption were unrelenting.

Gamblers' success in coopting police throughout the 1950s and 1960s also resulted from the way administrators coped with environmental pressures. To a significant degree the strategic failure of police executives to end collusion lay, according to McGregor's principles, in their choice of controls. Relying heavily on Theory X in directive and control strategies, officials sought to achieve honesty through external manipulation of the plainclothes force. Essentially, they followed the classic carrot-and-stick approach. They induced plainclothesmen into gambling enforcement through the detective incentive, assuming that honest policemen would not enter this field without coercion. Once assigned, plainclothesmen were compelled to produce arrests at any cost on the presumption that if they were required to arrest gamblers they could not form conspiracies. Finally, administrators used mechanisms of close supervision and discovery to keep a tight reign on all involved.

During the 1950s and 1960s police executives were unable, perhaps because they never really tried, to obtain plainclothesmen's commitment to honest gambling enforcement. There was no attempt to integrate this organizational goal with personal goals of individual plainclothesmen. In the absence of Theory Y commitment, Theory X strategies succumbed to the moral hazards. Only one control strategy, discovery, was really intended to cope directly with external pressures for cooptation. Even so, this application of Theory X was limited in scope to the case-by-case approach that ignored broader patterns of corruption and their causes. The strategy of close supervision failed, too, because it was limited to on-duty surveillance of plainclothesmen. Had the department even tried to apply Theory Y and achieve commitment for honest gambling enforcement, plainclothesmen would have been (at least in theory) self-directed in their pursuit of honesty.

Systems for control based on Theory X seem to be fundamentally flawed for successful application in a hostile environment. Experience shows that plainclothesmen resisted external controls, thereby enhancing gamblers' efforts at cooptation. These moral hazards of police work call for Theory Y management more than almost any other area of public administration. The compelling need to integrate organizational goals (honesty) with individual goals is based on the fact that only self-motivation can effectively prevent dishonesty. Thus the answer seems to lie in the development of individuals who are committed to achieving organizational goals in spite of public indifference and bribes proffered by interest groups.[25]

Conflicting Goals and Malfunctions of Theory X

A healthy environment for effective leadership exists when competing forces and pressures within an organization are more or less equal, so that no faction or goal dominates another. If one goal predominates or one group exerts excessive influence in pursuing its objectives, the imbalance often results in unanticipated, malfunctional consequences for management. The problem of conflicting goals within an organization is not unique to police or public bureaucracies; it plagues all organizations. Difficulty arises when the agency tries to achieve two goals that are inherently contradictory or become mutually exclusive because of managerial practices. More typically, goals come into conflict as a result of organizational operations.[26]

The classic case in public bureaucracies is the reversal of ends and means. That is, members subordinate the reason for the organization's creation (the end desired) to the organization's perpetuation (the means). This often happens when the agency is under attack or when its usefulness is over, its end having been achieved. A secondary but common form of displacement occurs when actual or apparent efficiency is substituted for the organization's objective. This problem is widespread, especially in public bureaucracies, because of the overemphasis on efficiency, the need to achieve the organization's goals with the least amount of resources. Where it is measured in dollars and cents, as in the profits of private industry, efficiency can be determined by accounting procedures. But where the organization provides abstract services–education, health, or public safety, for example–the only way to quantify efficiency is through general indicators such as reading levels or crime statistics.[27]

To provide concrete evidence of efficiency, public bureaucracies often amass impressive statistics as a measure of their good faith efforts. The danger of this practice is that numbers take precedence over actual performance, creating a disequilibrium between efficiency and desired objectives because the rank and file substitutes means for ends. As substitution occurs, top and middle management disregard intended goals in favor of the apparent achievement of objectives.[28] Thus an organization's leaders may introduce the mechanisms and incentives that undermine official policies, and create an internal environment antipathetic to their own strategies. Such was the case in the New York City Police Department, where leaders created administrative incentives that fostered unethical behavior.

Relying almost exclusively on the fundamental and pessimistic assumptions of Theory X, successive administrations maintained constant pressures on plainclothesmen to arrest as many gamblers as possible. Official policy that coupled honesty with "quality enforcement" against the higher echelon of organized gambling was displaced by administrative incentives to corruption. Arrests, however meaningless, became the end instead of remaining the means for suppressing illegal gambling; "covering the sheet" became the plainclothesman's objective. The department achieved apparent efficiency at the expense of honesty. Where they lacked guidance or found discrepancies in their superiors' orders and actions, plainclothesmen justified their behavior with unofficial norms. Indeed, unofficial norms helped to create unethical behavior whenever there was an administrative vacuum.

Because honest enforcement and high production could not coexist, plainclothesmen came to tolerate unethical conduct, which further nourished the growth of malpractice. Pressures to "produce" generated a series of unethical practices, including expedient arrests and "flaking," false reporting, falsification of affidavits, and perjury. Plainclothesmen sacrificed personal integrity for arrests and convictions. Under these circumstances, unscrupulous individuals probably earned the coveted gold shield while their superiors received recognition for jobs well done.

Efficiency also superseded honesty in policy decisions relating to personnel administration, such as in refusals to use rookie patrolmen in plainclothes, to limit tenure in plainclothes, and to transfer clerical men along with plainclothesmen. Administrators would not accept reduced effectiveness in investigations–that is, fewer arrests–as a tradeoff for possible increases in honesty. Rookie patrolmen, not yet exposed to the temptations and pressures that produced cooptation, lacked sufficient experience in law enforcement to be competent investigators. Moreover, by the time they became efficient in enforcement, their assignments might be ending. Although the Gambling Enforcement Inspection and Review Board recommended a two-year tenure to limit exposure to moral temptations, officials decried any loss in efficiency caused by constant turnover in personnel.

The department's failure to transfer clerical people when entire plainclothes units were flopped demonstrated how deeply officials were committed to the quest for productivity through stability in daily operations. Clerical men, with their monopoly of knowledge of illegal gambling, were likely if not essential parties to systemic malpractice in the plainclothes force. Whereas administrators knew that the clerical staff helped provide continuity for corruption, they felt compelled to place a higher premium on accumulating a high volume of arrests. Implausible as it may seem, statistics of arrests were officialdom's only evidence of the honest enforcement of gambling laws.

In addition to creating malfeasance, police reliance on Theory X had other adverse consequences for trying to achieve honesty. Specifically, the coercive assumptions of Theory X undermined the department's umbrella strategy for controlling corruption—supervision. Virtually every directive and control strategy applied to the plainclothes force was tied to close supervision. Officials reasoned that unless officers assigned to lead plainclothesmen were working under some compulsion, they would not do an effective job. Thus officials assigned only lieutenants awaiting promotion to a captaincy because those people stood to lose the most if they did not promote diligence and motivate integrity among their subordinates. Fear was the stimulus. But officials failed to appreciate the consequences of Theory X.

Because supervisors drafted into plainclothes were fearful and passive, most handled the assignment by "holding on" until they were promoted. The supervisors saw no evil, heard no evil, and spoke no evil. Their reluctance to become involved was reinforced by an unrealistic span of control and overwhelming work loads. There were simply too few hours in the day for commanders to meet administrative and field responsibilities as well as to oversee their subordinates at critical moments. Theirs was the scavenger model of enforcement with no directed investigations; superiors issued orders but never had time to ensure compliance. As a practical matter, plainclothesmen usually worked independent of their supervisors, who in turn were apparently content to be ignorant of the squad's activities. Although leaders knew that they compounded unethical practices through acquiescence, they were trapped by their own compromises to survive tenure in plainclothes. They felt that they were in the same predicament as their plainclothesmen, having had scant legal and technical training and having had to rely on past leadership experience. Although they were repeatedly warned of their accountability, commanders often were not trained to prevent or deal with malfeasance. Left to their own devices, most supervisors relied completely on the PCCIU and police headquarters while they yearned to escape from plainclothes untouched by scandal.

Even if they were inclined to achieve honest gambling enforcement, superiors had few effective means of controlling behavior. Corrupt schemes were arranged and executed after working hours, outside the commanders' jurisdiction. Corrupt plainclothesmen could still maintain appearances of diligent enforcement by arresting stand-ins supplied by organized gambling. The external controls developed from Theory X management were no match for collusive schemes of plainclothesmen and gamblers. Thus the department's almost exclusive reliance on the assumptions of Theory X created malfeasance within an environment antagonistic to honesty. Augmenting these systemic flaws, however, was a deep-seated instability within the police department's leadership.

Instabilities of Leadership

Crucial instabilities of leadership contributed to the long-term failure to achieve honesty. Even the best system for controlling behavior in an organization is bound to fail without forceful direction and execution. Frustrated and unable to fulfill their responsibilities as watchdogs, officials allowed their other role as the department's advocates to dominate their perspectives. This imbalance resulted from administrators' inability to maintain high priority for the achievement of honest enforcement, to execute their strategies, and to cope with the unpleasantness of crusading against corruption. Each of these failures contributed significantly to an environment favoring corrupt practice.[29]

A basic source of administrative instability was the department's political vulnerability. Because law enforcement was so sensitive, political leaders regarded the police as a perpetual problem, a source of crises. The department was continually scrutinized and subjected to more pressures than most other public bureaucracies. Thus a police commissioner's control over the department's priorities and goals was limited by powerful and fluctuating external demands.

In response to pressures and changing priorities, officials periodically reviewed overall demands of policing the city and structured the department's efforts accordingly. Organized gamblers benefited directly from the public's increased concern for civil liberties and individual safety, two issues of greater social and political importance than gambling in New York City during the 1950s and 1960s. As the public became more interested in how policemen enforced laws and protected citizens, the priority of gambling enforcement yielded to more urgent problems. Violent street crime, drug addiction, and serious disorders related to social and political issues came to dominate the department's energies. The resulting shift in resources diverted plainclothesmen and supervisors to other duties.[30]

Weakened priorities in gambling enforcement also took their toll on honesty and integrity because there developed a detachment from the issue and all its ramifications—a detachment based on the assumption that corruption in gambling was minimal. For decades police administrators proclaimed publicly that the vast majority of policemen were honest, dedicated, and self-sacrificing in comparison to a mere few dishonest rogue cops. Throughout the 1950s and 1960s most administrations held to this view of corruption in spite of scandals that evidenced continual malfeasance.[31] Thus integrity in enforcing gambling laws remained a concern rather than a major commitment for administrators.

Conforming to their official view of corruption, officials saw themselves waging never-ending war against malfeasance. The creation of the Gambling Enforcement Inspection and Review Board was hailed as a landmark in this struggle because all problems of integrity in gambling enforcement were under constant scrutiny by honest and dedicated administrators. Presumably the GEIRB provided better direction and tighter control of the plainclothes force. Unfortunately it underestimated its task, as it failed to overcome the influence of gamblers and never came to grips with the intricate pattern of administrative incentives that created and reinforced unethical practices. Because administrators never dealt with fundamental issues, they were optimistic that their house was in order, that corruption in gambling law enforcement was at an "irreducible minimum." More significantly, this confidence allowed successive administrations to keep problems of corrupt practice and unethical behavior at arm's length.[32]

Instability in leadership and policy making also diluted strategies for keeping the force honest and ethical. Leaders of noncontroversial public organizations, who benefit from low visibility, often enjoy long tenures that enable them to implant their policies. Given sufficient time, such administrators promote responsive subordinates to important positions within the hierarchy to reinforce acceptance of their programs. The opposite occurred in the NYCPD, where police commissioners usually had brief tenures. Frequent turnover in high-level posts following each change of administration made the department unstable. Strategies from preceding administrations were sometimes discarded or implemented with varying degrees of commitment by new administrations. Moreover, frequent turnover of leaders in the plainclothes force hindered officials from discovering cooptation or eliminating administrative incentives to corruption. Thus many directive and control strategies, whatever their conceptual strengths and weaknesses, never received the continuous application needed to make them take hold and achieve acceptance within the plainclothes structure.

Lack of stability affected leadership's power as well as its continuity. Leaders who are in power for prolonged periods amass sufficient administrative clout to implement and gain acceptance for policies that are unpopular with or even distasteful to the rank and file. Such was not the case in the NYCPD. Lacking a strong mandate to eliminate malfeasance, successive administrations in the 1950s and 1960s did not build up sufficient power to implement basic reforms within the department.

Because of these persistent frustrations and failures, the department's leaders resigned themselves to the status quo. For generations the department, from top to bottom, acceded to management based on tradition and precedent. Change had always been evolutionary, not revolutionary. Gradual transformation was reinforced by the belief that no one could really change the department anyway. Its bureaucracy was strong, having developed over a long period, and people with a lifetime of service continually rose to the highest ranks and perpetuated established patterns of thought.[33] Thus the assumptions and values of Theory X were ingrained and accepted as the only way to deal with cooptation and unethical practices.

Moreover, administrators were comfortable with the routine. Indeed, it was personally unpleasant and professionally unrewarding for officials to openly acknowledge and challenge malfeasance within the department. Police commissioners and their colleagues, who had risen professionally and were confident of their abilities, had no interest in turning the department asunder in search of a few rogue cops. They sought to cap their careers with achievement and leave with banners flying—not to be marked in history as those who betrayed the department or sullied its reputation. Nor did they wish to "bite the bullet" when they had to discipline former colleagues, perhaps even friends or previous on-the-job partners. Reformers also had to contend with adverse publicity and hostility from the rank and file, all of which decreased morale and output. "Corruption fighters," considered traitors by the force, also experienced significantly more bureaucratic resistance to their leadership. Such resistance could easily have affected areas unrelated to honesty and integrity and could have threatened the success of the administration's other programs.[34]

All these disadvantages led the department's leaders to accept their inability to achieve honesty. Resignation to failure reinforced itself over the years because new generations of officials accepted corruption in the plainclothes force as an inevitable fact of life.[35] No one was motivated to change the system. Continued reliance on Theory X offered police executives an easy rationalization for the department's record on corruption—the human nature of policemen. Theory Y, in contrast, points to failure of management. If the majority of police was indifferent to or tolerant of corruption, and if supervisors were unwilling to accept responsibility to end corrupt practices, Theory Y implies that the cause was ineffective leadership and control. More important, external controls based on Theory X offered a cheap, expedient, and viable solution. Their costs were minimal in terms of organizational resources and rank-and-file hostility. And the flurry of publicity over anticorruption campaigns went a long way in rebuilding public confidence and reducing political pressures for drastic reform. Given their brief tenures, what else could police leaders do to cope with the problem? Thus the hostile environment continued until the cycle of corruption was completed early in 1970, when another scandal in gambling enforcement burst forth into public view.

Backing into the Future: Theory X^n

Control Model X^n

Up to this point we have traced the application and failure of classic Theory X. What alternatives are left for police and other public bureaucracies who are undermined by collusive resistance to their organizational goals and programs? At the end of his book, Douglas McGregor notes that Theory X strategies "provide us with no standard except present accomplishment and thus encourage us . . . 'to face the past and back into the future.' "[36] For generations, police administrations faced the past, using the same strategies as their predecessors had used to achieve honesty. Continuity was the byword in controlling individual behavior. There were some slight variations, some shift in emphasis, but external controls based on Theory X were management's underlying assumptions.

Faced with these failures in early 1970, and caught up in the limelight of another cycle of corruption, the new administration undertook a dramatic turn in strategy to avoid backing into the future. Building on Theory X, officials extended the concept of external controls to the nth degree and coordinated a series of somewhat draconian strategies. I call this model for controlling behavior Theory X^n. As used by the New York City Police Department the model had four components: (1) heightened consciousness of control; (2) overt surveillance by peers; (3) covert programs for testing integrity; and (4) strict managerial accountability.

As the first step to implement Theory X^n, officials began by increasing the level of consciousness about corruption, making everyone in the department aware of its pervasiveness and the administration's determination to eliminate it. Officials wanted to arouse perceptions of the problem, increase concern, and raise tensions. In particular, they sought to destroy the confidence and trust among those involved in corrupt practices, as well as to promote hostility rather than tolerance toward them. To capitalize on this new awareness, two programs for surveillance were openly developed. Field associates were recruited from new plainclothesmen who agreed to report any misconduct of their peers. Also, selective amnesty was dispensed to encourage corrupt plainclothesmen, before or after they were discovered, to "turn around" and help incriminate former coconspirators. Both programs were designed to create an omnipresent fear of exposure and to heighten anxiety.[37]

Next, a series of covert tests of integrity were inaugurated. Using wiretaps and phony gambling enterprises, the new administration probed the depth and breadth of collusive resistance to develop information on which it could act as well as to measure its success at increasing fears of discovery.[38] Finally, to intensify pressure, officials imposed stricter rules that held superior officers accountable for the malfeasance of their subordinates.

The overall thrust of these programs, and the essence of Theory X^n, was the creation and use of functional anxiety to counter collusive resistance. The concept of functional anxiety is not new. One observer of organizational behavior has defined it as "a moderate degree of tension or sensitivity that tends to sharpen the individual's perception of behavioral alternatives appropriate to a given situation and to their probable consequences."[39] This view of the concept describes the psychological reaction to stimuli arising from pressures in the organization, such as interpersonal competition and fear of failure.[40] In our context, however, functional anxiety is the rational, consciously implemented policy to induce fear in subordinates and to use this fear as a means of control. Needless to say, administrators are not often likely to propose Theory X^n as an explicit policy or a legitimate means of advancing public affairs. It might seem incongruous—particularly in law enforcement, with its presumed norm of honesty—to advocate the use of fear to achieve organizational goals. The X^n model of control, however, bears an intriguing relationship to McGregor's X and Y theories.

One might wrongly assume that because model X^n is built on the assumptions and external controls of Theory X, that X^n is merely an extension or exaggeration of X to the nth degree. This is not the case. On careful examination one finds, paradoxically, that model X^n more closely approximates Theory Y than Theory X. That is, functional anxiety, the sum effect of X^n, is not an external control but rather an internal self-directing force not unlike the motivation envisioned in Theory Y. Fear substitutes for voluntary commitment to organizational goals. Although it is negative, it is self-directing. The crucial difference between X^n and Y is that according to Y, the individual is voluntarily committed to achieve the organization's goals because the goals are completely integrated—individuals achieve their personal aims while striving for the organization. Presumably, the commitment is self-determined, even though management might manipulate individuals through careful screening and selection to reinforce each one's dedication. Under Theory X^n, commitment is not voluntary; it is deliberately replaced by functional anxiety so that individuals work for organizational goals because they fear doing otherwise. Because workers are nonetheless self-directed, the need for external controls is reduced. Functional anxiety is effective twenty-four hours a day. Although the assumptions underlying Theory Y and Theory X^n are poles apart in their assessment of human relations, their operative effect is the same. Thus gambling and narcotics enforcement, which proceed under hostile conditions, appear to offer opportunities for the use of fear as avowed policy in police organizations. The following section considers why model X^n was needed and how effective it was; it also assesses the costs and benefits of using X^n in public affairs.

X^n Effectiveness and Limitations

Why should any organization apply Theory X^n to control the behavior of its members? In the case of the NYCPD, a scandal legitimized its use—the failure of previous administrations who relied on Theory X and pressure to improve the situation quickly. Because they took office during a crisis, administrators held a mandate to eliminate corruption, particularly in gambling enforcement. Indeed, the structure of external interests supporting strategies for honesty based on a system of X^n controls was a significant factor in their implementation and effectiveness.[41] An aggressive press and the Knapp Commission actively pursued the question of corruption, also creating an undeniable sense of urgency. Publicity in the media underscored the failure of previous administrations and highlighted the immediate need for effective solutions.

Although officials knew that honesty in gambling enforcement required long-term changes in policemen's attitudes, there was insufficient time to achieve commitment to honesty or to integrate organizational goals with the desires of individual plainclothesmen. Administrators needed an immediate substitute for commitment as a self-directing mechanism of control. Fear was used as the short-term substitute because it could be applied quickly and because it promised success.

After applying Theory X^n for only a few years, officials sought to measure its effectiveness toward the end of 1973 by undertaking a formal and unprecedented determination of the level of honesty throughout the force, especially in gambling enforcement. Known as the Integrity Assessment, the study comprised a series of self-assessments by senior commanders in gambling and narcotics enforcement, and by other commanders concerned with control of department-wide malfeasance. The final report contained extensive information gathered through interviews and covert tests of integrity. Indeed, the use of police and criminal informants as well as other confidential sources yielded significant data, lent credibility to the administration's evaluative effort, and gave the assessment greater validity.[42]

The most important conclusions of the Integrity Assessment were that the scope and degree of corruption had vastly diminished and that narcotics enforcement had replaced gambling as the major threat to integrity. The report, which included favorable and unfavorable information, was sobering but encouraging. Most of the findings regarding the impact of the new strategies on gambling enforcement were favorable. The principal determination was that in gambling enforcement, "organized systematic corruption had been virtually eliminated."[43] But this apparent success was all the more intriguing because of the finding that

> although much has been done to reduce actual corrupt conduct, much still remains to be done in the area of attitudes. The present improvement in corrupt practices is mainly the result of a fear of being apprehended as opposed to the preferred reason, that corruption is wrong. In the final analysis, it is the constant pressure produced by the current anti-corruption policies of the department, particularly the Field Associate Program, which is responsible for the decrease in corrupt activities. The attitudes and ethics of a great number of members of the service has not been substantially altered and any future reduction of anti-corruption pressure will probably result in a substantial increase in corrupt activities.[44]

Any cautious optimism in the report was further tempered by officials' suspicions that collusive resistance had become more sophisticated and that perhaps many were playing the "waiting game," hoping that the next administration would lessen Theory X^n controls.[45] At the end of 1974, officials conducted a second Integrity Assessment and found, as before, that there had been no resumption of organized corruption in gambling enforcement.[46] If we accept the principal determination of the two assessments–that organized corruption in gambling enforcement has been "virtually eliminated"–we must conclude that Theory X^n was the only strategy clearly successful in deterring malfeasance in gambling enforcement.

Assuming, then, that the X^n model can provide an effective system for controlling collusive resistance in an organization, we must now define its limitations and costs. The fundamental limitation is that functional anxiety in lieu of voluntary commitment to organizational goals offers, at best, a short-term solution. Theory X^n may curb malpractice but it does not alter attitudes underlying behavior. If strategies based on Theory X^n cannot be sustained until attitudes change, corruption will return. Because few bureaucracies function in an ideal environment, there is room for effective short-term solutions, provided their costs are not too high. Whereas management might continue to apply functional anxiety over a time that is sufficient to achieve a semblance of reform, it is doubtful that public officials can use fear long enough to change individual attitudes permanently.

Another limitation of Theory X^n is that it works only against collusive resistance or individually deviant behavior (such as organized cooptation or individual extortion or theft), and that it has limited impact on malfeasance caused by administrative incentives to corruption. To eliminate malfeasances such as false arrests and perjury, administrators must abandon the use of coercion and reduce their reliance on Theory X.

Coupled with these limitations are significant moral, practical, and political costs. Is it ethical for police, or other officials to use functional anxiety, to deliberately and indiscriminately induce fear to achieve goals? If we accept functional anxiety in law enforcement, will the use of fear spread to other agencies or to the private sector? I do not propose to answer these questions, not even in the limited context of balancing the competing interests of honest law enforcement against the rights of criminal conspirators; I merely raise some questions regarding the hazards of relying on Theory X^n.

In the practical administration of public bureaucracies I see other drawbacks in using a system of X^n controls. Officials will find it hard to recruit and keep capable people to do the necessary gambling and narcotics enforcement and the other unsavory tasks that lend themselves to the application of X^n. Fear of covert supervision may adversely affect performance. It would be extremely difficult to limit functional anxiety to those directly involved with corrupt practices without affecting everyone in corruption-prone parts of the department. And how can management prevent the hostility and resentment generated by Theory X^n from spilling into areas unrelated to collusive resistance and sabotaging other programs and policies?

Last, it seems dubious that public officials can openly advocate the use of X^n controls. Because they are political appointees, officials are subjected to indirect but powerful pressures, such as those generated by public employee organizations. Indeed, police unions and benevolent organizations have proved themselves to be among the most formidable political advocates when their vital interests are affected. At best, X^n appears viable only in a crisis, when expedience overrides other political costs and makes X^n appear to be a necessity.

Because of the ethical uncertainty, practical constraints, and other costs, Theory X^n would appear to have limited value to practitioners of public administration. But X^n does have an important relevance to public affairs now and for the forseeable future.

The Case for Theory X^n

Even a cursory review of the literature confirms that the thinking of the human relations school dominates both practical and theoretical concerns for managing people in organizations. Whereas management based on Theory X assumptions is probably the most prevalent model, there is evidence that the leaders of public and private organizations are seeking to develop their human resources. McGregor's ideas seem to be well accepted, at least to the extent that most administrators express concern about any loss of human potential.[47]

In spite of lip service about the concept, there are only a few examples of Theory Y management, particularly in public bureaucracies. Interestingly, some organizations that apparently succeeded in applying Theory Y did so before McGregor presented his thesis. The United States Forest Service is a case in point. Although it made some minor use of Theory X, its administrators used two strategies to achieve commitment and integration of organizational goals with individual goals. First, they carefully screened and selected applicants whose attitudes and goals were most compatible with those of the Forest Service. Second, leaders and peer groups reinforced this tendency toward integration through both planned and unstructured socialization within the agency. Whereas socialization could possibly have been used without selection controls to achieve conformity, the combination of the two proved highly effective.[48]

As for Theory X^n, no studies have documented the use of fear to achieve organizational goals as a matter of deliberate policy. Although many public agencies rely on Theory X controls to achieve their goals, and many have internal units to ensure integrity, these mechanisms represent only the application of Theory X's classic assumptions.[49]

What is particularly noteworthy about Theory X^n, however, is its application to police organizations. As I noted in Chapter 1, police today are under continuous scrutiny and their credibility is constantly questioned, especially in cities where collusive resistance is prevalent in gambling and narcotics enforcement. Given also the rapidly changing population of our urban centers and concomitant changes in political power, the trend for law enforcement seems to be toward more control rather than less. Even though Theory X management and external controls are decried in the literature, they may have greater relevance for police than ever before.[50] We seem unable to benefit from the experience of the last 25 years. Controls based on Theory X continue to offer expedient and sufferable solutions insofar as the public and police rank-and-file are concerned. And given their brief tenures, what else can police leaders do to cope with the problem?

Because of New York City administrators' apparent success in the early 1970s, police officials elsewhere might rely on a similar system of controls. The case for X^n is that if one can change behavior for a long enough period, one may eventually be able to change underlying attitudes. Although its effect may be transient and difficult to contain, a system of control based on X^n might still be effective. The short-term application of X^n in organizations could thus contribute to the creation of desirable attitudes as it nourishes new norms of behavior. Whether X^n could sustain those norms raises more complex questions. But there is a stong case for it as an emergency measure, especially when the political balance favors the immediate control of police malpractice. Probably the most likely future application in New York and elsewhere will be in narcotics enforcement, where public and police intolerance of corruption converge most closely. The use of X^n controls would be condoned because of urgent circumstances, when expedience overrides political costs and makes the use of fear an acceptable necessity. In the long run, however, public organizations need another, more effective and more acceptable means of achieving responsiveness.

Even if Theory X^n holds real possibilities for police administrators, there must be alternatives, because the inherent limitations of X^n keep us facing the past, causing us to back into the future. I suggest that for police forces and other organizations coping with collusive resistance to their goals, a solution must be found elsewhere. The solution may be highly reminiscent of Theory Y—of achieving commitment and integration of organizational and individual goals. And this integration is presented for consideration under the broad concept of professionalism.

Integrating Goals

A Long-Term Endeavor

As a first step in achieving meaningful reform, we might do well to acknowledge that police executives probably face an insurmountable task in eliminating corruption, given their limited tools (particularly their lack of knowledge of how to control subordinates' behavior) and the constraints under which they must use their tools. Where pressures for collusive resistance and other deviant behavior are likely to continue indefinitely, as in the demand for illegal goods and services, the achievement of durable organizational responsiveness must be viewed as a long-term endeavor. The system of X^n controls succeeded in changing only the behavior, not the attitudes, of the NYCPD plainclothesmen. Such success is transitory at best. Bureaucracies are not static—leaders come and go, goals are modified, and environments change. As old problems are solved, new ones appear—and as they are resolved, old difficulties are revived. Thus police and other public administrators who want to implement controversial policies need an enduring mechanism for achieving organizational responsiveness.

As we have already seen, management based on Theory X's external controls was overmatched by a hostile environment; it even created malpractices through administrative incentives to corruption. Theory X^n offers temporary solutions that are not sustainable because of their limitations and high costs. Moreover, continued reliance on X^n controls is an admission of management's failure in choosing a crisis response rather than an effective system for controlling behavior. Theory X^n attacks symptoms (deviant behavior) instead of causes (lack of commitment to organizational goals). What police and other public administrators need is a large-scale movement of the kind suggested by McGregor's Theory Y: commitment to and integration of organizational goals with individual goals. Unless their employees feel an individual commitment to honesty, to due process in law enforcement, or to other organizational goals, police and public agencies cannot fulfill their responsibilities. The most frequently proposed mechanism for obtaining a convergence of goals is professionalism. Professionalism is analogous to the positive, self-directing commitment of Theory Y management. Police in particular have advocated professionalism as the long-range solution to achieving organizational responsiveness.

Professionalism

The call to "professionalism" today reflects a broadly based quest for upward mobility. Socioeconomic forces shaping our society have created an increasing demand for occupational specialization, and rapid advances in knowledge and technology have helped to change the concept of professionalism, making it synonymous with expertise. As a result, the number of occupational groups seeking and claiming professional status has increased dramatically.[51]

Police and allied law enforcement agencies are prominent among these occupational groups. Unfortunately, professionalism has been advanced for various reasons by different groups within the law enforcement community, and this lack of unanimity has created both confusion and skepticism.[52] Different definitions with differing priorities have been put forward. As did other occupational groups, police first advocated professionalism to enhance demands for higher pay and other economic benefits, but now they seek social status and prestige. In recent years, as the legitimacy of police practices has come under closer scrutiny, critics of professionalism have seen the movement as a demand for independence, allowing law enforcement to avoid control by the public. Indeed, there is room for doubt. Professionals at times misuse power for self-regulation to take advantage of an uninformed public—price fixing and fee splitting are examples—and to conceal shortcomings of individual practitioners or the profession as a whole. Thus the nature of professionalism is significant because its attainment and usefulness is a function of its definition. Advocacy of professionalism has proceeded along three lines: expertise, higher education, and ethical practice.

Although policemen generally espouse the goal of professionalism, there is no consensus among them about its form or methods for attaining it. Until recently the practitioners' movement to professionalize police was based on improvements in providing public services and detecting crime through technological and administrative efficiency. Adoption of new practices for providing advanced training, using forensic laboratories, deploying patrol forces, and most recently, applying sophisticated systems of communication and computers has been hailed as professionalism. Thus this popular model of professionalism was essentially based on expertise, on performing duties more efficiently through technical and administrative innovations.[53] If people were to accept this model as the equivalent of professionalization, as some policemen do, the debate would soon end.

Many objective observers, as well as many police executives, look beyond the expertise model of professionalism because they see expertise as only an early stage in an evolutionary process. Optimistic administrators base hopes for professionalization on rapidly expanding academic programs in police science, public administration, and criminal justice. A small but perceptible movement is under way in several states to require policemen to undergo training in college. Higher education offers both the form and substance of professionalism, and a college degree is a credential traditionally associated with the established professions. College education offers policemen a broader perspective in their work, resulting from exposure to ideas and viewpoints from many disciplines. Higher education promises police executives better understanding of administrative processes and insights about controlling behavior in organizations.[54] Those who look beyond expertise see a fundamental shift of emphasis from organizational efficiency to improved individual performance.

To achieve enduring reform, other observers would build on higher education in their definition of professionalism. Their model of professionalism includes:

1. expertise based on substantial training in a body of knowledge
2. adherence to prescribed standards of ethical practices
3. public reliance based on trust in the policeman's knowledge and motivation

Proponents of this view of police professionalism acknowledge that right now theirs is only a skeletal model, with much of the substantive material still to be developed.[55] In particular, police have much to learn from the social sciences, from which they must continue to extract data relevant to law enforcement. Moreover, academicians must add to the literature of the social sciences and suggest alternatives to prevent and deal with crime. Police need to learn more about controlling their agencies, particularly how to introduce the ideas for management described in Theory Y. Administrators must expand their efforts to build a body of knowledge that will support ethical professionalism.

Although standards of ethical practice are not as nebulous as law enforcement's philosophical basis, they still require critical consideration before they can be used to prescribe behavior. Police need clear guidance in the exercise of discretion given the moral hazards they face. In recent years police, including the NYCPD, have adopted formal codes of ethics embodying uplifting values (see Exhibit Z in the appendix), but the codes have not been realized.[56] Advocates of professionalism, however, remain optimistic.

If police develop a body of knowledge, and if they apply it within bounds of ethical standards, the public may come to rely on them, trusting that officers will act unselfishly in the public's best interests. The foundation of this model of professionalism is a set of deeper humanistic values that would produce voluntary adherence to ethical standards. Among the most desirable of these values are the impartial enforcement of laws, commitment to enforcement through the rule of law, and belief in the dignity and worth of the individual regardless of race, sex, or social class.

Police executives do have reason to be optimistic in spite of their present lack of attainment because the overwhelming majority of people entering law enforcement believe in the traditional goals of police: the prevention of crime, the preservation of life and property, and the apprehension of wrongdoers. This disposition toward current organizational goals offers administrators a potential receptiveness to new directions for law enforcement.[57] Police administrators must now capitalize on this receptivity. Indeed, their failure during the past several decades has been to overemphasize technical-administrative efficiency at the expense of professional values. Police leaders must learn how to develop human resources and individual responsiveness. Professionalism will have its beginning when police and other bureaucratic leaders can achieve commitment to goals such as ethical practice. How and when leaders can achieve integration of individual and professional aims is considered in the next section, as part of professionalization.

Professionalization

As this study suggests, professionalism offers public administrators a *means* of achieving responsiveness to the organization's goals. But in a larger sense, professionalism is also an *end* in itself, particularly for organizations, such as police forces, that have failed to achieve mandated ethical practice. Keeping this distinction in mind, let us now move from professionalism, a description of behavior, to professionalization, the process of attaining that behavior. We will look at three relevant variables: the organizational setting, the effort required, and the time and distance to be covered.

The first important issue is the apparent tension between professionalism and organizations. Traditional professions such as medicine and law expect individuals to be responsible to only their parent profession and not to any organizational leaders. Control over the professional is exerted indirectly by his colleagues. Thus a potential conflict lies in the organization's demand for conformity and responsiveness, in contrast with the professional's independent exercise of judgment based on his code of ethics.[58] Clearly the concept of professionalism has been changing gradually as the United States has become an organizational society. The classic professions have become increasingly specialized, assuming many of the structural aspects of small firms in the traditional economic sense. The era of the independent practitioner is fast fading because professionals seek to provide more and better services through more organization and modern technology. The growth of health care, in particular, has brought doctors into a complex organizational setting not unlike police agencies—the urban hospital. But although doctors may struggle with bureaucracy, they do so with a long tradition of professional independence and ethical orientation.

Police agencies and other bureaucracies do not propose to imitate doctors or lawyers, but police do need the professional's ethical orientation. It should not be the occupational setting per se that determines professionalism, but whether the individual working in an organization is free to apply his knowledge and expertise in the exercise of judgment. Bureaucracy need not preclude professionalism. Organizational systems for directing and controlling behavior can be effective tools to achieve this goal. Judicious management in personnel administration, in operational procedures, in organizational structure, and in allocations of human and material resources can enhance professionalization.

Professionalization will not be achieved without a coordinated effort to change the institutions of law enforcement externally and internally. To a significant degree, achievement of professionalism will be a function of effective police leadership. Leaders who use their directive powers wisely can give legitimacy to the idea of professionalism, and in particular to its underlying attitudes. There is already a small but discernible movement underway among police executives who have taken the initiative, individually and collectively, to work for professionalization. While they acknowledge current inadequacies in the police service, they point with pride to significant improvements made during the last few decades, particularly to the development of new programs of higher education, the adoption of a formal code of "professional ethics," and the creation of responsible organizations to promote professionalism.[59]

Police leaders must continue to support professionalism by using higher standards to select personnel and to implement ethical practices. Hopefully, cumulative improvements in police performance will produce greater social acceptance for law enforcement. Receptive public attitudes and expectations, in turn, would reinforce the development of a more professional police force. Perpetuation of this cycle over a sufficient time might bring forth police professionalism based on actual ethical practice. Significantly, police leaders working for professionalization are receiving external support through the commitment of substantial public and private resources, particularly through federally sponsored revenue-sharing programs to improve the system of criminal justice.[60] Commitment to professionalism has also been reinforced by presidential and other nationally recognized commissions that are concerned with problems of criminal justice. Thus whereas police executives will be the active agents of change in the process of professionalization, their efforts will require continued psychological and financial support.

No doubt police have a long way to go to achieve the professionalism characterized by the ethical model. Thus it seems appropriate to conclude this consideration of professionalization in a sober perspective. Law enforcement today is a "semiprofession" that boasts considerable advances in technique and expertise but has an unfulfilled potential for ethical development.[61] No one can predict the progress towards fulfillment because the law enforcement community is not a monolithic institution. It is, in fact, an exceptionally diverse community of some forty thousand organizations with wide disparities in standards and performance. Among the significant differences are organizational jurisdiction (federal, state, and municipal), size, political environment, and degree of specialization and expertise. These variables substantially affect the professionalization process. Some organizations are already well ahead of others and enjoy significant advantages because of their internal and external resources.

The ethical model of professionalism also outlines the course of professionalization. People must first be trained in a body of knowledge that is relevant to law enforcement; the new expertise must be applied daily until ethical practice becomes the accepted norm—until finally the simultaneous growth of theory and practice reinforce each other to develop the highest degree of professionalism.

No timetable exists for this process. It extends over a long period, perhaps fifty years or more, even allowing for rapid growth in the social sciences and the "technology" of managing human behavior. Given the disparities in the law enforcement community, organizations with greater resources and expertise are likely to achieve results before less advantaged agencies, professionalization probably being a function of size. A "top-down" orientation is apt to develop internally as well because executives and middle management need to professionalize before the rank and file. This allows management to serve as a model for the rank and file, a traditional pattern. Top-down orientation is functional, too, because it provides incentives for subordinates to rise in the organization's hierarchy. Indeed, the desire for upward mobility within police agencies is probably the most useful mechanism available to leaders who want to enhance acceptance of professionalism.

Although it is realistic to think of professionalization as a gradual process, one should bear in mind that it has no well-defined point of attainment. It will be a slow, diffuse, and obscure process, with achievement varying considerably from organization to organization. Professionalism will come piecemeal, and its components will overlap as they slowly integrate within the law enforcement community.

Appendix: An Insider's View of Gambling Enforcement

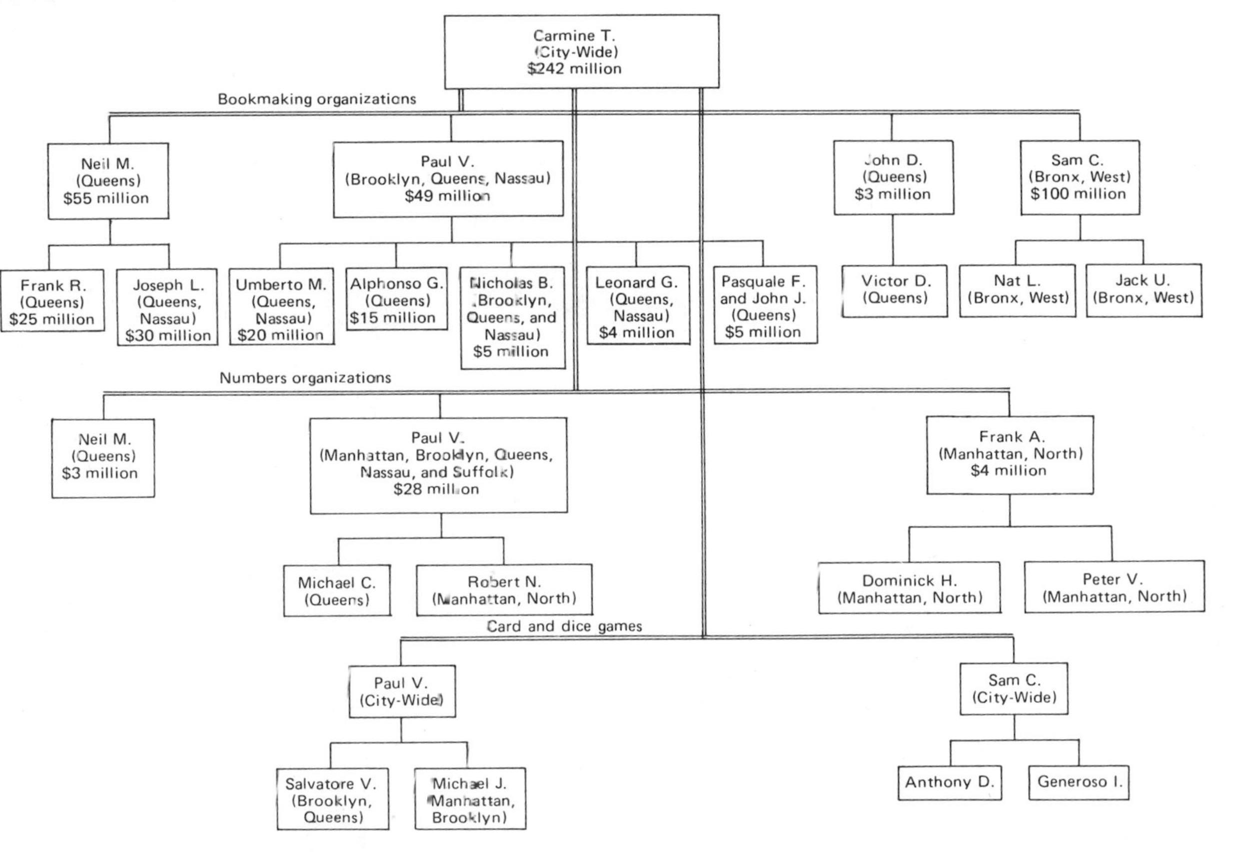

Note: Surnames have been abbreviated for confidentiality.

Source: New York City Police Department.

Exhibit A. Organized Crime Control of Bookmaking and Numbers.

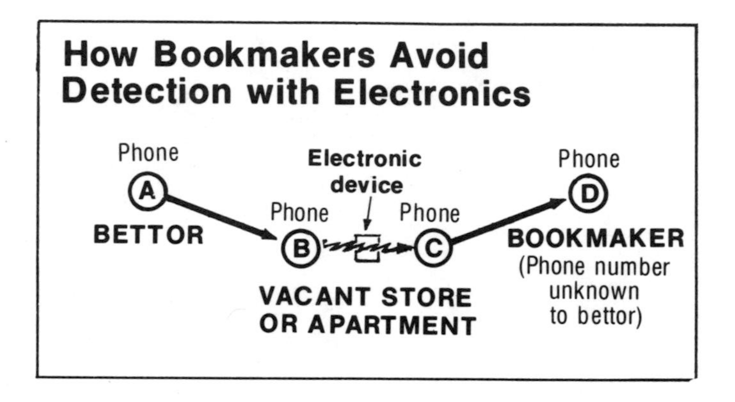

Source: *New York Times*, January 20, 1975, p. 1 © 1974/1975 by the New York Times Company. Reprinted by permission.

Exhibit B. A Cheese-box Security System.

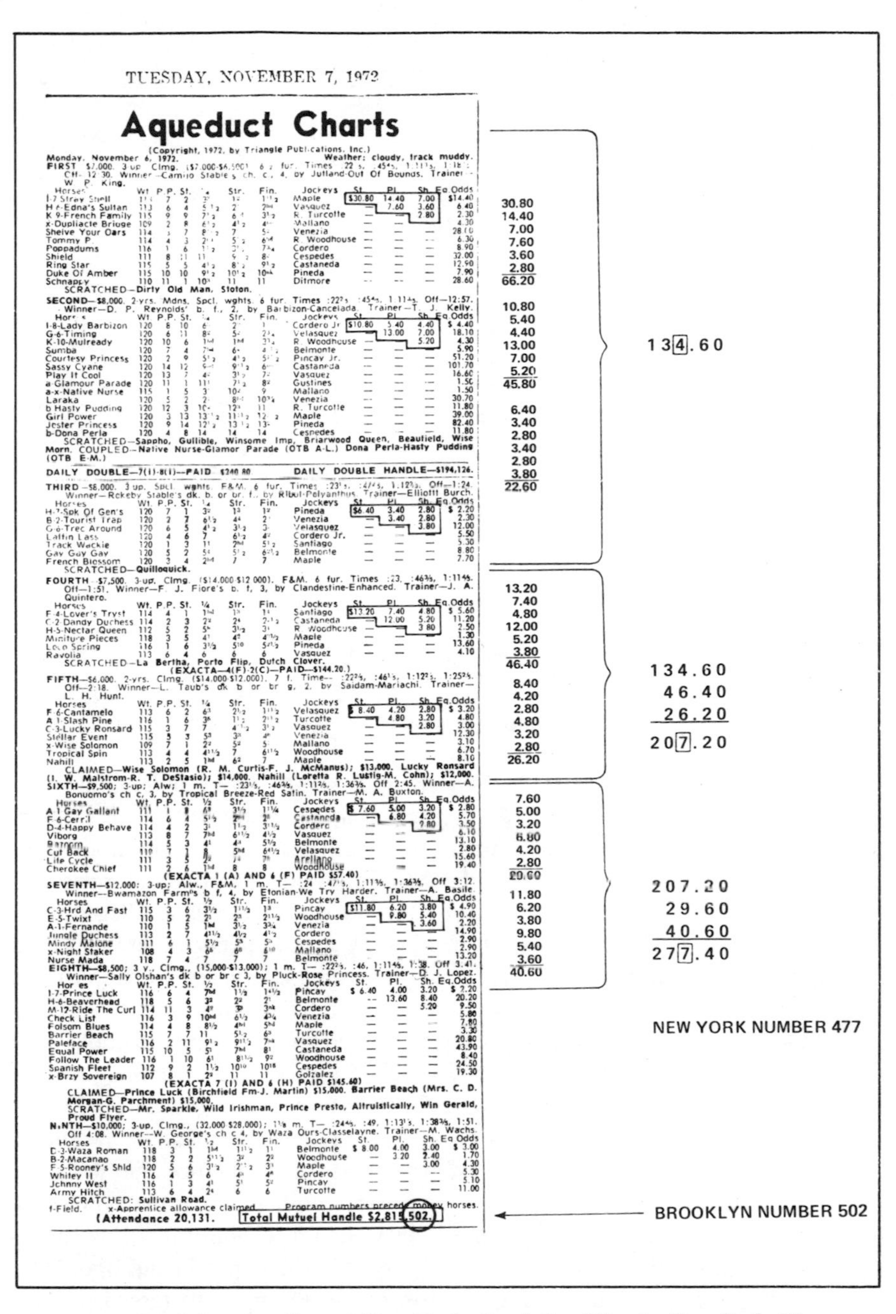

TUESDAY, NOVEMBER 7, 1972

Aqueduct Charts

(Copyright, 1972, by Triangle Publications, Inc.)

Monday, November 6, 1972. Weather: cloudy, track muddy.

FIRST $7,000. 3-up Clmg. ($7,000-$6,500) 6½ fur. Times :22⅗, :45⅘, 1:11⅗, 1:18. Off-12:30. Winner—Camilo Stable's ch. c., 4, by Jutland-Out Of Bounds. Trainer—W. P. King.

Horses	Wt.	P.P.	St.	¼	Str.	Fin.	Jockeys	St.	Pl.	Sh.	Eq. Odds
I-7-Stray Shell	11[illegible]	7	2	3	1	$1^{1½}$	Maple	$30.80	14.40	7.00	$14.40
H-6-Edna's Sultan	113	6	4	$5^{1½}$	2	2^{hd}	Vasquez	—	7.60	3.60	6.40
K-9-French Family	115	9	9	$7^{1½}$	6	$3^{1½}$	R. Turcotte	—	—	2.80	2.30
x-Dupliacte Briuge	109	2	8	$6^{1½}$	$4^{1½}$	4	Mallano	—	—	—	4.30
Sheive Your Oars	114	3	7	$8^{1½}$	7	5	Venezia	—	—	—	28.00
Tommy P.	114	4	3	2	$5^{1½}$	6^{hd}	R. Woodhouse	—	—	—	6.30
Poppadums	116	1	6	$1^{1½}$	3	$7^{¾}$	Cordero	—	—	—	8.90
Shield	111	8	11	11	$9^{1½}$	8	Cespedes	—	—	—	32.00
Ring Star	115	5	5	$4^{1½}$	$8^{1½}$	$9^{1½}$	Castaneda	—	—	—	12.90
Duke Of Amber	115	10	10	$9^{1½}$	$10^{1½}$	10^{nk}	Pineda	—	—	—	7.90
Schnappy	110	11	1	10	11	11	Ditmore	—	—	—	28.60

SCRATCHED—**Dirty Old Man, Stoton.**

SECOND—$8,000. 2-yrs. Mdns. Spcl. wghts. 6 fur. Times :22⅖, :45⅘, 1:11⅘. Off—12:57. Winner—D. P. Reynolds' b. f., 2, by Barbizon-Cancelada. Trainer—T. J. Kelly.

Horses	Wt.	P.P.	St.	¼	Str.	Fin.	Jockeys	St.	Pl.	Sh.	Eq. Odds
I-8-Lady Barbizon	120	8	10	6	2	1	Cordero Jr.	$10.80	5.40	4.40	$ 4.40
G-6-Timing	120	6	11	8	5	$2^{¾}$	Velasquez	—	13.00	7.00	18.10
K-10-Mulready	120	10	6	1^{hd}	1^{hd}	$3^{¾}$	R. Woodhouse	—	—	5.20	4.30
Sumba	120	7	4	7^{hd}	6	$4^{1½}$	Belmonte	—	—	—	5.90
Courtesy Princess	120	2	9	$5^{1½}$	$4^{1½}$	$5^{1½}$	Pincay Jr.	—	—	—	51.20
Sassy Cyane	120	14	12	9	$9^{1½}$	6	Castaneda	—	—	—	101.70
Play It Cool	120	13	7	4	$3^{1½}$	7	Vasquez	—	—	—	16.60
a-Glamour Parade	120	11	1	11	$7^{1½}$	8	Gustines	—	—	—	1.50
a-x-Native Nurse	115	1	5	3	10	9	Mallano	—	—	—	1.50
Laraka	120	5	2	2	8	$10^{¾}$	Venezia	—	—	—	30.70
b-Hasty Pudding	120	12	3	10	12	11	R. Turcotte	—	—	—	11.80
Girl Power	120	3	13	$13^{1½}$	$11^{1½}$	$12^{1½}$	Maple	—	—	—	39.00
Jester Princess	120	9	14	$12^{1½}$	$13^{1½}$	13	Pineda	—	—	—	82.40
b-Dona Perla	120	4	8	14	14	14	Cespedes	—	—	—	11.80

SCRATCHED—**Sappho, Gullible, Winsome Imp, Briarwood Queen, Beaufield, Wise Morn.** COUPLED—**Native Nurse-Glamor Parade (OTB A-L.) Dona Perla-Hasty Pudding (OTB E-M.)**

DAILY DOUBLE—7(I)-8(I)—PAID $240.80 DAILY DOUBLE HANDLE—$194,126.

THIRD—$8,000. 3-up. Spcl. wghts. F&M. 6 fur. Times :23⅕, :47⅘, 1:12⅗. Off—1:24. Winner—Rokeby Stable's dk. b. or br. f., by Ribot-Polyanthus. Trainer—Elliott Burch.

Horses	Wt.	P.P.	St.	¼	Str.	Fin.	Jockeys	St.	Pl.	Sh.	Eq. Odds
H-7-Spk Of Gen's	120	7	1	3	1	1	Pineda	$6.40	3.40	2.80	$ 2.20
B-2-Tourist Trap	120	2	7	$6^{1½}$	4	2	Venezia	—	3.40	2.80	2.30
G-6-Trec Around	120	6	5	$4^{1½}$	$3^{1½}$	3	Velasquez	—	—	3.80	12.00
Laffin Lass	120	4	6	7	$6^{1½}$	4	Cordero Jr.	—	—	—	5.50
Track Wackie	120	1	3	1	2^{hd}	$5^{1½}$	Santiago	—	—	—	5.30
Gay Guy Gay	120	5	2	5	$5^{1½}$	$6^{1½}$	Belmonte	—	—	—	8.80
French Blossom	120	3	4	2^{hd}	7	7	Maple	—	—	—	7.70

SCRATCHED—**Quilloquick.**

FOURTH—$7,500. 3-up. Clmg. ($14,000-$12,000). F&M. 6 fur. Times :23, :46⅗, 1:11⅘. Off—1:51. Winner—F. J. Fiore's b. f, 3, by Clandestine-Enhanced. Trainer—J. A. Quintero.

Horses	Wt.	P.P.	St.	¼	Str.	Fin.	Jockeys	St.	Pl.	Sh.	Eq. Odds
F-4-Lover's Tryst	114	4	1	1^{hd}	1	1	Santiago	$13.20	7.40	4.80	$ 5.60
C-2-Dandy Duchess	114	2	3	2	2	$2^{1½}$	Castaneda	—	12.00	5.20	11.20
H-5-Nectar Queen	112	5	2	5	$3^{1½}$	3	R. Woodhouse	—	—	3.80	2.50
Miniture Pieces	118	3	5	4	4	$4^{1½}$	Maple	—	—	—	1.30
Loco Spring	116	1	6	3½	5^{10}	$5^{1½}$	Pineda	—	—	—	13.60
Ravolia	113	6	4	6	6	6	Vasquez	—	—	—	4.10

SCRATCHED—**La Bertha, Porto Flip, Dutch Clover.**

(EXACTA—4(F)-2(C)—PAID—$144.20.)

FIFTH—$6,000. 2-yrs. Clmg. ($14,000-$12,000). 7 f. Time— :22⅗, :46⅕, 1:12⅖, 1:25⅗. Off—2:18. Winner—L. Taub's dk b or br g, 2, by Saidam-Mariachi. Trainer—L. H. Hunt.

Horses	Wt.	P.P.	St.	¼	Str.	Fin.	Jockeys	St.	Pl.	Sh.	Eq. Odds
F-6-Cantamelo	113	6	2	6	2½	$1^{1½}$	Velasquez	$ 8.40	4.20	2.80	$ 3.20
A-1-Slash Pine	116	1	6	3	$1^{1½}$	$2^{1½}$	Turcotte	—	4.80	3.20	4.80
C-3-Lucky Ronsard	115	3	7	7	$4^{1½}$	$3^{1½}$	Vasquez	—	—	2.80	3.00
Stellar Event	115	5	3	5	3	4	Venezia	—	—	—	12.30
x-Wise Solomon	109	7	1	2	5	5	Mallano	—	—	—	3.10
Tropical Spin	113	4	4	$4^{1½}$	7	$6^{1½}$	Woodhouse	—	—	—	6.70
Nahill	113	2	5	1^{hd}	6	7	Maple	—	—	—	8.10

CLAIMED—**Wise Solomon (R. M. Curtis-F. J. McManus); $13,000. Lucky Ronsard (I. W. Malstrom-R. T. DeStasio); $14,000. Nahill (Loretta R. Lustig-M. Cohn); $12,000.**

SIXTH—$9,500; 3-up; Alw; 1 m. T— :23⅕, :46⅗, 1:11⅖, 1:36⅗. Off 2:45. Winner—A. Bonuomo's ch c, 3, by Tropical Breeze-Red Satin. Trainer—M. A. Buxton.

Horses	Wt.	P.P.	St.	½	Str.	Fin.	Jockeys	St.	Pl.	Sh.	Eq. Odds
A-1-Gay Gallant	111	1	8	6	3½	$1^{1¼}$	Cespedes	$ 7.60	5.00	3.20	$ 2.80
F-6-Cerril	114	6	4	5½	2^{hd}	2	Castaneda	—	6.80	4.20	5.70
D-4-Happy Behave	114	4	2	3	1½	$3^{1½}$	Cordero	—	—	2.80	3.50
Viborg	113	8	7	7^{hd}	$6^{1½}$	4½	Vasquez	—	—	—	6.10
Batgorn	114	5	3	4	4	5½	Belmonte	—	—	—	13.10
Cut Back	119	7	1	8	5^{hd}	$6^{1½}$	Velasquez	—	—	—	2.80
Life Cycle	111	3	5	2	7	7	Arellano	—	—	—	15.60
Cherokee Chief	111	2	6	1^{hd}	8	8	Woodhouse	—	—	—	19.40

(EXACTA 1 (A) AND 6 (F) PAID $57.40)

SEVENTH—$12,000; 3-up; Alw., F&M, 1 m. T— :24, :47⅕, 1:11⅗, 1:36⅗. Off 3:12. Winner—Bwamazon Farm's b f, 4, by Etonian-We Try Harder. Trainer—A. Basile.

Horses	Wt.	P.P.	St.	½	Str.	Fin.	Jockeys	St.	Pl.	Sh.	Eq. Odds
C-3-Hrd And Fast	115	3	6	3½	$1^{1½}$	1	Pincay	$11.80	6.20	3.80	$ 4.90
E-5-Twixt	110	5	2	2	2	$2^{1½}$	Woodhouse	—	9.80	5.40	10.40
A-1-Fernande	110	1	5	1^{hd}	3½	$3^{¾}$	Venezia	—	—	3.60	2.20
Jungle Duchess	113	2	7	$4^{1½}$	4½	$4^{1½}$	Cordero	—	—	—	14.90
Mindy Malone	111	6	1	5½	5	5	Cespedes	—	—	—	2.90
x-Night Staker	108	4	3	6	6	6^{10}	Mallano	—	—	—	2.90
Nurse Mada	118	7	4	7	7	7	Belmonte	—	—	—	13.20

EIGHTH—$8,500; 3 y., Clmg., (15,000-$13,000); 1 m. T— :22⅗, :46, 1:11⅘, 1:38. Off 3:41. Winner—Sally Olshan's dk b or br c 3, by Pluck-Rose Princess. Trainer—D. J. Lopez.

Horses	Wt.	P.P.	St.	½	Str.	Fin.	Jockeys	St.	Pl.	Sh.	Eq. Odds
I-7-Prince Luck	116	6	4	7^{hd}	1½	$1^{4½}$	Pincay	$ 6.40	4.00	3.20	$ 2.20
H-6-Beaverhead	118	5	6	3	2	2	Belmonte	--	13.60	8.40	20.20
M-12-Ride The Curl	114	11	3	4	3	3^{nk}	Cordero	—	—	5.20	9.50
Check List	116	3	9	10^{hd}	6½	$4^{¾}$	Venezia	—	—	—	5.80
Folsom Blues	114	4	8	8½	4^{hd}	5^{hd}	Maple	—	—	—	7.80
Barrier Beach	115	7	7	11	$5^{1½}$	6	Turcotte	—	—	—	3.30
Paleface	116	2	11	$9^{1½}$	$9^{1½}$	7^{nk}	Vasquez	—	—	—	20.80
Equal Power	115	10	5	5	7^{hd}	8	Castaneda	—	—	—	43.90
Follow The Leader	116	1	10	6	$8^{1½}$	9	Woodhouse	—	—	—	8.40
Spanish Fleet	112	9	2	1½	10^{10}	10^{18}	Cespedes	—	—	—	24.50
x-Brzy Sovereign	107	8	1	2	11	11	Golzalez	—	—	—	19.30

(EXACTA 7 (I) AND 6 (H) PAID $145.60)

CLAIMED—**Prince Luck (Birchfield Fm-J. Martin) $15,000. Barrier Beach (Mrs. C. D. Morgan-G. Parchment) $15,000.**

SCRATCHED—**Mr. Sparkle, Wild Irishman, Prince Presto, Altruistically, Win Gerald, Proud Flyer.**

NINTH—$10,000; 3-up. Clmg., (32,000-$28,000); 1⅛ m. T— :24⅘, :49, 1:13⅕, 1:38⅗, 1:51. Off 4:08. Winner—W. George's ch c 4, by Waza Ours-Classelayne. Trainer—M. Wachs.

Horses	Wt.	P.P.	St.	½	Str.	Fin.	Jockeys	St.	Pl.	Sh.	Eq. Odds
D-3-Waza Roman	118	3	1	1^{hd}	$1^{1½}$	1	Belmonte	$ 8.00	4.00	3.00	$ 3.00
B-2-Macanao	118	2	2	$5^{1½}$	3	2	Woodhouse	—	3.20	2.40	1.70
F-5-Rooney's Shld	120	5	6	$3^{1½}$	$2^{1½}$	3	Maple	—	—	3.00	4.30
Whitey II	116	4	5	6	4	4	Cordero	—	—	—	5.30
Johnny West	116	1	3	4	5	5	Pincay	—	—	—	5.10
Army Hitch	113	6	4	2	6	6	Turcotte	—	—	—	11.00

SCRATCHED: **Sullivan Road.**

f-Field. x-Apprentice allowance claimed. Program numbers precede money horses.

(Attendance 20,131. Total Mutuel Handle $2,815,502.)

Source: Fund for the City of New York, *Legal Gambling in New York* (New York: January 1972), p. 21. Reprinted with permission.

Exhibit C. How the Winning Number is Figured from Horse Race Results.

Year	Volume of policy play (millions of dollars)[a]	Mean value of a bet (cents)	Population (thousands)	Percent black	Per-capita income	Business profit plus wages (millions of dollars)	Number of		
							Banks	Controllers	Collectors
1963	8.61	16.18	285	76	1066	252.1	7	35	762
1964	9.36	18.12	281	76	1137	262.7	7	40	892
1965	9.55	22.28	282	77	1190	272.7	7	64	1039
1966	11.38	21.55	285	80	1276	287.9	7	72	1068
1967	10.75	29.41	285	80	1481	331.9	6	72	1140
1968	11.95	32.23	281	81	1618	341.7	6	73	1239
1969	16.25	36.04	281	81	1763	381.6	6	74	1269
1970	26.06	37.08	280	82	1847	412.4	5	76	1345

Note: This data applies to Bedford-Stuyvesant, a New York City neighborhood.

[a]All dollar figures are in constant New York City dollars (1957-1959 = 100).

Source: Harold D. Lasswell and Jeremiah B. McKenna, *The Impact of Organized Crime on an Inner City Community* (New York: The Policy Sciences Center, 1972), p. 112. Reprinted with permission.

Exhibit D. Economics of the Policy Business.

1		2		3		4		5	
123	100	376	25	398	25	066	50	411	75
210	25	291	25	752	25	612	50	239	50
161	25	291	(90	447	25	828	200	906	25
806	25	936	25	587	50	207	25	348	50
303	50	427	50	330	300	401	25	555	500
711	100	660	100	806	50	411	25	707	(75
605	25	331	40	182	(60	871	25	356	50
612	50	113	50	245	25	724	25	161	50
337	100	211	100	245	100	384	(30	611	100
751	50	427	50	324	25	087	100	185	25
678	(30	714	50	101	(30	156	50	926	25
329	25	881	100	606	50	069	25	761	25
013	50	070	25	851	50	124	25	245	25
609	25	121	25	581	75	112	25	488	50
157	25	121	25	131	25	220	(75	330	(30
202	25	121	150	321	25	678	25	710	25
222	200	121	25	775	25	890	25	525	100
389	50	875	25	625	50	315	50	707	25
560	25	278	50	999	50	424	200	711	25
490	25	612	50	884	50	528	25	200	25
440	100	440	100	274	25	696	100	117	25
317	100	713	80	300	100	777	50	616	25
414	50	250	25	123	25	312	50	297	25
355	25	610	25	402	(30	844	50	814	50
320	40	707	150	767	25	579	250	391	25
980	(60	616	(60	152	50	112	25	101	100
246	25	795	25	301	25	317	75	543	25
711	100	500	25	328	50	210	100	152	100
114	50	700	100	711	25	164	25	616	50
939	100	042	25	604	100	143	50	504	50
670	25	101	25	317	25	080	50	219	100
227	25	776	100	052	50	101	100	625	(60
	17.30		18.20		16.45		21.05		19.90

17.30
18.20
16.45
21.05
19.90
92.90

ANK 1-21-66

Note: Numbered columns list digits selected by bettors, and unnumbered columns list amounts wagered. Player's names were retained by the collector and discarded the next day.

Exhibit E. A Collector's Sheet with Daily Bets Totaling $92.90.

Ro 1409—

Jerry, TT, SR, PW, Monte, T.T., Joe, Al, Tony, Jack, Manny, Albie, Blimp, J.D., Sal, P.T.

463•11 +
209•75 +
245•00 +
152•63 +
1,645•89 +
146•00 +
364•60 +
37•50 +
102•56 +
474•40 +
30•00 +
888•25 +
150•25 +
45•10 +
147•60 +
75•70 +
1,258•36 +
6,436•70 *

Ray N00

7

Motty, El, JX, Sam, Ben, Ro, R, 2, CBL, Paul

5,963•40 +
3,507•95 +
107•10 +
355•65 +
1,709•65 +
725•10 +
1,806•75 +
2,679•59 +
1,114•00 +
3,690•75 +
6,150•00 +
27,809•94 *

Wom 463 209

7

Sal 2,315•00 +
El 929•50 +
Valle 240•00 +
82•50 +
500•65 +
R 1,540•80 +
274•00 +
26 355•00 +
CBC 6,237•45 *

7 463 209

1– 117•50 +
3– 125•50 +
4– 375•25 +
5– 137•50 +
6– 327•55 +
7– 399•00 +
8– 365•40 +
9– 615•57 +
10– 36•60 +
FL 370•16 +
SS 272•00 +
AA 264•35 +
18 1,145•63 +
20 895•00 +
21 564•00 +
23 256•10 +
24 4,568•25 +
25 1,110•50 +
30 1,235•30 +
31 888•00 +
34 456•32 +
RF 4,589•50 +
35 644•25 +
36 500•50 +
38 2,645•00 +
CK 966•00 +
F2 1,234•50 +
Joe 25,105•23 *

Source: Harold D. Lasswell and Jeremiah B. McKenna, *The Impact of Organized Crime on an Inner City Community* (New York: The Policy Sciences Center, 1972), p. 90. Reprinted with permission.

Exhibit F. A Controller's Ribbon with Total Wagers of Several Collectors.

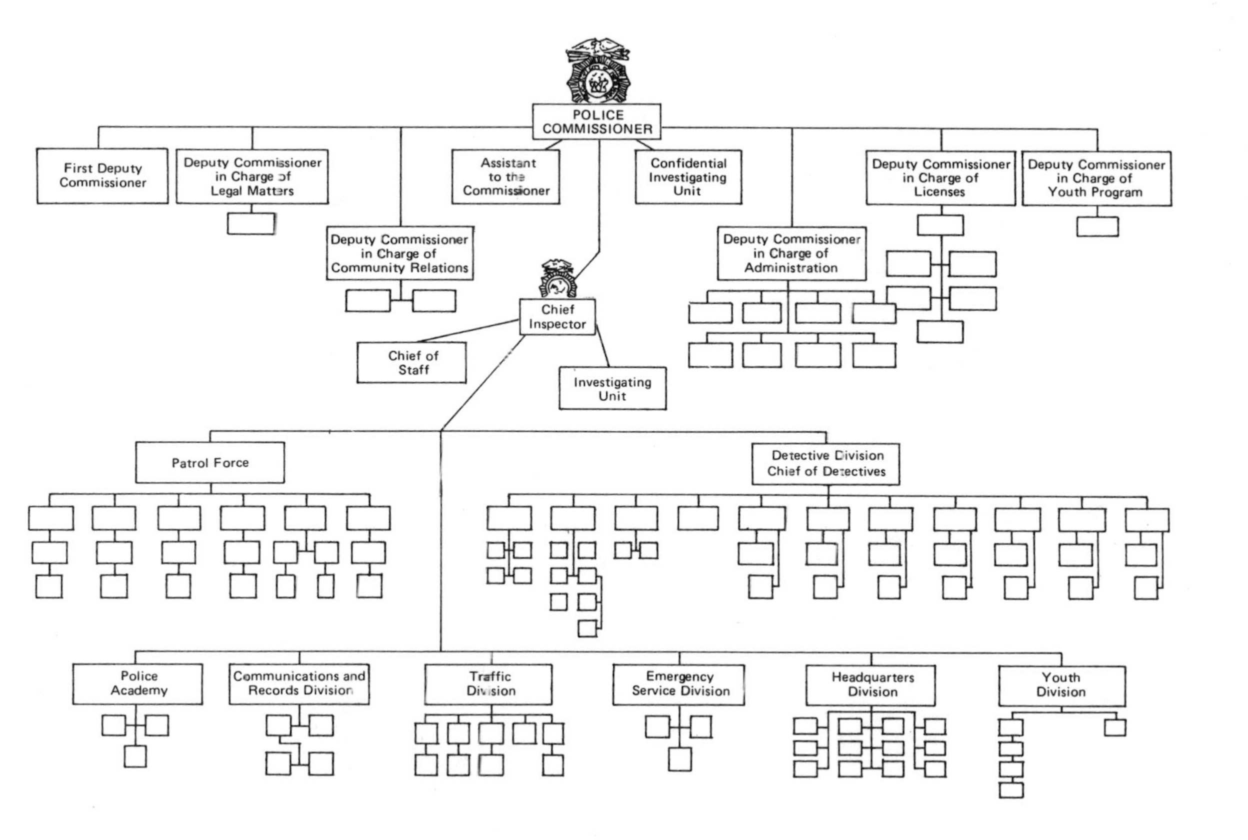

Source: New York City Police Department.

Exhibit G. Structure of the New York City Police Department, 1957.

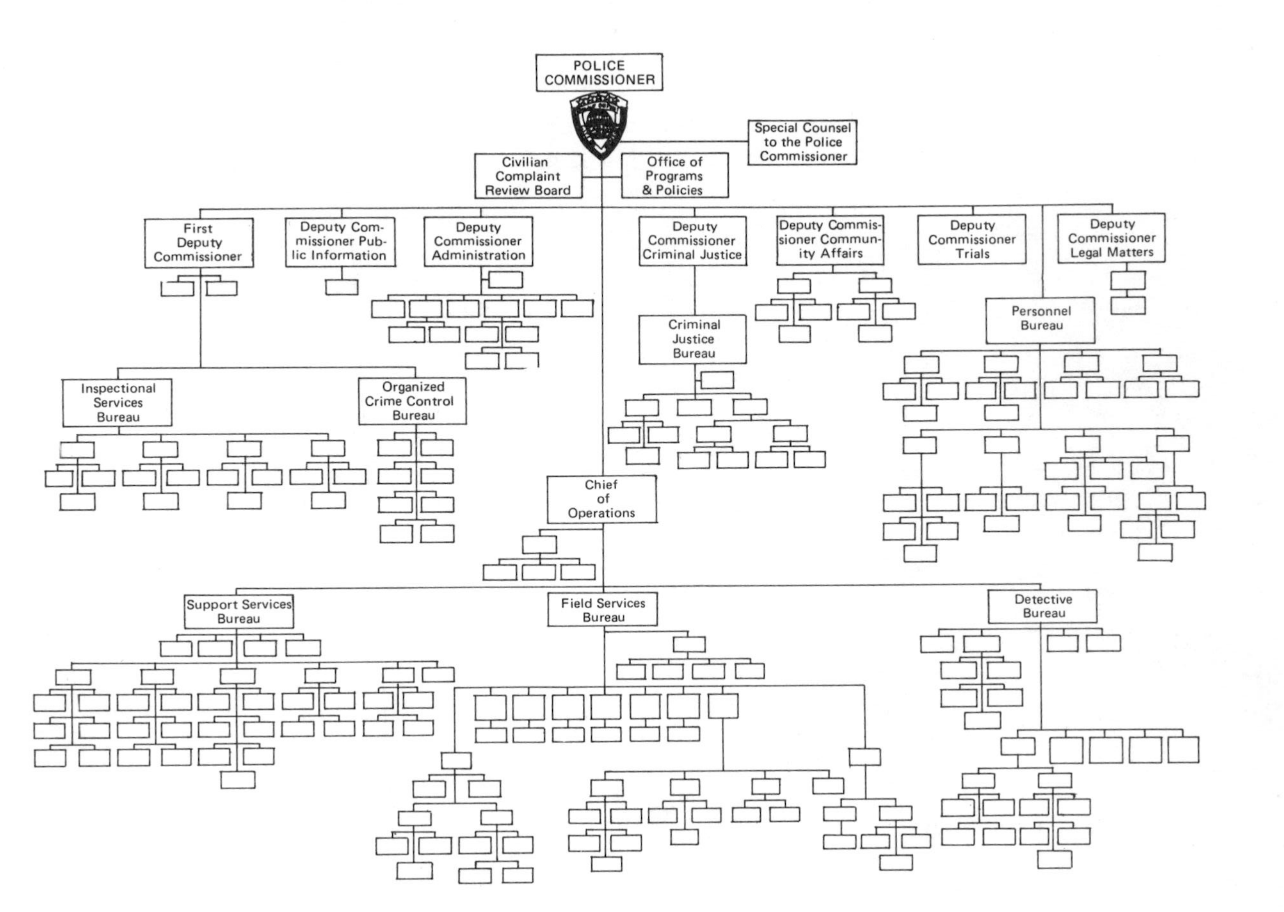

Source: New York City Police Department.

Exhibit H. Structure of the New York City Police Department, 1974.

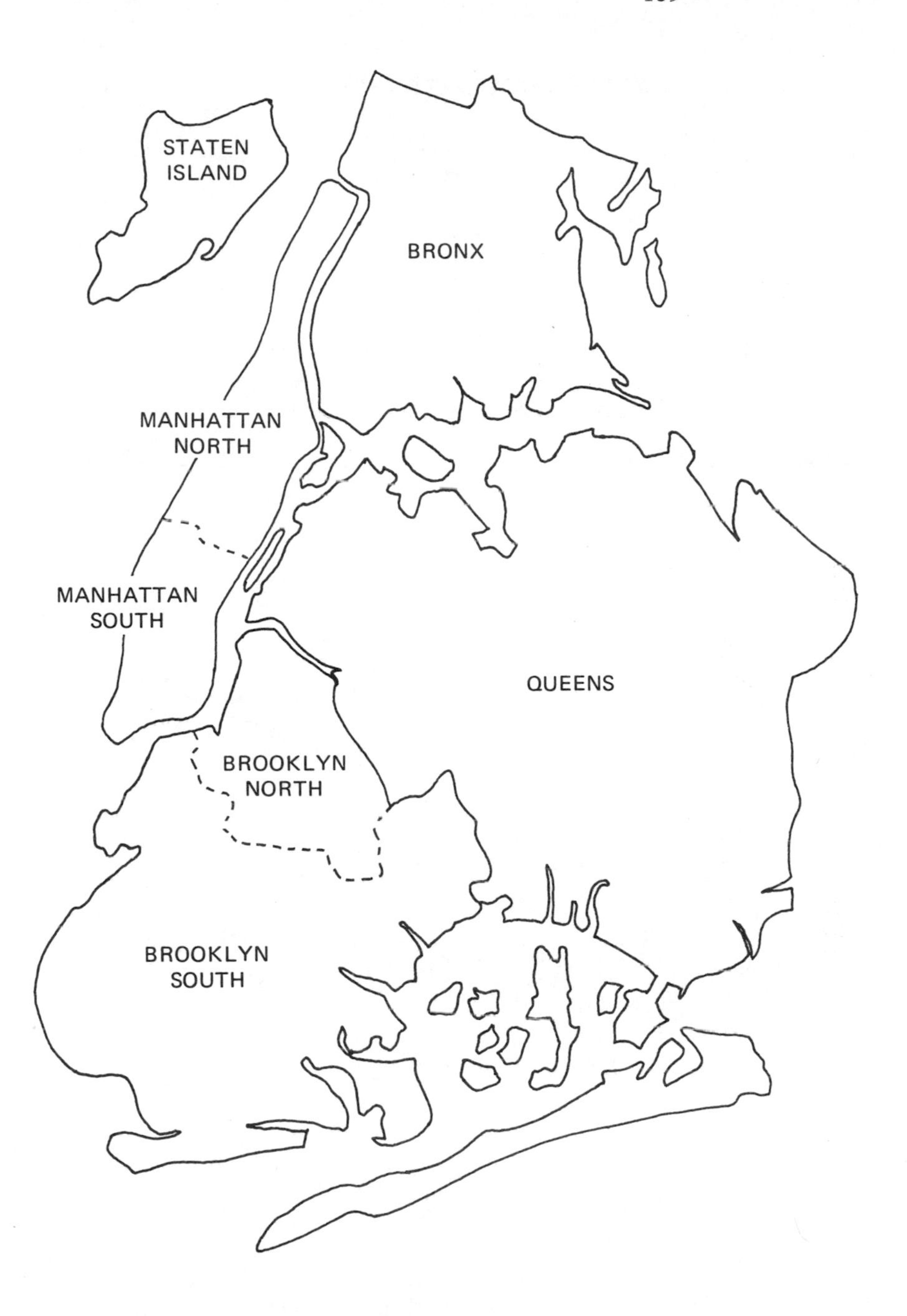

Source: New York City Police Department.

Exhibit I. Police Borough Commands in New York City.

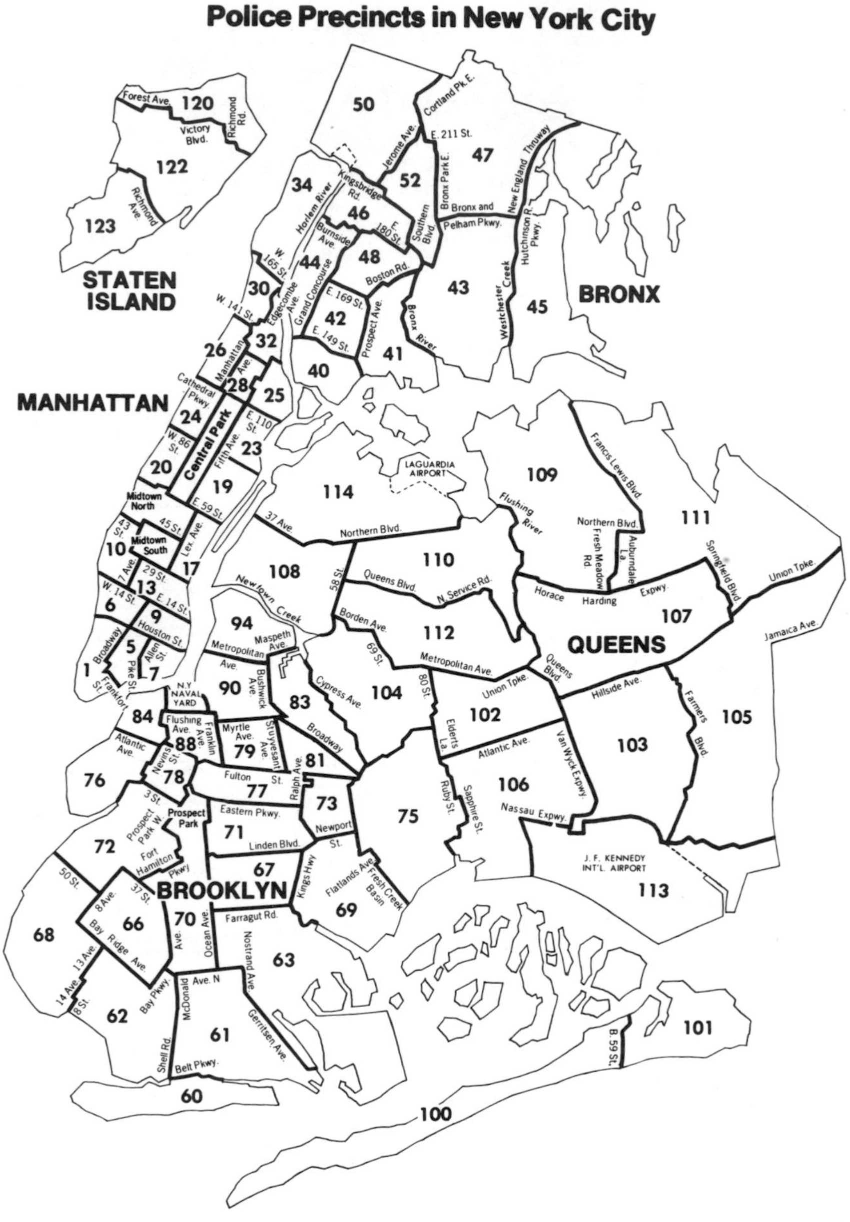

Police Precincts in New York City

Source: *New York Times*, December 2, 1974, p. 38. © 1974/1975 by the New York Times Company. Reprinted by permission.

Exhibit J. Police Precincts in New York City.

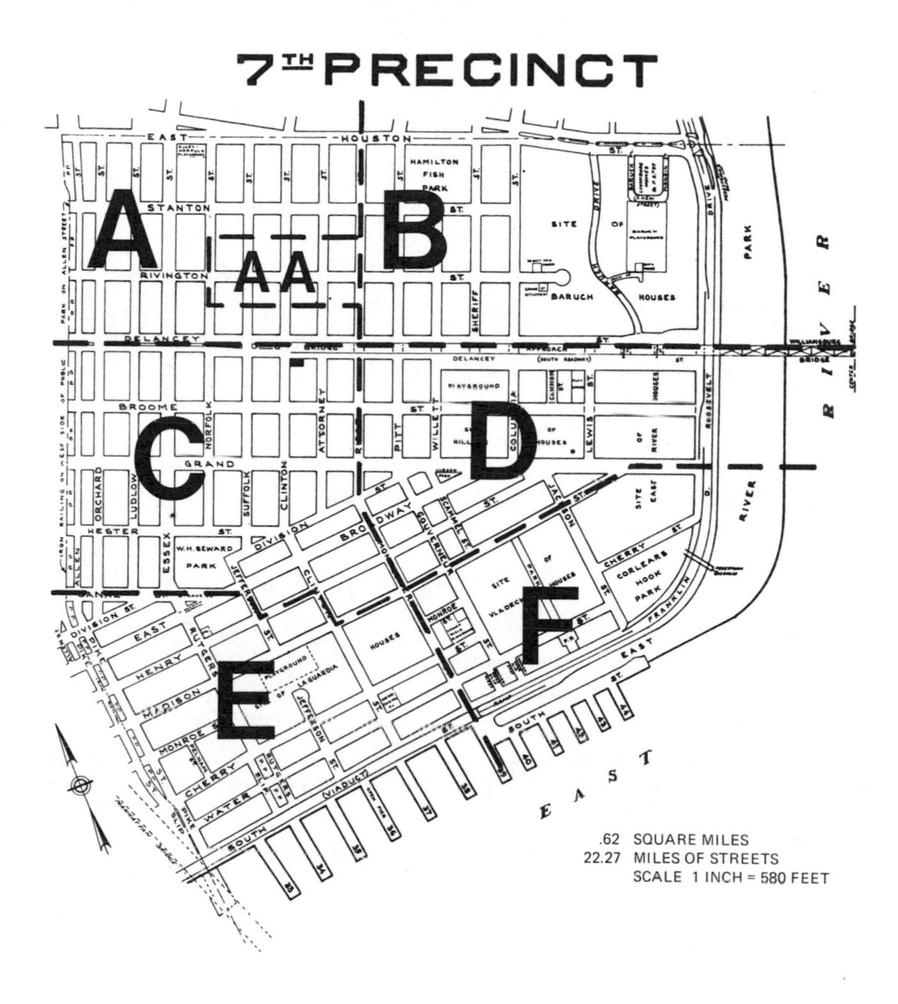

Note: Each radio car patrol sector is made up of several foot posts, or "beats," which usually run along main streets or avenues and extend one-half block in each direction from the main thoroughfare. In this figure the foot post (AA) runs east-west along Rivington Street, extending north and south for one-half block.

Source: New York City Police Department.

Exhibit K. Typical Patrol Car Sectors and Foot Patrol "Beats."

PRECINCT ______________

DIVISION ______________

POLICE DEPARTMENT

CITY OF NEW YORK

______________ Date

REPORT OF INVESTIGATION BY PLAINCLOTHESMEN

To Commanding Officer, ______________ (Division, Borough or Part Thereof)

In answer to complaint number ______ complaining of ______________

____

we report as follows: LOCATION ______ (Number) ______ (Street or Avenue)

Apartment No. ______ Floor ______ Description of Building ______________

Does premises investigated differ from that given in complaint as to the exact location? ______

Nature of business at particular place complained of ______________

Name and address of occupant of premises ______________

Name and address of manager of premises ______________

Name and address of owner or lessee of premises ______________

Was arrest made? ______ Number of prisoners ______ Specific Charge ______________

Has condition been suppressed? ______ Was writer of complaint interviewed: ______

Detailed result of investigation ______________

____

____

____

____

Penalty for Falsification: Falsification of any statement made herein is an offense punishable by a fine or imprisonment or both. (N.Y.C. Admin. Code. Sect. 982-9.0).

Recommendation as to continued surveillance of premises ______________

____

____

Ptl. ______________ Ptl. ______________

Shield No. ______ Command ______ Shield No. ______ Command ______

(Rank) ______ (Supervisor of Plainclothes Squad) ______ (Command)

Note: Warning about falsification was not used on other departmental forms. The reverse side of the form has been reduced to fit this page.

Source: New York City Police Department.

Exhibit L. Report of Investigation by Plainclothesmen (U.F. 128).

PUBLIC MORALS INVESTIGATION REPORT

U.F. 128 (Rev. 8-64)

REPORT CONCERNS COMPLAINT OF ☐ GAMBLING ☐ A.B.C. VIOLATION ☐ PROSTITUTION ☐ OTHER (Describe)

DIV. | PCT. | U.F. 46 NO.

RECEIVED FROM ☐ PUBLIC ☐ MEMBER OF FORCE ☐ OTHER AUTHORITY (Describe)

RECEIVED BY ☐ TELEPHONE ☐ LETTER ☐ PERSON ☐ U.F. 47 ☐ OTHER (Describe)

COMMUNICATION No.
P.C.
C.I.
P.M.
BORO
DIV.
PCT.

NAME AND ADDRESS OF COMPLAINANT (If M.O.F., indicate rank, shield no. and command) | APT./FLOOR | TELEPHONE NO.

NAMES AND ADDRESSES OF PERSONS DESCRIBED IN COMPLAINT | "KG", "B" or "E" No.

LOCATIONS DESCRIBED IN COMPLAINT	TYPE OF PREMISES	NAMES AND ADDRESSES OF OWNERS

GAMBLING COMBINE NO. | STATE LIQUOR AUTH LIC. NO. (If any) | CURRENT U.F. 45 SERIES NO. | TWO YEAR HISTORY | COMPLAINTS | ARRESTS

DETAILS OF INITIAL INTERVIEW WITH COMPLAINANT OR MEMBER OF FORCE

IF SEARCH WARRANT OBTAINED	DATE	COURT	JUDGE	RESULTS OF WARRANT

RECORD OF POLICE ACTION TAKEN

DATE	SUMMONS OR ARREST NO.	PCT.	DEFENDANT	VIOLATION	LOCATION	TYPE OF EVIDENCE

INSTRUCTIONS:
1. Investigating officers shall prepare this report in their own handwriting.
2. Plainclothes patrolmen assigned to precincts shall prepare this report in duplicate. The original shall be forwarded to the patrol division concerned. The duplicate shall be filed. One copy shall be prepared by plainclothes patrolmen assigned to patrol divisions to be filed thereat.
3. Daily memorandum book entries and information recorded on this report shall correspond.

Note: Warning about falsification is not used on other departmental forms.

Source: New York City Police Department.

Exhibit M. Public Morals Investigation Report (U.F. 128).

OBSERVATIONS MADE TO EFFECT ANY POLICE ACTION. (Record only positive observation results. Terms "No Violations Observed" etc. will not be used. List in chronological order, including dates, times, locations, persons and events observed, vehicles used, associates, etc.)

RANK	SIGNATURES OF INVESTIGATING OFFICERS	SHIELD NO.	COMMAND	DATE
RANK	SIGNATURE OF IMMEDIATE SUPERVISOR	SHIELD NO.	COMMAND	DATE

PENALTY FOR FALSIFICATION:
Falsification of any statement made herein is an offense, punishable by a fine or imprisonment or both. (N.Y.C. Administrative Code, Section 1151-9.0)

REVIEW BY PUBLIC MORALS DEPUTY INSPECTOR OR PUBLIC MORALS INSPECTOR:

RANK	SIGNATURE OF PUBLIC MORALS DEPUTY INSPECTOR OR PUBLIC MORALS INSPECTOR	COMMAND	DATE

Exhibit M. (cont.)

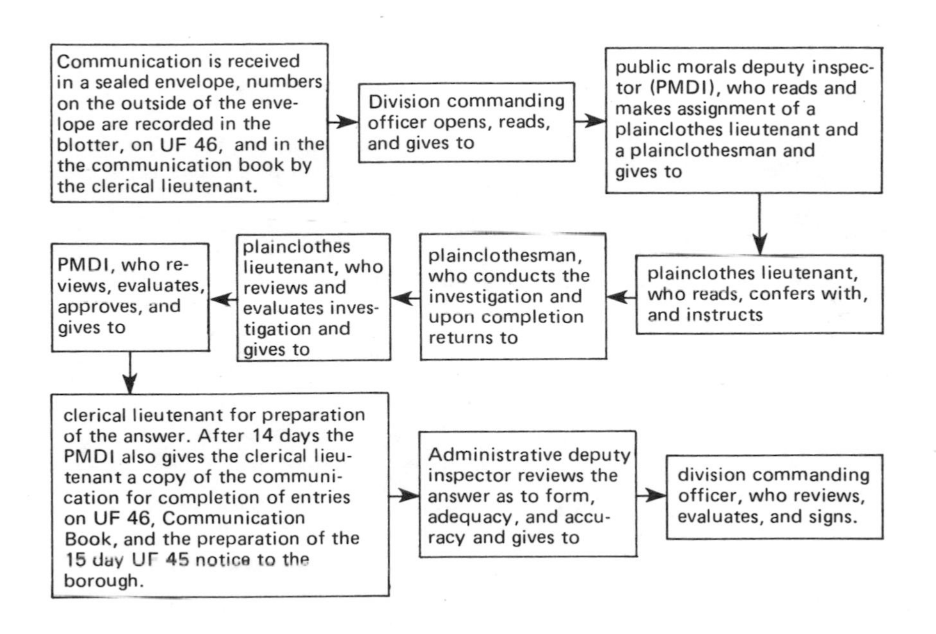

Source: New York City Police Department.

Exhibit N. Public Morals Communications–Flow Chart.

Commissioner	Dates of Tenure	Prior experience	
Bernard J. York	Jan. 1898-Feb. 1901	Clerk of Court Special Sessions	NC
John B. Sexton	Jan. 1898-Feb. 1901	Under-Sheriff, New York County	NC
Theodore L. Hamilton	Jan. 1898-May 1898	contractor and builder	NC
William E. Philips	Jan. 1898-May 1898	produce business	NC
Jacob Hess	May 1898-Feb. 1901	member, Board of Electrical Control	NC
Henry E. Abell	Jan. 1899-Feb. 1901	member, New York State Assembly	NC
Michael Murphy	Feb. 1901-Dec. 1901	member, New York State Senate	NC
John N. Partridge	Jan. 1902-Dec. 1902	State Superintendent of Public Works	NC
Francis J. Greene	Jan. 1903-Dec. 1903	Major General, U.S. Army, retired; corporate director	NC
William McAdoo	Jan. 1904-Dec. 1905	U.S. Congress, Assistant Secretary of the Navy	NC
Theodore A. Bingham	Jan. 1906-July 1909	Brigadier General, U.S. Army, retired	NC
William F. Baker	July 1909-Oct. 1910	member, City Civil Service Commission	NC
James C. Cropsey	Oct. 1910-May 1911	private law practice	NC
Rhinelander Waldo	May 1911-Dec. 1913	Deputy Police Commissioner	NC
Douglas I. McKay	Jan. 1914-Apr. 1914	First Deputy Police Commissioner	NC
Arthur Woods	Apr. 1914-Dec. 1917	Fourth Deputy Police Commissioner; cotton broker	NC
Frederick H. Bugher	Jan. 1918-Jan. 1918	First Deputy Police Commissioner	NC
Richard E. Enright	Jan. 1918-Dec. 1925	Police Captain	C
George V. McLaughlin	Jan. 1926-Apr. 1927	Deputy State Bank Superintendent	NC
Joseph A. Warren	Apr. 1927-Dec. 1928	Attorney for State Health Department; Commissioner of Accounts	NC
Grover A. Whalen	Dec. 1928-May 1930	business manager; Commissioner of Public Works	NC
Edward P. Mulrooney	May 1930-Apr. 1933	Assistant Chief Inspector	C
James S. Bolan	Apr. 1933-Dec. 1933	Deputy Inspector	C
John F. O'Ryan	Jan. 1934-Sept. 1934	Major General, U.S. Army, retired; member of State Transit Commission	NC
Lewis J. Valentine	Sept. 1934-Sept. 1945	Chief Inspector	C
Arthur W. Wallander	Sept. 1945-Mar. 1949	Deputy Chief Inspector	C
William P. O'Brien	Mar. 1949-Sept. 1950	Third Deputy Commissioner	C
Thomas F. Murphy	Sept. 1950-July 1951	Assistant U.S. Attorney, Southern New York District	NC
George P. Monaghan	July 1951-Dec. 1953	Fire Commissioner	NC
Francis W.H. Adams	Jan. 1954-July 1955	Assistant U.S. Attorney General; lawyer	NC
Stephen P. Kennedy	Aug. 1955-Feb. 1961	Chief Inspector	C
Michael J. Murphy	Feb. 1961-June 1965	Chief Inspector	C
Vincent L. Broderick	June 1965-Feb. 1966	Third Deputy Commissioner	NC
Howard R. Leary	Feb. 1966-Oct. 1970	Police Commissioner, Philadelphia	NC
Patrick V. Murphy	Oct. 1970-Apr. 1973	Deputy Chief Inspector	C
Donald F. Cawley	May 1973-Jan. 1974	Chief of Patrol	C
Michael J. Codd	Jan. 1974 to date	Chief Inspector	C

C = career; NC = noncareer.

Source: Adapted from Wallace Sayre and Herbert Kaufman, *Governing New York City*, (New York: Russell Sage Foundation, 1960) p. 286 and Theodore J. Lowi, *At the Pleasure of the Mayor*, (New York: The Free Press, 1960) p. 160.

Exhibit O. New York City Police Commissioners, 1898-1975.

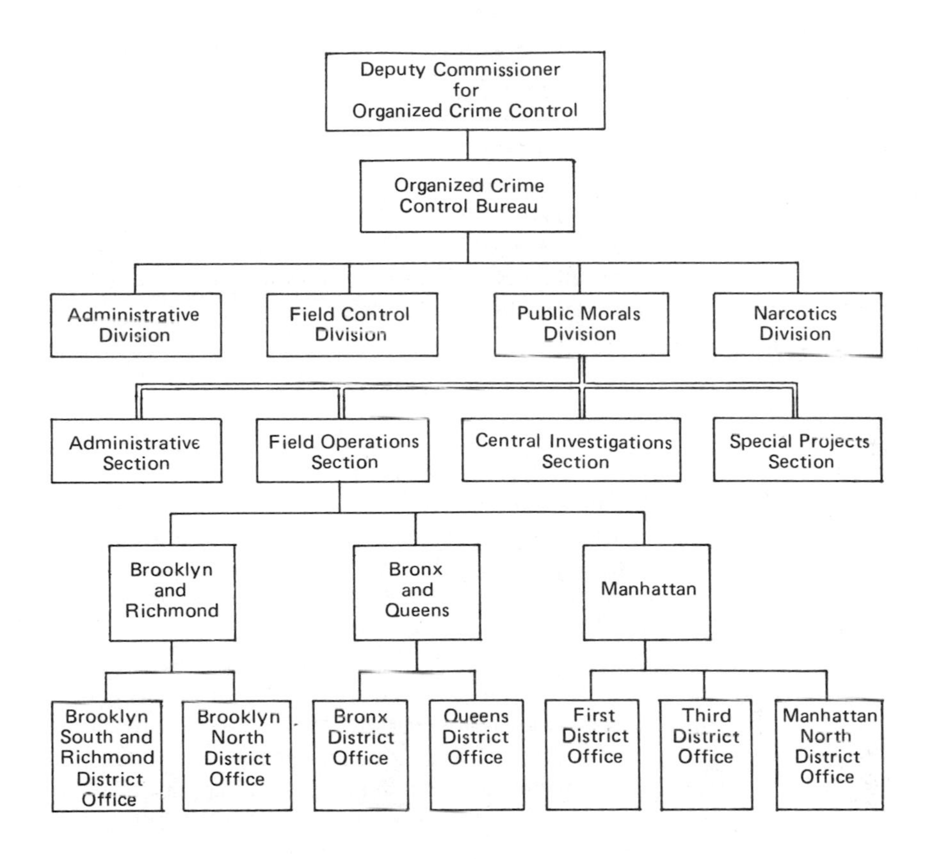

Source: New York City Police Department.

Exhibit P. The Organized Crime Control Bureau and its Public Morals Division.

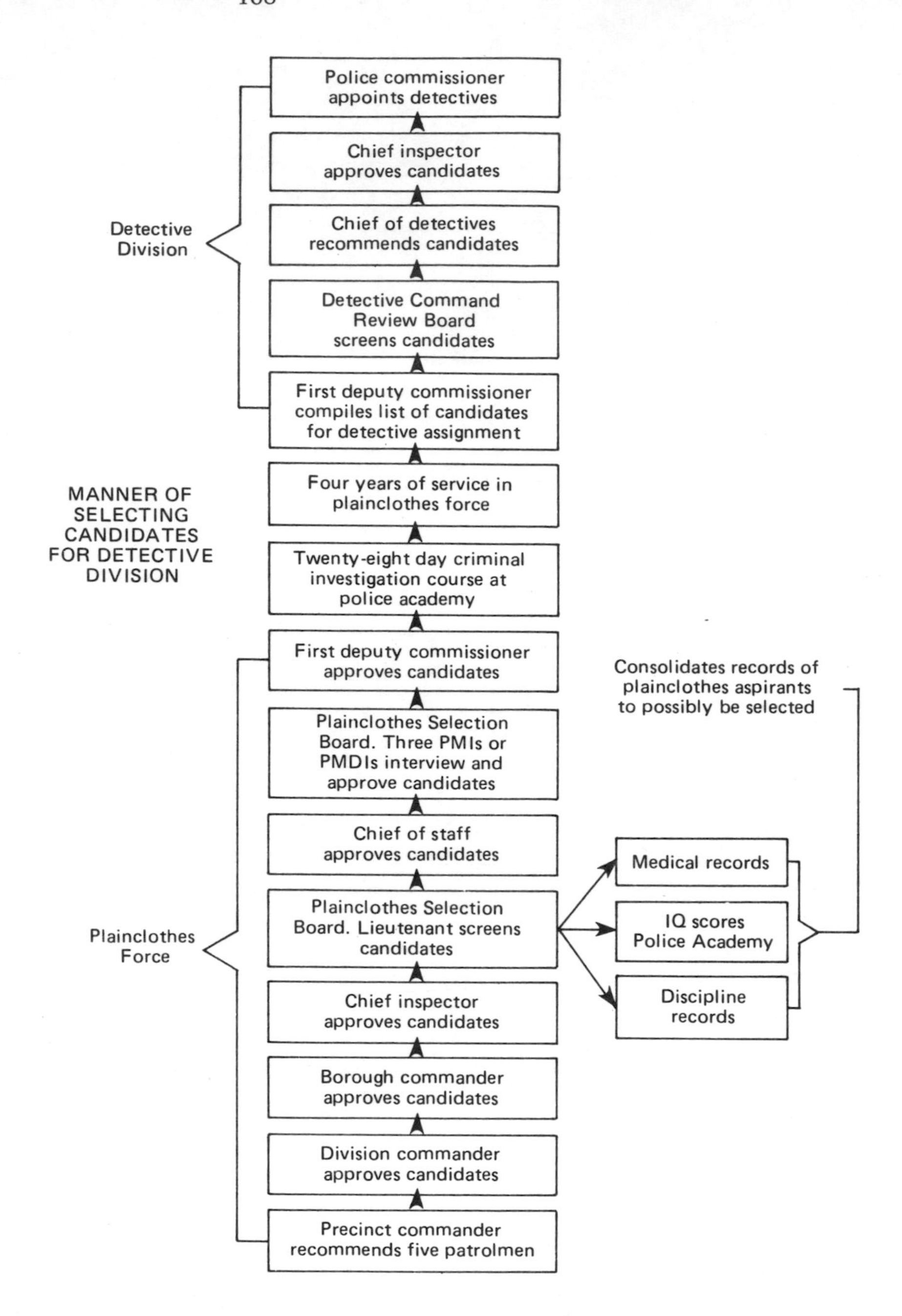

Source: New York City Police Department.

Exhibit Q. Detective Incentive—Flow Chart.

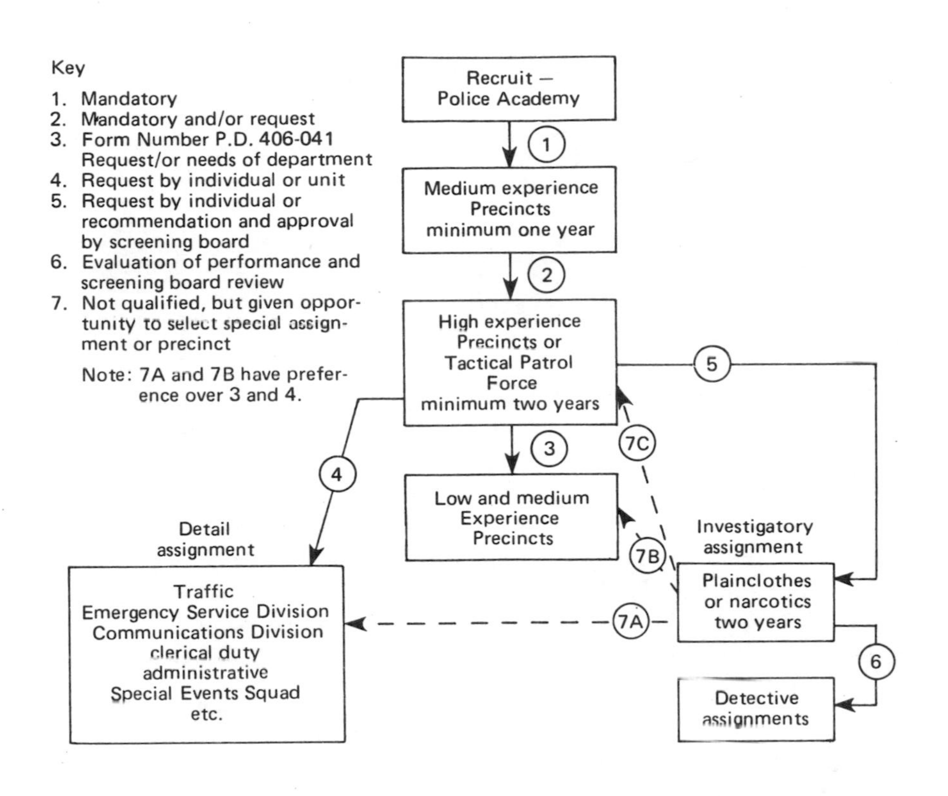

Source: New York City Police Department.

Exhibit R. Career Path—Flow Chart.

October 6, 1972

From: Police Commissioner

To: Narcotic District Commanders
Special Investigation Unit Squad Commanders
Intelligence and Undercover Units Commanders
Public Morals Borough District Unit Commanders
Central Investigation Section Unit Commanders
Public Morals Administrative; Special
Operations; and Intelligence Sections
Commanders

Subject: CORRUPTION ASSESSMENT

1. You are requested to complete the enclosed questionnaire by October 17, 1972.

2. One copy will be returned by you direct to the Office of the First Deputy Commissioner in a sealed envelope marked "confidential." At the same time that you forward this copy, a second copy will be forwarded to the next level in your chain of command, also in a sealed envelope marked "confidential."

3. You are not to confer about or discuss the contents of this questionnaire with any other unit commanding officer, or with the Section or Division commanders or any officer of their staffs until such time as you have forwarded the completed copy to the First Deputy Commissioner. Any violation of this directive will be considered to be a serious violation of Department policy.

4. If, prior to the time that you forward the completed copy of the questionnaire to the First Deputy Commissioner, you are approached in any fashion by any officer, other than a member of your own staff, concerning your reply to the questionnaire, you will immediately notify me by telephoning 577-7466, 7, 8.

md POLICE COMMISSIONER

Note: All names and other identifying data have been deleted.
Source: New York City Police Department.

Exhibit S. Corruption Assessment Questionnaire.

THE FOLLOWING IS A LIST OF POSSIBLE TYPES OF POLICE CORRUPTION

Type	In Your Assessment Do They Exist In Your Command?		To What Degree			Who Is Involved?						Is It Organized?					
	Yes	No	High	Medium	Low	Lts		Sgts		Dets & Ptl.		Lts		Sgts		Dets & Ptl.	
						Yes	No	Yes	No	Yes	No	Yes	No	Yes	No	Yes	No
Prostitution																	
Pornography																	
Bars & Grills																	
Social Clubs																	
Free Meals																	
After-Hr. Spots																	
Narcotics & Gambling Operations																	
Flaking Defendants																	
Scores or Shakedowns																	
Falsifying Affidavits																	
Withholding Drugs																	
Selling Drugs																	
Selling Evidence																	
Evidence Substitution																	
Falsifying Expense Accounts																	
Disclosing Confidential Info.																	
Illegal Eavesdropping																	
Informants																	
Non-Registering																	
Giving Drugs for Info.																	
Falsifying Records																	
Court Process																	
False Testimony																	
Selling Cases																	
Illegal Dealing with: Bondsmen																	
Attorneys																	
Other (Specify)																	

Exhibit S (cont.)

Do you suspect or believe or is there a possibility that any member of your staff might be involved in any of the following?

	Yes	No	Don't Know
Selling Days Off	____	____	____
Accepting or Requesting Remuneration for:			
• Favorable Assignments	____	____	____
• Preparing Departmental Recognition Requests	____	____	____
• Other Clerical Favors	____	____	____

Do you think there might be a sergeant's club in your unit?

		Degree of Involvement by Sgts		
Yes	No	All	Most	Some
____	____	____	____	____

Do you think there might be solicitation of Christmas gratuities:

	Organized		Not Organized		Degree of Involvement		
	Yes	No	Yes	No	All	Most	Some
Sergeants	____	____	____	____	____	____	____
Lieutenants	____	____	____	____	____	____	____
Dets & Ptl.	____	____	____	____	____	____	____
Clerical Staff	____	____	____	____	____	____	____
Other Ptl.	____	____	____	____	____	____	____

Exhibit S (cont.)

II

Indicate for each type of corruption the basis on which you have made the preceding assessment? (Attach additional sheets if necessary)

III

What steps are you taking to verify your assessment?

IV

Based on your assessment what programs have you or are you developing to address these problems.

Exhibit S (cont.)

OPERATIONS DIVISION

December 21, 196X

MEMORANDUM FOR THE POLICE COMMISSIONER:

Subject: GAMBLING ARRESTS FOR FRIDAY, DECEMBER 20, 196X.

COMMAND		1 DC	CIIU	Boro	Div	Pct	Others	Vio.	Specific Charge
MANHATTAN SOUTH									
1 Division					*1			225.05	Collector-out
MANHATTAN NORTH									
4 Division					*1			225.05	Collector-in
5 Division				*1				225.05	Collector-out
6 Division					*2		*1(25	225.05	Collector-in
				*3			Precinct)	225.10	Banker-in (Fel)
BRONX									
7 Division	(40Precinct)					*2		225.05	Collector-in
	(42Precinct)					*2		225.05	Collector-in
8 Division	(41Precinct)				*2		*1(41	225.05	Collector-out
	(41Precinct)			*1			Squad)	225.05	Collector-in
BROOKLYN SOUTH									
11 Division	(76Precinct)						*2(76	225.05	Pickup-in
	(76Precinct)				*1		Precinct)	225.05	Collector-in
	(84Precinct)				*1			225.05	Collector-in
12 Division	(75Precinct)			*1				225.05	WireRoom-in
	(71Precinct)			*3				225.05	Collector-in
BROOKLYN NORTH									
13 Division	(77Precinct)					*1		225.05	Collector-in
	(79Precinct)			*2				225.05	Collector-in
14 Division	(81Precinct)				*1			225.05	Collector-in
	(81Precinct)				*1			225.10	Collector-out (Fel)
	(92Precinct)								
					*2			225.10	Collector-in (Fel)
QUEENS									
16 Division				*1				225.05	Collector-out
RICHMOND									
120Precinct				*1				225.05	Handbook-out
		0	0	13	12	5	4	TOTAL ARRESTS . . . 34	

*additional charges

RECAPITULATION

225.10 (Fel.)		225.05		TOTAL ARRESTS
Banker	3	Collector . . .	24	34
Collector . . .	3	Handbook . .	1	
		Pickup	2	
		WireRoom . .	1	

Lieutenant
OPERATIONS SECTION

Note: All names and other identifying data have been deleted.
Source: New York City Police Department.

Exhibit T. "The Sheet" for December 20, 196X.

Affidavit for Search Warrant
Sec. 797-a C.C.P.

Criminal Court of the City of New York

Part One, County of Kings

State of New York } ss.:
County of Kings }

PLAINCLOTHESMAN EAGER BEAVER, SHIELD #13246, 6th DIVISION

being duly sworn, deposes and says:

1. I am a police officer assigned to plainclothes duty with the 6th Division of the New York City Police Department.
2. I have information based upon the following:

I have received information from a confidential informant, known to me, that one Joseph Bettorsman, of 2552 Nonexistent Place, Brooklyn, N.Y., is accepting, receiving and transporting records of bets in the vicinity of Buffalo Avenue and St. Johns Place from his automobile, License number BK 1234 (1965), a dark green Mercury sedan, 4-door, registered in his name. The information was received within the past seven days.

On Monday, June 13, 1965, at approximately 11:15am, in the vicinity of Buffalo Avenue and St. Johns Place, I observed Joseph Bettorsman drive up in the aforementioned Mercury automobile, license #BK 1234, and after a brief conversation with four unknown males, Joseph Bettorsman did accept a slip of paper from each of the four males at separate intervals and then drive off.

On Monday, June 13, 1965, at approximately 12:10pm, in the vicinity of Ralph Avenue and St. Johns Place, I observed an unknown male studying a National Horseracing Program. After a short while the unknown male did make a notation on a slip of paper and after folding same he did place two bills of United States currency in with the slip of paper. At this point in time, approximately 12:14pm, Joseph Bettorsman did drive up in the aforementioned Mercury sedan and he was approached by the unknown male who handed Joseph Bettorsman the slip of paper with the money, which slip he did accept. Two other males also approached Joseph Bettorsman and handed him slips of folded paper at separate intervals which he also accepted, following which Bettorsman drove away in the aforementioned Mercury sedan.

Note: All names and other identifying data have been changed.
Source: New York City Police Department.

Exhibit U. A Search Warrant Affidavit.

Information from this same informant has been relaible in the past, and has resulted in the arrest of one Harry Horseplayer, arrested on January 23, 1965., and convicted in this court on March 4, 1965.

3. Based upon the foregoing reliable information and upon my personal knowledge there is probable cause to believe that such property namely, written records of horse bets and other paraphernalia commonly use in bookmaking, is being used and/or transported in violation of 986PL, and 970 (b) PL.

and may be found in the possession of Joseph Bettorsman (described above) or in automobile license #BK 1234 (1965)

or at premises in the vicinity of St. Johns Place between Buffalo and Ralph Avenues, in the County of Kings, State of New York.

WHEREFORE, I respectfully request that the court issue a warrant and order of seizure, in the form annexed, authorizing the search of said person and/or vehicle.

and directing that if such property or evidence or any part thereof be found that it be seized and brought before the court; together with such other and further relief that the court may deem proper.

No previous application in this matter has been made in this or any other court or to any other judge, justice or magistrate.

EAGER BEAVER	13246	Plcl.	6th Division
Police Officer	*Shield*	*Rank*	*Command*

Eager Beaver

Sworn to before me

June 14, 1965

A. Nonymous

Judge

Exhibit U (continued)

EVALUATION OF PLAINCLOTHES PATROLMAN

U.F. 85 (6-62)

Report for Period from.....................................through.......................................

Surname	First Name	Initial	Shield No.	Command

Date Assigned to Plainclothes Duty in This Command	Date Originally Assigned To Plainclothes Duty	Date Granted Extra Compensation	Date Appointed to Police Department

	Vacation	Sick	Other Leave	Special Assignment	Total
NO. OF DAYS ABSENT FROM REGULAR ASSIGNMENT DUE TO:					

PART I—PERSONAL AND PERFORMANCE FACTORS (Mark E-Excellent; G-Good; F-Fair; P-Poor)

RATING	FACTOR	DESCRIPTION
	DEPENDABILITY	(Consistently accomplishes desired action with minimum supervision)
	JUDGMENT	(Thinks logically and makes practical decisions)
	INITIATIVE	(Takes necessary and appropriate action on his own)
	KNOWLEDGE	(Acquires knowledge and grasps concepts readily)
	JOB INTEREST	(Enthusiasm for his work; takes action to improve self)
	LOYALTY	(The quality of rendering faithful and willing service and unswerving allegiance)
	INVESTIGATIVE PERFORMANCE	(Complaint investigations, procurement and use of information, obtaining of evidence)
	ARREST ACTIVITY	(Interest displayed through arrests and summonses in eradication of professional gambling and vice)
	REPORTS	(Particularly U.F. 128, U.F. 44, Memo Book, K.G. investigations)
	COURT AFFIDAVIT PREPARATION	(Essentials of crime; relevancy of evidence)
	OVERALL EVALUATION OF ABOVE FACTORS	

RATER'S REMARKS (To be used for additional pertinent information or comment re: Parts I & II)

Note: This form has remained essentially unchanged since it was issued in 1962.
Source: New York City Police Department.

Exhibit V. Plainclothes Evaluation Form.

PART II—ARREST AND SUMMONS ACTIVITY

CLASSIFICATION	CURRENT PERIOD			RECAPITULATION ALL ARRESTS			DISPOSITION OF ARRESTS			SUMMONSES	
	PLACES	ARRESTS	KNOWN GAMBLERS	PLACES	ARRESTS	KNOWN GAMBLERS	CONVICTIONS	NON-CONVICTIONS	PENDING	CURRENT PERIOD	RECAPITU-LATION
POLICY											
Banker											
Controller											
Pick Up Man											
Collector											
Player											
Other (A & P, K & M, etc.)											
TOTALS											
BOOKMAKING											
Wire Room											
Telephone Seized											
Handbook IN											
Handbook OUT											
Other (A & P, K & M, etc.)											
TOTALS											
MISCELLANEOUS GAMBLING											
Art. 130 P.L. (Lottery)											
973 P.L.											
982 P.L.											
970 P.L											
580 P.L.											
722 P.L. (Dice)											
722 P.L. (Cards)											
722 P.L. (Misc. Gambling)											
PROSTITUTION											
887 C.C.P. (Female)											
887 C.C.P. (Male)											
1146 P.L. (Dis. House)											
DEGENERATES											
A.B.C. LAW & RULES											
NARCOTICS											
MISCELLANEOUS											
GRAND TOTALS											

Total Number of Patrolmen Rated.................. This Patrolman's Standing in Group..................

(Date) (Rank) (Rater's Signature) (Command)

COMMANDING OFFICER'S RECOMMENDATION: (Statement to include specific recommendation for retention, extra compensation, transfer or other personnel action with justification therefor.)

(Date) (Commanding Officer's Signature) (Command)

Exhibit V. (cont.)

Thursday, June 13, 1966
Day Duty - Ring 30
9 15 a - 10 05 a Vicinity Eastern Parkway + Utica Ave - possible 486 PL - NVO
10 20 a - 10 45 a Vicinity 1614 St. Johns Pl. re KG Elusive - not observed
10 55 a 11 45 a At Division Office
11 50 a 2 15 p On patrol with Lieutenant Smart in Division areas, NVO
2 30 p - 3 15 p Observed KG Fictitious vicinity Duffy's Tavern, 385 Ralph Ave, NVO
3 30 p - 3 45 p Issued ABC summons at Crown Heights Bar, 283 Vernon Ave, "No soap in Washroom" - SS 246.001
4 00 p - 5 00 p At Division Office, conferred with clerical ptl. Jones
Ptl Eager Beaver # 13246

UF-16-6,500M-701846(66) 114 № 40

Lt. J.S.

Monday, July 2, 1966
Day Duty - Ring 35
9 00 a 12 15 p Brooklyn Gamblers Court part #6, case of Harry Horseplayer, $10 fine - Judge Easy - case of J. Bettorsman adjourned till July 28th by Judge Crater in part #3 -
12 15 p - 12 45 Brooklyn Property Clerk's Office to return evidence
12 55 p - 1 45 p Vicinity 2552 Park Place re Complaint # 372665 - NVO
2 05 p - 3 50 p Arrest of Mary Smith - soliciting for purposes of prostitution
4 15 - 4 30 Chez Lounge, 275 Pitkin Ave - ABC summons - "dim lighting"
4 35 5 45 At Division Office - UF128s with clerical patrolman Jones
Ptl. Eager Beaver # 13246

UF 16-6 500M-701846(66) 114 № 49

D.I. J.K.

Note: All names and other identifying data have been changed.

Source: New York City Police Department.

Exhibit W. Typical Entries in a Plainclothesman's Memorandum Book.

Name of Defendants and Charges	Date of Arrest	Time of Arrest	Defendant Arrested Before?	Age	Previous Charges	Amount Money Seized	Amount Work Seized	Court Sentence
BIG JOE J. 974 PL	8/14/65	2:30pm	Yes	49	974 PL	$1450	1630 plays	$250 Fine
BEN GREEN 974a PL	8/22/65	3:30pm	Yes	56	974 PL	$ 825	1245 plays	$175 Fine
PHIL WHITE 986c PL	9/4/65	1:15pm	Yes	47	986 PL	$1865	280 bets	$450 & 30 days-SS
JOHN SMITH 974a PL	10/13/65	11:30am	Yes	23	Possession of Heroin	$12.50	125 plays	$10 Fine
JOHN JONES 974 PL	10/30/65	12:15pm	No	26	None	$56.00	140 plays	$50 Fine-SS
	Too Early!			Stand-ins?			Old Work?	

Note: This shows an unofficial survey that was used to discover patterns indicating cooptation by gamblers, such as when arrests were made too early in the day for maximum effectiveness, or when defendants had previous arrests for narcotics violations indicating that they might be "stand-ins." All names and other identifying data have been changed.

Source: New York City Police Department.

Exhibit X. A Plainclothesman's Pattern of Gambling Arrests.

OFFICE OF THE [ ] DIVISION

DAILY ASSIGNMENT SHEET

DATE: 10-15-73
TOUR: 10 00 am - 6 00 pm
RING: 35

PTL. Eager Beaver
PTL. John Sheetsman
PTL.

COMM. # COMB. # ETC.	LOCATION	SUBJECT	TIME FROM	TIME TO	INSTRUCTIONS OR RESULTS
	Office - complete DARs + briefing	New Penal law sections	10 00 am	10 40 am	See me
#195	Flemmy's Candy Store - Grand St. + Essex St.	Big Joe K	11 00 am	1 45 pm	Tail Cadillac
#238	Madison Cafeteria - East 26th St.	Unknown	2 15 pm	4 15 pm	Identify controller
	Office	surveillance reports — be specific!	4 40 pm	6 00 pm	See me

Sgt Preston
SUPERVISOR

Note: All names and other identifying data have been changed.

Source: New York City Police Department.

Exhibit Y. Daily Assignment Sheet for Plainclothesmen.

As a Law Enforcement Officer, my fundamental duty is to serve mankind; to safeguard lives and property; to protect the innocent against deception, the weak against oppression or intimidation, and the peaceful against violence or disorder; and to respect the Constitutional rights of all men to liberty, equality and justice.

I will keep my private life unsullied as an example to all; maintain courageous calm in the face of danger, scorn, or ridicule; develop self-restraint; and be constantly mindful of the welfare of others. Honest in thought and deed in both my personal and official life, I will be exemplary in obeying the laws of the land and the regulations of my department. Whatever I see or hear of a confidential nature or that is confided to me in my official capacity will be kept ever secret unless revelation is necessary in the performance of my duty.

I will never act officiously or permit personal feelings, prejudices, animosities or friendships to influence my decisions. With no compromise for crime and with relentless prosecution of criminals, I will enforce the law courteously and appropriately without fear or favor, malice or ill will, never employing unnecessary force or violence and never accepting gratuities.

I recognize the badge of my office as a symbol of public faith, and I accept it as a public trust to be held so long as I am true to the ethics of the police service. I will constantly strive to achieve these objectives and ideals, dedicating myself before God to my chosen profession . . . law enforcement.

Note: This code was originally adopted by the International Association of Chiefs of Police (IACP) in 1957.

Source: President's Commission on Law Enforcement and Administration of Justice, *Task Force Report: The Police* (Washington, D.C.: Government Printing Office, 1967, p. 213.

Exhibit Z. Law Enforcement Code of Ethics.

Notes

Notes

Chapter 1
Ethical Police Practice

This manuscript is based on extensive interviews and records of the New York City Police Department as well as on other sources that are available to the public. Because of a need for confidentiality, names of persons interviewed and references to some police department materials have been omitted from the notes.

1. The President's Commission on Law Enforcement and Administration of Justice, *Task Force Report: The Police* (Washington, D.C.: Government Printing Office, 1967), p. 208.

2. See, for example, David Bordua, ed., *The Police: Six Sociological Essays* (New York: John Wiley & Sons, 1967); Jameson W. Doig, James Q. Wilson, and Herman Goldstein, a symposium, "The Police in a Democratic Society," *Public Administration Review* 28 (September/October 1968): 393-423; John A. Gardiner, *Theft of a City* (Bloomington: Indiana University Press, 1974); Albert J. Reiss, Jr., *The Police and the Public* (New Haven: Yale University Press, 1971); Jonathan Rubinstein, *City Police* (New York: Farrar, Straus and Giroux, 1973); Lawrence W. Sherman, ed., *Police Corruption* (New York: Anchor Books, 1974); Jerome H. Skolnick, *Justice Without Trial* (New York: John Wiley & Sons, 1966); and James Q. Wilson, *Varieties of Police Behavior* (Cambridge, Mass.: Harvard University Press, 1968).

3. For a review of police problems with minorities, see "The Police and the Community," *Report of the National Advisory Commission on Civil Disorders* (Washington, D.C.: Government Printing Office, 1968), pp. 157-169.

4. *Mallory* v. *United States*, 354 U.S. 449 (1957).

5. *Mapp* v. *Ohio*, 367 U.S. 643 (1961).

6. *Escobedo* v. *Illinois*, 378 U.S. 478 (1964).

7. *Miranda* v. *Arizona*, 384 U.S. 436 (1966). Though commonly known as the "Miranda decision," this was actually four similar cases decided in one opinion.

8. See, for example, Yale Kamisar, "Public Safety v. Individual Liberties: Some 'Facts' and 'Theories,'" *Journal of Criminal Law, Criminology and Police Science* 53 (June 1962): 171-193; Yale Kamisar, "Some Reflections on Criticizing the Courts and 'Policing the Police,'" *Journal of Criminal Law, Criminology and Police Science* 53 (December 1962): 453-462; Yale Kamisar, "On the Tactics of the Police–Prosecution Oriented Critics of the Courts," *Cornell Law Quarterly* 49 (Spring 1964): 436-477; William H. Parker, "A Lawman's Lament," *The Los Angeles Bar Bulletin* (October 1965): 642; Yale Kamisar, "When the Cops Were

Not Handcuffed," *The New York Times Magazine*, November 7, 1965, p. 34; Herbert L. Packer, Richard H. Kuh, Theodore Souris, Fred E. Inbau, Vincent L. Broderick, Robert E. English, O.W. Wilson, Charles S. Desmond, and David W. Craig, "A Symposium on the Supreme Court and the Police," *Journal of Criminal Law, Criminology and Police Science* 57 (September 1966): 238-311; Irving R. Kaufman, "Miranda and the Police–The Confession Debate Continues," *The New York Times Magazine*, November 2, 1966, p. 37.

9. See Jerome Skolnick, *The Politics of Protest*, a staff report to the National Commission on the Causes and Prevention of Violence (Washington, D.C.: Government Printing Office, 1969); and David P. Stang, "The Police and Their Problems," in *Law and Order Reconsidered*, a staff report to the National Commission on the Causes and Prevention of Violence (Washington, D.C.: Government Printing Office, 1969), pp. 285-308.

10. For discussion of these issues see, for example, Joseph Goldstein, "Police Discretion Not to Invoke the Criminal Process: Low Visibility Decisions in the Administration of Justice," *Yale Law Journal* 69 (1960): 543-594; Wayne R. LaFave, *Arrest: The Decision to Take a Suspect into Custody* (Boston: Little, Brown, 1965); Paul Chevigny, *Police Power–Police Abuses in New York City* (New York: Vintage Press, 1969); Algernon D. Black, *The People and the Police* (New York: McGraw-Hill, 1968), pp. 1-50; "Interrogations in New Haven," *Yale Law Journal*, 76 (July 1967): 1519-1677; William A. Westley, *Violence and the Police* (Cambridge, Mass.: The MIT Press, 1970); Skolnick, "The Police in Protest," in *The Politics of Protest*, pp. 183-222; and Skolnick, "The Informer System," in *Justice Without Trial*, pp. 112-138.

11. Stang, "The Police and Their Problems," in *Law and Order Reconsidered*, p. 293.

12. For an analysis of the root causes of unethical police behavior, see the comparison of the "crime control" and "due process" models of law enforcement by Herbert L. Packer, *The Limits of the Criminal Sanctions* (Stanford, Calif.: Stanford University Press, 1968), pp. 149-246.

13. *Task Force Report: The Police*, pp. 208-210.

14. See James Q. Wilson, "The Police and Their Problems: A Theory," in James R. Klonoski and Robert Mendelsohn, eds., *The Politics of Local Justice*, (Boston: Little, Brown, 1970), pp. 161-174.

15. There is, for example, far more consensus among the police and public about the need for nondiscriminatory law enforcement than there is about means for achieving this goal. Police have vigorously contested civilian review boards and other proposals designed to increase citizen involvement in police management. See, for example, Black, *The People and the Police*, pp. 69-238, for an account of the short-lived Civilian Complaint Review Board in New York City.

16. Public policy toward legalizing gambling varies among the states. The Commission to Review National Policy Toward Gambling, which comprises

congressional and presidential appointees, has held public hearings to "shape new Federal policies and guidelines on sports betting and other forms of gambling." Hearings were held in nine different cities throughout the country during 1975, and transcripts are scheduled to be published in early 1976. See the *New York Times*, "Sports Betting: States Act to Legalize It but U.S. Opens Inquiry," January 19, 1975, p. 1; "States Ignore Bet Laws in Split on U.S. Policy," January 20, 1975, p. 1; "Sports Betting: What Are the Reasons," January 21, 1975, p. 27; "Sports Betting: States Plan 'No Risk' Future," January 22, 1975, p. 29; and "Extensive Hearings to Open on Betting," January 26, 1975, p. N.J. 3; also See Walter H. Waggoner, "Bettors Will Pick Own Numbers In New Daily Lottery in Jersey," May 9, 1975, p. 1, and "New Jersey's New Tax Is a Numbers Game," May 11, 1975, IV, p. 5.

17. See Harold D. Lasswell and Jeremiah B. McKenna, *The Impact of Organized Crime on an Inner City Community* (New York: The Policy Sciences Center, 1972), pp. 238-242; *Increased Legal Gambling In New York*, Hudson Institute Report to the New York State Gambling Commission (New York, January 1973); Fund for the City of New York, *Legal Gambling in New York* (New York, 1972), and "Legalized Numbers–A Plan," a discussion paper prepared by the New York City Off-Track Betting Corporation (1973).

18. See *The Knapp Commission Report on Police Corruption* (New York: George Braziller, 1973), pp. 61-90; *Report on Police Corruption and the Quality of Law Enforcement in Philadelphia* (The Pennsylvania Crime Commission, 1974), pp. 166-216; and William F. Whyte, "Gambling and The Police in Boston," in Sherman, ed., *Police Corruption*, pp. 108-128.

19. For an overview of the range of external control mechanisms see "Securing Police Compliance With Constitutional Limitations," in *Law and Order Reconsidered*, pp. 365-409, and "Control Over Police Authority," in *The Urban Police Function* (New York: American Bar Association, 1973), pp. 144-170. See also Leonard Ruchelman, ed., *Who Rules the Police*? (New York: New York University Press, 1973).

20. See note 8.

21. See *Law and Order Reconsidered*, pp. 386-390, and *The Urban Police Function*, pp. 160-161.

22. For example, U.S. Congress, Senate Special Committee to Investigate Crime in Interstate Commerce, *Investigation of Organized Crime in Interstate Commerce*, Reports 1-18 (Washington, D.C.: Government Printing Office, 1950-1951); and the New York State Commission of Investigation, Report of the Commission, *Syndicated Gambling in New York State* (Buffalo: State of New York, 1961), which cited widespread corruption in gambling enforcement in hearings held as a result of the meeting of "underworld" leaders held at Apalachin, New York, in 1957.

23. Indeed, the American Bar Association concluded that "The process of administrative rule-making . . . and strong internal procedures hold the greatest

promise of being the basis for effective review and control of police conduct." See *The Urban Police Function*, p. 167.

24. For studies of behavior in bureaucracies, see Gene W. Dalton and Paul R. Lawrence, *Motivation and Control in Organizations* (Homewood, Ill.: The Dorsey Press, 1971); Anthony Downs, *Inside Bureaucracy* (Boston: Little, Brown, 1967); Douglas McGregor, *The Human Side of Enterprise* (New York: McGraw-Hill, 1960); Charles Perrow, *Complex Organizations* (Glenview, Ill.: Scott Foresman, 1972); Robert Presthus, *The Organizational Society* (New York: Random House, Vintage Books, 1962); and Herbert A. Simon, *Administrative Behavior*, 2nd ed. (New York: The Free Press, 1957).

25. See, for example, V.A. Leonard, *Police Organization and Management*, 2nd ed. (Brooklyn: The Foundation Press, 1964); *Municipal Police Administration*, 6th ed. (Chicago: International City Manager's Association, 1969); Jim L. Munro, *Administrative Behavior and Police Organization* (Cincinnati: W.H. Anderson Company, 1974); and O.W. Wilson and Roy McLaren, *Police Administration*, 3rd ed. (New York: McGraw-Hill, 1972).

26. Herbert Kaufman, *The Forest Ranger* (Baltimore: The Johns Hopkins Press, 1967), p. x.

27. Ibid., pp. 91-200. Strategies and procedures identified by Kaufman also were applied in the New York City Police Department.

28. Ibid. For a more detailed discussion of these obstacles, see also Simon, *Administrative Behavior*; Presthus, *The Organizational Society*; Downs, *Inside Bureaucracy*; and Wilson, *Varieties of Police Behavior.*

29. For an overview of the full range of corrupt practice by police, see *The Knapp Commission Report*, pp. 65-192.

30. For an analysis of the socialization process, see Lawrence W. Sherman, "Becoming Bent: Moral careers of corrupt policemen," in his *Police Corruption*, pp. 191-208.

31. See Norman Weiner, "The Effect of Investigations on the Enforcement of the Gambling and Public Morals Laws Within the Police Department" (unpublished master's thesis, Bernard M. Baruch School of Business and Public Administration, The City College of New York, June 1960); and Gerald Astor, *The New York Cops–An Informal History* (New York: Charles Scribner's Sons, 1971), pp. 54-167.

32. See the series of articles by Ed Reid in the *Brooklyn Eagle*, December 1949: "Lucrative Borough Rackets Feed Vast Crime Syndicate," December 11, 1949, p. 1; "Huge Payoffs for Protection," December 12, 1949, p. 1; "Who is the Top Brass of Brooklyn Rackets?" December 14, 1949, p. 1; "Police Inspectors Get Paid Off, Bookie Charges," December 15, 1949, p. 1; "Dockmen Enslaved by Crime Boss," December 16, 1949, p. 1; "Policy Bosses Prey on Rich and Poor Alike," December 19, 1949, p. 1.

33. For a contemporary account of the Gross case and its disclosures, see the following highlights in the *New York Times*: "O'Brien to Press Drive on

Gambling," January 8, 1950, p. 46:1; "City Backs Inquiry into Police Links to Gaming in Kings," February 9, 1950, p. 1:5; "McDonald Seeks Blue-Ribbon Grand Jury in Gambling Case," April 12, 1950, p. 1:4; "Gambling Inquiry to be Broadened," May 1, 1950, p. 17:2; "McDonald Wants $92,030 for Inquiry," June 10, 1950, p. 34:1; "Jury at Brooklyn Gambling Trial Hears About Ruses of Policy Ring," June 16, 1950, p. 26:3; "McDonald to Press Gambling Inquiry," August 1, 1950, p. 46:5; "Gaming Protection for $350 a Week Laid to Policemen," September 16, 1950, p. 1:1; "Bookie Chief Held in Bail of $250,000; 24-Hour Guard Set," September 20, 1950, p. 1:1; "Gross Won't Name Police Associates," September 21, 1950, p. 1:2; "Ouster of O'Brien Imminent; Bookie Names Graft Takers," September 23, 1950, p. 1:4; "O'Brien Out as Police Head; Murphy of Hiss Case Named; Jury Asks Reform of Police," September 26, 1950, p.1:1; "Bookies Big Business: $3-10 Billion a Year," October 8, 1950, IV p. 10:1; $50,000 A-Day Bets Made With Gross," October 11, 1950, p. 1:1; "A Who's Who of New York's Gambling Inquiry," October 29, 1950, IV p. 6:1; "Bookies Aide Puts Monthly Payoffs at $1500 to $2500," October 31, 1950, p. 1:1; " 'Cheesebox' Remote Control Phone Device Leads to Raid on Bookmaking Headquarters," November 18, 1950, p. 33:2; "Gross's Guilty Plea Cuts Trial Short, Girl Breaks Case," January 24, 1951, p. 1:1; " 'Hush-Hush' Police All to Face Jury," March 8, 1951, p. 32:3; "77 Policemen Cited by Jury in Bet Racket," May 10, 1951, p. 1:1; "Top Police Linked to Gross Pay-Off as Trial Resumes," September 18, 1951, p. 1:1; "Gross Defiance Ends Trial; 18 Police Freed of Charges; Bribery is Seen by McDonald," September 20, 1951, p. 1:7; "Gross Gets 12-Year Term; Police Graft Story Bared," September 28, 1951, p. 1:6; "Gross Said Bookies Had O'Dwyer Fund; Listed $20,000 Gifts," September 29, 1951, p. 1:8; "12 More Policemen Accused by Gross in Gambling Graft," April 26, 1952, p. 1:1; "Gross Lists O'Brien, Moran and Bals as Bribe Takers; Names 120 Police in Pay-Offs," May 8, 1952, p. 1:6; "Gross Adds Whalen, Flath, Former Top Line Officers, to His Police Pay-Off List," May 9, 1952, p. 1:8; "Police Trial Ends," May 13, 1952, p. 1:4; "Bookies and Police: Continued Story," May 18, 1952, IV, p. 9:7; "Gross Accuses 9 More at Trial; Tells of Pay-Offs to Bals's Squad," September 26, 1952, p. 16:5; "Gross Calls Graft Vital in His Trade," October 9, 1952, p. 64:5; "Monaghan Ousts 23 Accused by Gross; 6 Men Are Cleared," February 25, 1953, p. 1:1; "Police Alter Plan to Fight Gambling," March 7, 1953, p. 1:3; "70 Policemen Fired in 5 Months," June 5, 1953, p. 28:3.

34. For some discussions of control mechanisms in organizations see Downs, *Inside Bureaucracy*, pp. 144-157, and Amitai Etzioni, *Modern Organizations* (Englewood Cliffs, N.J.: Prentice-Hall, 1964).

Chapter 2
The Environment of Gambling: 1950-1975

All technical information relating to organized gambling, except for secondary sources cited below, was obtained through a series of personal interviews at the

New York City Police Department (NYCPD). Departmental experts furnished all facts and estimates from their personal experience and from current reports.

1. In 1967, profits from illegal gambling were estimated at $50 billion. See The President's Commission on Law Enforcement and Administration of Justice, *Task Force Report: Organized Crime* (Washington, D.C.: Government Printing Office, 1967), pp. 1-24. For indication of a new trend see Nicholas Gage, "Organized Crime Reaps Huge Profits From Dealing in Pornographic Films," *New York Times* October 12, 1975, p. 1.

2. See *Legalized Gambling*, Report to the New York State Commission on Gambling (New York, February 1973); *Increased Legal Gambling in New York*, Hudson Institute Report to the New York State Gambling Commission (New York, January 1973); and Fund for the City of New York, *Legal Gambling in New York* (New York, 1972).

3. See note 16, Chapter 1. Also see the *New York Times*, "Bookies Who Pay Taxes Promised Immunity," January 14, 1975, p. 72:4; "Betting Cards: Too Small for Big Bettors, Just Right for Millions," January 21, 1975, p. 28:3; and "Tax Cut Gives Legality a Chance Against Illegality in Nevada Betting," January 22, 1975, p. 30:5; and "OTB Called No Handicap to Bookmakers," *New York Daily News*, May 11, 1975, p. 1K.

4. An individual bettor selects a number of his choice instead of purchasing a prenumbered ticket used in the state lotteries. In addition, he can bet on any one-, two-, or three-digit numbers or on each of the six possible combinations of any three-digit number.

5. See Thomas C. Schelling, "Economic Analysis of Organized Crime," in The President's Commission, *Task Force Report: Organized Crime*, p. 119; and Clarence M. Kelley, "Are There Victimless Crimes?" *New York Daily News*, Sunday Magazine, May 11, 1975.

6. See "The Bookmaker Always Wins," in *Syndicated Gambling in New York State*, Report of the New York State Commission of Investigation (Buffalo: February, 1961), pp. 53-55.

7. By the early 1950s bookmaking had assumed the structure and operating procedures still characteristic today. For a concise historical presentation of organized bookmaking, see Michael J. Murphy, *The Gambling Situation–1964*, A Report by Police Commissioner Michael J. Murphy, On the Status of Illegal Gambling and Gambling Enforcement in New York City, To the Select Committee on Off-Track Betting (New York: New York City Police Department, February 1964), pp. 32-34. See also Frederick W. Egen, *Plainclothesmen* (New York: Arco, 1959), pp. 27-59; and *Legal Gambling in New York*, pp. 35-44.

8. Murphy, *The Gambling Situation–1964*, pp. 34-37.

9. "Professional Handicapping of Events: The Line," in *Syndicated Gambling in New York State*, p. 28.

10. For other discussions of the numbers game, see Murphy, *The Gambling Situation–1964*, pp. 51-55; Egen, *Plainclothesmen*, pp. 60-82; and *Legal Gambling in New York*, pp. 20-34.

11. The policy player, however, faces some discrimination in the winning payoff. Instead of being paid at the legitimate odds of 1000 to 1, he collects winnings at odds of 550 or 600 to 1, depending on the practice of the numbers organization and the type of bet. Two-digit "bolita" bets are usually paid at odds of 70 to 1, while "single action" players receive only 6 to 1 payoffs. In addition, "cut numbers" are paid at greatly reduced odds of 250 or 300 to 1, and bets on specified numbers are not accepted on certain days. This is done to prevent major losses when a number such as 317 is played by thousands of people on St. Patricks Day. Because of increased competition in 1975, however, store-front signs in some neighborhoods openly advertised "No Cut Numbers In Here." A typical cut card is shown in Figure N-1.

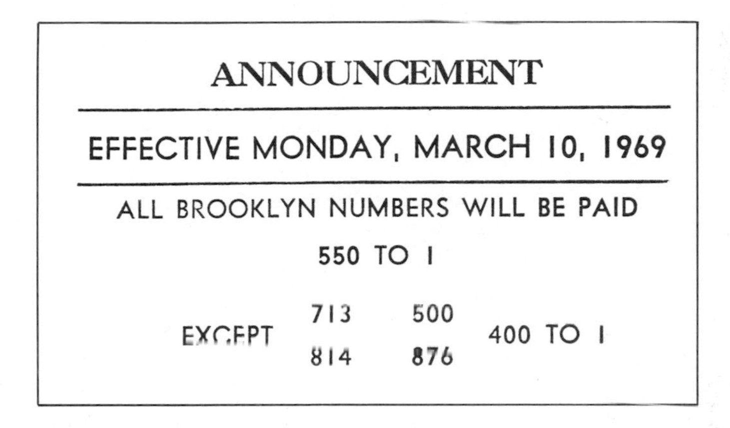
ANNOUNCEMENT

EFFECTIVE MONDAY, MARCH 10, 1969

ALL BROOKLYN NUMBERS WILL BE PAID

550 TO 1

EXCEPT 713 500 814 876 400 TO 1

Figure N-1. Cut Card.

12. Collectors accept bets as early as 6:00 a.m. every racing day from people on their way to work. Closing time is approximately 1:00 p.m. They carry betting records and cash on their persons or store them in a safe place. But the work must be transferred to the next echelon before post-time of the day's first race, usually between 12:30 and 1:00 p.m. This time limit on forwarding bets prevents collectors from acting in collusion with players by accepting bets after the results of the first race are known, giving bettors an advantage in determining the first digit of the day's number.

13. Collectors package the 3-digit "straight" bets for transfer by separate couriers and different routes, but retain "single action" and "bolita" wagers which they "book" themselves. Sometimes they make the actual delivery; but

most often, the transporting is done by pickup men, who generally are part-time employees paid salaries of $50 to $100 per week for an hour or two of work each day. They play a limited role and are easily replaced in the organization. At most, pickup work requires a person of ordinary appearance and enough intelligence to recognize a police surveillance. Using some caution, these couriers bring the materials to the next level of the organization, the controller.

14. The pickup man working for the bank takes them from the controller's spot for delivery to an intermediate drop or another courier. The envelopes remain there until a trusted bank clerk retrieves them, perhaps several hours later. With utmost care, this clerk delivers the work to the policy bank. He may spend hours making sure he is not observed by the police; if necessary, he will abandon the work rather than take it to the bank under possible surveillance. As a precaution there are usually separate couriers going to the policy banks, one to carry the money and the other to carry the records.

15. For example, if $50 were bet on a New York number that hit, the bank would have to pay off $30,000 at 600 to 1. Thus any time $30 or more is bet on a number, policy banks contact other banks within their organization to lay off bets. A small or independent bank goes to a larger organization for help and must pay for this layoff service. Inability to cover major losses is the principal cause of bankruptcy and takeover by larger numbers organizations, who refinance and reestablish failures.

16. Robert Presthus, *The Organizational Society* (New York: Random House, 1962), p. 4.

17. Although the police department's duties and responsibilities are outlined in the first paragraph of its *Rules and Procedures*, no mention is made of its role in safeguarding public morality. The department's responsibilities for public morals enforcement are set out in a separate chapter of the *R & P.* The *Rules and Procedures*, 1957 ed., Chapter 8, pp. 99-108a as amended. See note 27.

18. Under the New York City Charter the police commissioner has plenary authority for the "cognizance and control of the government, administration, disposition and discipline of the Police Department and its Police Force." The police force, which comprises only sworn policemen, is distinguished from the overall police department, which includes policemen, civilian employees, and administrators. Career policemen appointed as police commissioner or deputy commissioner must resign from the force to accept these civilian posts. See *Rules and Procedures*, 1957 ed., Chapter 1/2.0, p. 9 as amended, taken from New York City Charter.

19. A former noncareer commissioner (1954-1955), stated that one of the main reasons he resigned after only eighteen months in office was that his role as champion of the department began to dominate his perspective. For a discussion of how police commissioners deal with their internal and external constituencies, see Wallace S. Sayre and Herbert Kaufman, *Governing New York City* (New York: Russell Sage Foundation, 1960), pp. 285-292.

20. Deputy commissioners for licenses and youth affairs have been eliminated, as has the department's primary role in both of these areas. The new post of Deputy Commissioner for Criminal Justice has been added.

The other deputies become acting police commissioner only if specifically designated by the commissioner. No provision is made for automatic assumption of the police commissioner's duties beyond the first deputy. Like the commissioners, first deputies have come from within the force and from nonpolice backgrounds. Between April 1961 and September 1971, the first deputy commissioner exercised special responsibility for gambling enforcement, which was transferred to the newly appointed deputy commissioner for organized crime control.

21. Seniority of rank among members of the force of the same rank is determined by date of appointment to that rank; and if the date is the same, seniority is determined by numerical order on the promotion list. Detective and plainclothes are "detail" assignments, not formal ranks.

22. The uppermost ranks of the hierarchy have been in a state of flux during recent years. Chief of planning, created in 1963, was abolished shortly thereafter, as was chief of staff. Chief of personnel, created in 1967, was civilianized in 1972 when new ranks—chief of inspectional services and chief of organized crime control—reflecting the commissioner's concerns were created. See *Rules and Procedures*, 1957 ed., Chapter 1/16.0 as amended by General Orders #3, s. 1963, (February 8, 1963), #14, s. 1968 (July 2, 1968), and Temporary Operating Procedure (TOP) #251, s. 1972, (September 4, 1972).

The Patrol Bureau and the new rank of chief of patrol (subordinate only to the police commissioner and chief inspector) were created April 29, 1966, in TOP #139, s. 1966. The new designations of Patrol Services Bureau and uniformed service were made in TOP #50, s. 1972 (March 6, 1972).

In 1973 numerous rank and organizational titles were changed. Chief of personnel was made a police, no longer a civilian, job. The chief inspector became the chief of operations; chief of patrol became chief of field services; the Patrol Bureau and Patrol Precincts became Field Service Bureau and Precincts. See Interim Orders #45, s. 1973 (April 23, 1973), and #62, s. 1973 (June 1, 1973).

23. Since the late 1960s the department has tried to increase the uniformed service's responsibilities, hoping to enhance the patrol function. First, patrolmen were given limited authority to investigate minor burglaries, the first step toward freeing detectives for work against more serious crimes. Now patrolmen "conduct field investigations of most of the complaints received by the New York City Police Department." Limited authority for investigations was established in 1969 and expanded in TOPs #47, s. 1970 (February 25, 1970), #110, s. 1970 (April 22, 1970), and #469, s. 1971 (December 29, 1971).

24. For an historical account of the development of the Detective Division (Bureau), see Edward P. Mulrooney, "On the Trail Since The '90's," *Spring 3100* (April 1930), p. 8.

The Detective Bureau has also experienced its share of reorganizations. Detective districts, comparable to patrol divisions, were established in the 1920s, abolished in 1954, and reestablished in 1961, only to be replaced in 1972 by specialized homicide and other commands as precinct detective squads were phased out. In 1973, however, Precinct Investigation Units (similar to the squads just abolished) were established under the direction of the precinct commander. See TOP #468, s. 1971 (December 29, 1971), reorganizing the Detective Bureau effective January 1, 1972. Also see Interim Orders #117, s. 1973 (August 27, 1973), #133, s. 1973 (October 1, 1973), and #143, s. 1973 (October 16, 1973).

25. In 1973 a new "full service" management concept was adopted that gave major commanders responsibility for all law enforcement efforts in their territories. The seven geographic borough commands were redesignated "areas," and a new staff was created to assist "area commanders" in administration and corruption control. See Interim Order #45, s. 1973 (April 23, 1973).

26. The number of patrol divisions has remained fairly constant (around sixteen) in recent years, although their precinct subunits have been drastically realigned. Community groups have opposed the recent trend to consolidate patrol precincts.

In 1973 divisions were retitled "zones," and inspectors became "field service inspectors." More important, their role was changed from commanders to staff officers for the area commander. The intermediate layer of command (divisions) was eliminated to shorten the chain of command and to speed the flow of paper work. Precinct captains now reported directly to the area commander. See Operations Order #9173, s. 1973 (July 3, 1973).

27. Originating with a pocket-sized volume of *Rules and Regulations* in 1853, new editions appeared in 1898, 1901, and 1908. In 1924 a supplemental *Manual of Procedure* was added, and these two volumes were published in 1929, 1937, and 1949. In February 1957 the single-volume *Rules and Procedures* was published (Department Directive #8, s. 1957, January 10, 1957) and underwent considerable amendment thereafter. A new multivolume edition replacing the *Rules and Procedures* was prepared in the early 1970s. The *Patrol Guide* superseded the *R & P* in December 1972; the *Detective Guide* in July 1974; the *Organizational Guide* in July 1975; and an *Administrative Guide* scheduled for publication in 1975 has been delayed. See TOP #340-1, s. 1972 (December 7, 1972), and Press Release #136, s. 1972 (December 11, 1972).

28. All directions, supervisory responsibilities, and prohibitions are set forth in the *Rules and Procedures*, 1957 ed., Chapters 1, 2, and 3, as amended.

Policemen may not:

1. disobey the lawful orders of a superior officer
2. disclose official business of the department to unauthorized persons
3. use confidential information to advance their own financial interests
4. belong to political clubs or take active parts in campaigning

5. join or associate with any person or organization that fosters racial or religious hatred
6. knowingly associate with criminals, racketeers, gamblers, or persons engaged in unlawful activities
7. drink intoxicants while in uniform, or at any time to an extent making them unfit for duty
8. use their police shield or identification except for official business
9. use personal cards listing their department rank, assignment, or telephone number
10. accept rewards for police service without the approval of the police commissioner
11. solicit or accept gratuities for police service
12. recommend any professional service or commercial product
13. play games of cards or chance in a department building, or engage in illegal gambling anywhere
14. engage in a business transaction that conflicts with their official duties

29. In 1961 through General Order #67 (November 24, 1961), the two existing departmental memoranda–Department Directives and Local Orders (which were created in Department Directive #1, s. 1955, April 20, 1955)–were replaced by Standard Operating Procedures (SOPs) and Temporary Operating Procedures (TOPs), respectively. Since then the number of administrative memoranda has mushroomed almost to the point that every bureau chief issues a separate set of personal directives.

In 1973 SOPs, TOPs, and General Orders (GOs) were replaced by a new series of directives, including Interim Orders, Operations Orders, Personnel Orders and the Department Bulletins. See TOP #379, s. 1972 (December 20, 1972).

30. Until 1967, bookmaking and policy were considered distinct offenses. A long-standing misdemeanor statute sought to restrict organized bookmaking by forbidding anyone to: (1) record or forward bets placed with him; (2) accept or forward money to be wagered; (3) knowingly possess betting records; (4) assist in any of the above acts; or (5) allow premises under his ownership or control to be used for any of the above acts. (N.Y. Penal Law, Art. 88, Sec. 986.)

These provisions were broad enough to affect not only people within the organization from top to bottom, but also those outside it who provided support services. To differentiate between lower and higher echelons of bookmaking hierarchies, however, a felony statute was added in 1960 that established greater liability for anyone accepting more than five bets representing more than $5000 wagered in any one day. (N.Y. Penal Law, Art. 88, Sec. 986-c.)

Policy was proscribed by a series of similar provisions. A misdemeanor statute aimed at the lowest organizational level, the collector, forbade anyone to: (1) keep or use any room or place for numbers playing; (2) deliver or receive money, or other valuable consideration in furtherance of playing policy; (3) allow premises under his ownership or control to be used for numbers operations; or (4) aid or abet any of the preceding acts. (N.Y. Penal Law, Art. 88, Sec. 974.)

Pickup men, controllers, bank clerks, and bankers were the target of a complementary felony statute that prohibited anyone to: (1) receive $500 in numbers plays in any one day; (2) receive 100 numbers plays over any period; (3) receive any amount of money or any amount of numbers plays from a person other than a player; or (4) keep, occupy, or use a place or room for any of the preceding purposes. (N.Y. Penal Law, Art. 88, Sec. 974-a.)

31. Instead they require proof only that "(1) . . . the game or scheme in issue constitutes gambling, and (2) if so, whether the defendant's conduct is that of the indicated promotional character than that of a 'player.' " Thus a new offense of "promoting gambling" was created, encompassing all forms of gambling activity, and this was supplemented by narrower prohibitions carried over from old statutes, including possession of gambling records and paraphernalia and more serious felony offenses. See New York, Penal Law, art. 225, commission staff notes, *New York State Penal Law Annotated* (Rochester, N.Y.: Consolidated Law Service, 1967), pp. 4-56.

32. The more formal selection process for plainclothesmen grew out of suggestions made by several grand juries in Kings County (Brooklyn) and Richmond (Staten Island) investigating police corruption in gambling enforcement beginning in 1950 with the Harry Gross case. By 1955, the police commissioner had ended the practice of allowing plainclothesmen to transfer to new commands with their inspectors. It was not until 1960, however, that the formal procedure beginning with recommendations by precinct commanders was instituted. See Department Directive #38, s. 1960 (March 4, 1960).

33. Police academy reports, memoranda, and syllabuses, 1954-1964.

34. Information on the work of the plainclothes force was garnered from a series of personal interviews conducted with former plainclothesmen and superior officers who had been assigned as PMIs, PMDIs, lieutenants, and sergeants supervising plainclothes squads of all levels throughout the city. Documentary materials were extensively used also.

35. Begun in 1946, the KG program did not receive major emphasis until the police commissioner in the late 1950s sought to increase investigative efforts against known gamblers. Under his direction all members of the force were made responsible for gambling enforcement. In 1961 the newly formed Gambling Enforcement Inspection and Review Board helped issue the department's first Standard Operating Procedure, the known gamblers file, which has been updated three times. In spite of this administrative effort, the KG program and the KG file stagnated.

The file burgeoned sevenfold in little more than a decade, as shown by statistics taken from miscellaneous departmental materials, 1961. In 1948, there were 631 KGs; that number increased to 1000 in 1950, 2087 in 1955, 3231 in 1958, and 4262 in 1961.

The effort of the GEIRB to salvage the file by dividing it into active and inactive sections (SOP #1, November 24, 1961) also proved unsuccessful.

36. Known as the "Suspected Place," or 'UF 45' (Uniformed Force Report #45) file, this record system was even more elaborate than the KG file. All complaints from the public and referrals from the patrol force were cross-indexed in the file, along with results of plainclothes investigations. As with the KG file, it became necessary to divide the file into active and reference (inactive) sections. There were complex procedures for processing all Suspected Place reports, paralleling procedures for KGs.

37. Insight on the functioning of the plainclothes force was obtained through personal interviews of former plainclothesmen and superior officers. Many of the subjects (that is, selection, training, production quotas, supervision, false reporting, and so forth) will be discussed in greater detail in succeeding chapters, because this chapter introduces the reader to the ethos and complexities of plainclothes.

Chapter 3
The Directive Strategies: 1950-1975

Much of the material in this chapter was obtained during a series of interviews with former plainclothesmen and supervisors of the plainclothes force.

1. The strategies of "preforming decisions" and "developing the will and capacity to conform" were described in Herbert Kaufman's study of the U.S. Forest Service, *The Forest Ranger* (Baltimore: The Johns Hopkins Press, 1967), pp. 91-125, 161-200.

2. The police commissioner has plenary authority "and control of the government, administration, disposition and discipline of the Police Department and its Police Force." *Rules and Procedures*, 1957 ed., Chapter 1/2.0, p. 9 as amended, taken from the New York City Charter.

3. See David Burnham, "City Opens Study of Policing Police," *New York Times*, April 24, 1970, p. 1:7; David Burnham, "Graft Paid to Police Here Said to Run Into Millions," *New York Times*, April 25, 1970, p. 1:1; David Burnham, "Gamblers' Links to Police Led to Virtual Licensing," *New York Times*, April 26, 1970, p. 1:2; David Burnham, "Police Corruption Fosters Distrust in Ranks Here," *New York Times*, April 27, 1970, p. 1:2; Martin Tolchin, "City Opens Study of Police Graft," *New York Times*, April 28, 1970, p. 1:2; William E. Farrell, "Leary Assails Articles in Times on Police Corruption as 'Unfair,' " *New York Times*, April 29, 1970, p. 1:2; David Burnham, "Panel on Police Corrup-

tion Asks Mayor to Supersede It," *New York Times*, May 15, 1970, p. 1:6; and Douglas Robinson, "Leary Links Graft to Hypocrisy," *New York Times*, June 8, 1970, p. 1:1.

4. This idea concerning insight of agency heads was described by Herbert Kaufman in *Administrative Feedback* (Washington, D.C.: The Brookings Institution, 1973), p. 51.

5. By the late 1960s, however, corruption in the enforcement of the narcotics laws became the dominant concern of police administrators.

6. Initial statements of policy by recent Police Commissioners include those of Francis F.W. Adams, in Press Release #1A, s. 1954 (January 6, 1954); Stephen P. Kennedy, in Press Release #62, s. 1955 (August 8, 1955); Michael J. Murphy, in Press Release #13, s. 1961 (March 9, 1961); Vincent L. Broderick, in Press Release #56, s. 1965 (June 7, 1965); Howard R. Leary, in Press Release #20, s. 1966 (March 10, 1966); "Remarks of Police Commissioner Patrick V. Murphy to Superior Officers Above the Rank of Captain, At a Police Academy Conference," on October 28, 1970; and Michael J. Codd in Press Release #32, s. 1974 (June 16, 1974).

7. See Press Release #97, s. 1971 (October 7, 1971), which challenged the Knapp Commission, and Press Release #120, s. 1971 (December 20, 1971), which rebuked the "entire court system." Also see Press Release #55, s. 1974 (October 10, 1974), which refuted allegations of "rampant misconduct" by police.

8. For an account of the Knapp Commission's history and investigative procedures, see *The Knapp Commission Report on Police Corruption* (New York: George Braziller, 1973), pp. 35-60.

For a contemporary account of the controversy surrounding the creation and powers of the Knapp Commission, see David Burnham, "Lindsay Appoints Corruption Unit," *New York Times*, May 22, 1970, p. 46:1; David Burnham, "PBA Urges City to Curb Inquiry," *New York Times*, May 27, 1970, p. 94:3; Edward Ranzel, "Police Panel Gets Subpoena Powers," *New York Times*, May 28, 1970, p. 1:8; David Burnham, "PBA Moves to Bar Corruption Inquiry," *New York Times*, July 2, 1970, p. 1:7; Maurice Carroll, "Mayor, Still Fought by Garelik, Wins Funds for Police Inquiry," *New York Times*, July 25, 1970, p. 1:1; and Edward Ranzel, "Lindsay Hails the Police Force, But Extends The Corruption Inquiry," *New York Times*, January 8, 1971, p. 38:4.

9. See David Burnham, "Murphy Says He Was Appalled By Police Graft He Found in '70," *New York Times*, May 17, 1972, p. 1:7; and David Burnham, "Murphy Warns Top Aides Fight On Corruption Lags," *New York Times*, August 28, 1972, p. 1:1.

10. Overzealousness by the city's investigations commissioner and the Knapp Commission enabled the police commissioner to impose more radical strategies. See David Burnham, "PBA Fights Plea to Jail 3 Police," *New York Times*, August 8, 1970, p. 14:2; Robert E. Tomasson, "Court Rebuffs City's

Investigation Chief," *New York Times*, October 1, 1970, p. 28:1; David Burnham, "Two Inspectors Demoted in Inquiry on Corruption," *New York Times*, November 11, 1970, p. 1:6; Robert E. Tomasson, "5 Police Officers Sue Over Inquiry," *New York Times*, December 1, 1970, p. 1:2; David Burnham, "Inquiry Charges Payoffs to Police on the East Side," *New York Times*, December 4, 1970, p. 1:5; McCandlish Phillips, "Notebook Seizure Irritates Police," *New York Times*, December 7, 1970, p. 33:1; and David Burnham, "Police Inspector Fights Subpoena," *New York Times*, December 9, 1970, p. 1:2.

11. Information about the GEIRB's planning and policy making was obtained through interviews of senior officials and through a review of pertinent departmental materials, 1961-1967.

12. See Department Directive #82, s. 1961 (April 19, 1961).

13. Personal interviews with former plainclothesmen and superior officers.

14. The principal staff officer of the GEIRB was Lt. William H.T. Smith, who became first deputy commissioner. His hand-picked assistant was Sgt. Donald F. Cawley, later police commissioner from 1973 to 1974. Thus senior officials in the early 1970s were knowledgeable about problems of honesty and ethical behavior in gambling enforcement.

15. See Temporary Operating Procedure #231, s. 1970 (July 28, 1970), which limited the GEIRB's responsibility for determining procedures and assignments, and TOP #318, s. 1972 (October 27, 1972), which abolished the GEIRB.

16. See Press Releases #88, s. 1971 (September 10, 1971), and #111, s. 1971 (November 18, 1971).

17. The so-called "rotten apple" theory, in which corruption within the department was accepted as an inevitable but limited problem, was expressly rejected by the first deputy commissioner. See James F. Clarity, "Murphy's Deputy Says 'Rotten Apple' Concept Cuts Public Confidence in Police," *New York Times*, October 28, 1971, p. 45:1.

18. For an account of the "policy themes" underlying these strategies, see William P. Brown, *The New York City Police Department Anti-Corruption Campaign, October 1970-August 1972* (Albany: State University of New York at Albany, 1972), pp. 43-56. Brown, formerly an inspector in the department, was invited by the staff of the first deputy commissioner's office to conduct his study.

19. Interviews with former senior officials, New York City, October 13, 1972, and Washington, D.C., May 23, 1973.

20. See *Rules and Procedures*, 1957 ed., Chapter 8 as amended.

21. Departmental materials, 1954 and 1955.

22. Local Order #40, s. 1955 (June 1, 1955).

23. Departmental materials, 1956. Also reported in *New York Times* of April 16, 1960, p. 1:1; April 19, 1960, p. 1:1; April 20, 1960, p. 1:1; and June

7, 1960, p. 46:1. When the 183 men in the Bureau of Criminal Investigation responsible for preparing the criminal records ("yellow sheets") were being screened during this investigation, the digits "183" were reportedly bet heavily by numbers players. See *New York Times*, April 23, 1960, p. 45:8.

24. Departmental materials, 1966, and Chief Inspector Memo #35, s. 1966 (June 2, 1966).

25. Departmental materials, 1966.

26. See General Order #52, s. 1958 (November 17, 1958); TOP #357, s. 1966 (November 18, 1966); GO #17, s. 1967 (July 14, 1967); TOP #280, s. 1969 (August 28, 1969); and GO #2, s. 1970 (January 23, 1970).

27. This was a sharp reversal of the long-standing policy of involving all members of the force in gambling enforcement. See "City Police Changing Enforcement in Gambling and Narcotics, With Purpose of Focusing on Major Dealers," *New York Times*, January 13, 1972, p. 33:1. Also see TOP #216, s. 1972 (August 3, 1972).

28. Departmental materials, 1963.

29. Murphy, *The Gambling Situation–1964*, A Report by Police Commissioner Michael J. Murphy, On the Status of Illegal Gambling and Gambling Enforcement in New York City, To the Select Committee on Off-Track Betting (New York: New York City Police Department, February 1964). Also see departmental materials, 1965, and Chief Inspector Memo #38, s. 1969 (June 20, 1969).

30. Departmental materials, 1962 and 1964-1966, and interviews with former plainclothesmen.

31. See *New York Times* articles of April 14, 1950, p. 47:2; June 17, 1952, p. 36:6; December 25, 1952, p. 1:1; February 12, 1953, p. 29:2; April 9, 1954, p. 17:5; August 4, 1954, p. 10:3; February 18, 1956, p. 1:3; March 30, 1957, p. 74:5; February 13, 1959, p. 1:1; March 6, 1959, p. 27:8; April 26, 1960, p. 1:2; December 3, 1960, p. 15:2; May 4, 1961, p. 1:3; October 21, 1961, p. 23:1; December 4, 1961, p. 33:3; and April 27, 1962, p. 27:2. The policy of mass transfer continued throughout the 1960s with the support of the GEIRB (see departmental materials, 1961-1966).

32. The Interim Presentment of the Kings County ("hold over") Grand Jury for the term of December 1949, quoted in "Grand Jury's Warning on Police Graft," *New York Times*, September 26, 1951, p. 26:3.

33. Departmental materials, 1966.

34. Department Directive #141, s. 1956 (June 21, 1956), and "Recommendations of the Second Additional 1958 Kings County Grand Jury, Relative to Enforcement of the Gambling Laws," Second Additional 1958 Kings County Grand Jury.

35. One squad was responsible for Brooklyn East, whereas in Brooklyn West a three-tiered system was created, with plainclothes squads in patrol precincts, divisions, and borough headquarters. When the structure of Brooklyn's patrol

force was again realigned in late 1960, Brooklyn East became Brooklyn North and Brooklyn West became Brooklyn South. During the experiment, the department continued to rely on plainclothes squads in patrol divisions in the other boroughs. See Press Release #80, s. 1959 (December 5, 1959); Department Directives #176, s. 1959 (December 15, 1959) and #190, s. 1960 (November 22, 1960).

36. Departmental materials, 1961 and 1962.

37. Press Release #75, s. 1962 (August 22, 1962); TOP #274, s. 1962 (August 22, 1962); GO #46, s. 1962 (December 12, 1962); and TOP #27, s. 1963 (January 25, 1963).

38. Departmental materials, 1961-1967.

39. Departmental materials, 1962 and 1963. Also, Press Releases #82, s. 1966 (August 15, 1966) and #110, s. 1966 (November 10, 1966), and TOP #139, s. 1966 (April 29, 1966).

40. Departmental materials, 1967.

41. The CIIU's responsibility for investigating gambling was transferred to the PMAD in TOP #141, s. 1971 (April 23, 1971). The structure of the public morals enforcement program was reorganized in TOP #185, s. 1971 (May 20, 1971). In June 1971, the CIIU was redesignated as the Chief Inspector's Investigation and Evaluation Division (CIIED) to reflect its new responsibilities. See TOP #235, s. 1971 (June 23, 1971). In spite of PMAD's new responsibilities and the more centralized structure, field commanders were told that they were still responsible for the integrity of their people. See GO #19, s. 1971 (June 24, 1971).

42. See Press Releases #88, s. 1971 (September 10, 1971) and #111, s. 1971 (November 18, 1971); TOPs #423, s. 1971 (November 18, 1971), which created the OCCB, and #432, s. 1971 (November 30, 1971), which established new departmental procedures relative to the OCCB; and OCCB Memo #1 (December 2, 1971), which further detailed the OCCB's procedures for investigating and reporting.

43. See Interim Order #107, s. 1973 (August 10, 1973), and Exhibit H in the appendix of this book. In 1974 the structure of the Public Morals Division was streamlined, reducing the commander's span of control to his deputies for field operations and central investigations. See *1974 Public Morals Division Annual Report* (January 8, 1975), p. 16.

44. See TOP #4, s. 1961 (November 28, 1961).

Evolution of the GEIRB's policies for plainclothes selection can be traced through departmental directives. See Department Directives #38, s. 1960 (March 4, 1960); #38-1, s. 1960 (June 25, 1960); #38-2, s. 1960 (December 2, 1960); and #73, s. 1961 (April 7, 1961). Continued in TOPs #4, s. 1961 (November 28, 1961); #219, s. 1962 (June 14, 1962); #19, s. 1963 (January 18, 1963); #70, s. 1964 (February 19, 1964); #131, s. 1965 (April 28, 1965); #244, s. 1966 (July 19, 1966); #70, s. 1967 (March 1, 1967); #109, s. 1968 (March

19, 1968); #74, s. 1969 (March 10, 1969); #74-1, s. 1969 (July 10, 1969); #362, s. 1969 (November 7, 1969); and #28, s. 1970 (January 29, 1970).

In the early 1960s a debt limit of $200 per month was established for plainclothes candidates, so that patrolmen with financial obligations exceeding this standard were automatically eliminated from consideration. Examinations to measure intelligence quotients were also used as screening devices. Throughout the 1960s, the selection board accepted minimum scores of 90 to 95, although there was some effort to raise the standard to 110. But the dearth of otherwise qualified candidates made it impractical to require higher scores.

45. Departmental materials, 1961.

46. Police Commissioner Francis F.W. Adams, quoted by Charles Grutzner, "Adams Bids City Study Gambling and Youth Crime," *New York Times*, May 2, 1955, p. 1:1.

47. Departmental materials, 1961, 1963-1965.

48. In July 1967, only about 15 percent of the 3000 members of the Detective Division had prior experience as plainclothesmen. Departmental materials, 1967.

49. See TOP #70, s. 1964 (February 19, 1964).

50. See OCCB Memo #1 (December 2, 1971) and Interim Order #105 (August 8, 1973).

51. See Chief of Personnel Memos #60, s. 1971 (August 27, 1971); #60-1, s. 1971 (December 1, 1970); #60-2, s. 1971 (January 12, 1972). See also Bob Knightly, "The Hook is Dead," *Spring 3100* (May 1972), p. 15.

52. Personal interviews, 1973, and Press Release #85, s. 1973 (November 2, 1973).

53. Departmental materials, 1961, and personal interviews.

54. See the series of TOPs cited in note 45.

55. Personal interviews, 1972.

56. See *1974 Public Morals Division Annual Report*, p. 28.

57. Departmental materials, 1961-1965.

58. See OCCB Policy Memo #5 (May 19, 1972).

59. Departmental materials, 1961 and 1962. Also in Department Directive #89, s. 1961 (May 5, 1961).

60. Departmental materials, 1960-1966; see also "In-Service Plainclothes Training Commences," *Spring 3100* (December 1950), p. 8.

61. Personal interviews with former plainclothesmen. In an effort to improve the criminal investigation course, the academy surveyed all precinct commanders who directed plainclothesmen in 1965. Because many plainclothesmen were sent to precincts upon completion of the course, weaknesses in training were most visible at this level. When commanders were asked to evaluate plainclothes training, they cited "corruption" as the most serious "personal shortcoming." The captains recommended more thorough screening and more supervision, but they did not mention a need for more preparation for the moral temptations involved in plainclothes duty.

62. Departmental materials, 1964-1966; Murphy, *The Gambling Situation–1964.*

63. Departmental materials 1961, 1963-1966, and personal interviews with former plainclothes commanders.

64. Departmental materials, 1970-1972. See also Lacey Fosburgh, "Police Rookies Warned on Corruption," *New York Times*, October 26, 1971, p. 45.

65. Interviews with departmental officials in New York City, August 10, 1972. Also see "An Invitation to Understanding–Law Enforcement Integrity," *Police Chief* 39, 5 (May 1972): 34-44. Reported in Press Releases #9, s. 1972 (January 27, 1972), and #55, s. 1972 (June 12, 1972).

66. Departmental materials, 1970-1972, and interview with former senior official, Washington, D.C., May 23, 1973.

67. See OCCB Policy Memo #6 (July 20, 1972).

68. Interview with former senior official, Washington, D.C., May 23, 1973. See also David Burnham, "Murphy Warns Top Aides Fight on Corruption Lags," *New York Times*, August 28, 1972, p. 1:1.

69. Interview with a senior official, in New York City, December 11, 1973.

70. See OCCB Policy Memo #4 (May 2, 1972), p. 1.

71. For a more detailed discussion of the various corruption hazards, see *The Knapp Commission Report on Police Corruption* (New York: George Braziller, 1973), pp. 61-195.

72. A similar idea was expressed by Michael Armstrong, former chief counsel to the Knapp Commission: "10% of the department is unalterably corrupt, 10% is unalterably honest, and 80% wish to be honest," in a speech given on December 8, 1975, in Washington, D.C., before the American Association for Professional Law Enforcement.

73. Interviews with former senior officials, New York City, October 13, 1972, and Washington, D.C., May 23, 1973.

74. Departmental materials, 1970-1972. For one insider's account, see Robert Daley, *Target Blue* (New York: Dell, 1974), p. 431.

75. Departmental materials, 1970-1972.

76. Ibid. See also TOP #369, s. 1971 (October 5, 1971).

77. Ibid. For a contemporary account see David Burnham, "250 Police Officials Get Corruption Questionnaire," *New York Times*, October 7, 1972, p. 1.

78. See Martin Arnold, "Murphy's Drive on Graft Is Deeply Affecting Police," *New York Times*, September 20, 1971, p. 1:3. Also interviews with four plainclothesmen, New York City, March 1974.

79. Ibid. Also see Daley, *Target Blue*, pp. 300-320.

80. "Confidential Memorandum for the Executive Corps," dated August 17, 1971, quoted in part by William P. Brown, *The New York City Police Department Anti-Corruption Campaign*, p. 84.

81. Departmental materials, 1971. This standard of accountability was enunciated publicly by the commissioner in an address before the American

Society of Public Administration. See Press Release #25, s. 1972 (March 22, 1972).

82. Statistics on implementation of the policy of accountability are not available; however, on May 23, 1973, a former senior official cited a 90-percent turnover in the department's executive corps during 1970-1972. For some contemporary accounts, see "A Deputy Inspector in Morals Division Demoted to Captain," *New York Times*, February 4, 1972, p. 36:1; David Burnham, "22 Top Policemen May Be Demoted," *New York Times*, April 14, 1972, p. 1:3; Robert D. McFadden, "17-High Ranking Police Officers Are Shifted in a New Shake-Up," *New York Times*, October 21, 1972, p. 15:4; and David Burnham, "10 High Policemen Directed to Quit or Face Demotion," *New York Times*, November 17, 1972, p. 1:1.

83. Accountability was extended to the process of recommendation in TOP #31, s. 1972 (February 7, 1972). The new system of personnel records was established in Chief of Personnel Memos #69, s. 1971 (September 28, 1971) and #69-2, s. 1971 (November 2, 1971). See also Knightly, "The Hook is Dead," p. 15.

84. A departmental study in early 1972 showed that in the five-month period from September 1, 1971 to February 29, 1972, bribery arrests had increased from 75 to 345, 335 percent over the same period a year before. See Press Release #30, s. 1972 (April 4, 1972).

On September 20, 1972, 4 patrolmen were promoted to detective for making outstanding bribery arrests, and 630 others were granted waivers in the Career Path requirements, enabling them to move more rapidly toward the detective assignment. The action was taken through the newly established Bribery Arrest Evaluation Board. See TOP #274, s. 1972 and Press Release #101, s. 1972, both published September 20, 1972.

85. See Interim Orders #140, s. 1973 (October 16, 1973) and #153, s. 1973 (December 3, 1973), which created the Integrity Review Board and new commendations. Also see Press Releases #38, s. 1974 (July 16, 1974), and #68, s. 1974 (November 27, 1974), which announced the promotion of ten "incorruptable" policemen to detective.

86. Departmental materials, 1954, 1956, 1958, and 1960. Also Department Directive #39, s. 1959 (February 23, 1959).

87. Departmental materials, 1961, 1962, and 1964.

88. Standard Operating Procedure (SOP) #20, s. 1962 (June 1, 1962), revised and reissued on June 7, 1967, and again on April 9, 1970.

89. Interview with senior official, New York City, July 19, 1972.

90. Departmental materials, 1962-1965, and interviews of former plainclothesmen. Also see Chief Inspector Memo #63, s. 1965 (December 1, 1965) condemning the "splitting" of arrests and other practices in the plainclothes force.

91. Interview with former senior official, New York City, July 13, 1972.

92. In 1969, borough commanders were cautioned about erroneous reporting and recording of statistics at plainclothes commands. In some instances improper counts were made or arrests were improperly classified. Departmental materials, 1969.

93. In 1969, commanders of plainclothesmen were told that in spite of the 100-person reduction in the plainclothes force on June 18, 1969, it was essential that they intensify the enforcement efforts of the remaining plainclothes force. The level of enforcement must be maintained. Moreover, borough commanders were told that plainclothesmen had to increase the number of arrests for narcotics, but that the intensification of narcotics enforcement had to be accomplished in a manner that would not result in a letdown in enforcement efforts against gamblers and other public morals violators. Departmental materials, 1969.

94. Information obtained in personal interviews with former plainclothesmen.

95. Departmental materials, 1965 and 1967, and interviews with former plainclothesmen.

96. See Chief Inspector Memo #47, s. 1970 (September 15, 1970), which established the confidential informants file.

97. See OCCB Memo #51 (June 27, 1973), which revised procedures for registering informants.

98. Departmental materials, 1971.

99. See OCCB Policy Memo #1 (March 10, 1972).

100. Personal interviews and departmental materials, 1962-1965.

101. Departmental materials, 1961, 1962, 1964, and 1965. Also TOP #231, s. 1962 (May 10, 1962).

102. The department's entire procedure for evaluation was revamped. As of November 1971, all sergeants were required to attend a one-day training course to learn new procedures for rating. In March 1972, the Personnel Bureau prepared a seventeen-page "Evaluator's Guide" for the "Performance Evaluation System." Departmental materials, 1971-1972.

103. See OCCB Memo #16 (April 28, 1972), which outlined the complete evaluation procedure.

104. Departmental materials, 1965-1967.

105. Departmental materials, 1961, 1962, and 1964. Also confirmed by a senior official, in New York City, August 1, 1972.

106. See OCCB Memos #5 (December 31, 1971); #5-1 (January 28, 1972); #5-2 (February 17, 1972); and #5–Revision #1 (May 5, 1972). Also see OCCB Memos #32 (October 5, 1972), which established the $200 advance of funds; #35 (October 11, 1972) and #35-1 (December 20, 1972), which provided for reimbursement for damage to private automobiles used on official business; #37 (October 25, 1972), which provided for cash advances for the purchase of equipment; #43 (February 7, 1973), which established procedures for paying

confidential informants; and #45 (February 26, 1973), which provided instructions for reporting payments to informants.

Chapter 4
The Control Strategies: 1950-1975

Much of the material in this chapter was obtained during a series of interviews with former plainclothesmen and supervisors of the plainclothes force.

1. The strategy of "detecting and discouraging deviation" was described in Herbert Kaufman, *The Forest Ranger* (Baltimore, Maryland: The Johns Hopkins Press, 1967), pp. 126-160.

2. *Rules and Procedures*, 1957 ed., Chapter 2, paragraph 35.0 provided that "A member of the force shall report to his commanding officer any violation of the *Rules and Procedures* which he observes or of which he has knowledge." Similar provisions were contained in the *Rules and Regulations* as far back as the first edition (sec. 26), which was published in 1853.

3. In 1960 a senior official reported that most members of the department were extremely reluctant to report other members' derelictions in enforcing laws relating to public morals, particularly gambling. He recommended to his superiors that paragraph 35.0 (see note 2) be strengthened by a supplementary paragraph providing that a member of the force having knowledge of another member's corruption should report by telephone or in writing directly to the police commissioner, and that such information should be treated as confidential. The senior official thought his suggestion might help to overcome the reluctance of members of the department to report cases of outright corruption. See departmental materials, 1960. Although this proposal was never adopted, paragraph 35.0 was subsequently amended by the addition of the New York City Code of Ethics regulating conflicts of interest. See General Order #22, s. 1962 (June 8, 1962).

4. The teletype message authorizing direct reporting to the district attorney or Department of Investigation was published in Press Release #45, s. 1970 (May 16, 1970). Also see Press Release #45, s. 1970 (May 16, 1970); Temporary Operating Procedure #251, s. 1970 (August 26, 1970); TOP #251-1, s. 1970 (September 18, 1970); and other departmental materials, 1970.

5. TOP #251-3, s. 1970 (December 7, 1970).

6. See TOPs #251-4, s. 1970 (April 21, 1971) and #358, s. 1971 (September 29, 1971).

7. Set out in OCCB Policy Memo #1 (March 10, 1972).

8. Reportedly, OCCB investigators were not accepting and recording telephone complaints alleging malfeasance. Instead they were referring callers to the Internal Affairs Division, contrary to official policies.

9. GOs #16, s. 1954 (March 30, 1954) and #10, s. 1965 (April 2, 1965). Also TOP #259, s. 1970 (September 7, 1970) regarding vague entries and "two sets of memorandum books."

10. General Order #4, s. 1968 (March 11, 1968). The use of memorandum books was questioned by DCI Patrick V. Murphy, who recommended instead the use of multiple precarbon forms. After becoming police commissioner in 1970, Murphy discontinued plainclothesmen's use of memorandum books.

11. See PMD Order #2, s. 1972 (February 3, 1972), which established ring schedules; also see TOP #432, s. 1971 (November 30, 1971) and OCCB Memo #4 (January 1, 1972) which discuss DARs. The unofficial rule called for DARs to be at the Administrative Division of the OCCB within five working days.

In mid-1972 the Administrative Division of the OCCB was designated as the repository for all memorandum books of the defunct plainclothes force. The books were retained for a five-year period as required by the *Rules and Procedures*, 1957 ed., Chapter 8, paragraph 10.4. Borough and Division commanders were directed to forward the books to the OCCB for safekeeping. See TOP #137, s. 1972 (May 15, 1972).

12. A revised directive was issued to the OCCB's personnel after inspections of Daily Activity Reports revealed a pattern of non-specific reporting. New guidelines required more detailed DARs. See OCCB Memo #1-1 (undated, but issued in approximately mid-1972).

13. GO #4, s. 1955 (February 4, 1955); Department Directive #218, s. 1956 (October 24, 1956); and GO #14, s. 1957 (April 18, 1957). See also Exhibits L and M (Form U.F. 128) in the appendix.

14. See Department Directives #39-1, s. 1959 (March 17, 1959) and #104, s. 1959 (July 18, 1959); and GO #43, s. 1960 (September 28, 1960). Requirements for reporting arrests of KGs extended in GOs #10, s. 1966 (April 12, 1966); #10, s. 1968 (May 10, 1968); #22, s. 1968 (September 16, 1968); and #23, s. 1968 (October 10, 1968).

15. Set out in GOs #52, s. 1958 (November 17, 1958); #34, s. 1963 (August 26, 1963); and #17, s. 1967 (July 14, 1967); and in TOPs #357, s. 1966 (November 18, 1966) and #280, s. 1969 (August 28, 1969).

16. Departmental materials, 1964, and interviews with former plainclothesmen. (See Exhibit M expressly prohibiting use of phrase "No Violations Observed.")

17. This belief was reinforced by official requirements in reporting that were intended to present a statistical portrayal of the contribution of a specific command to the overall enforcement of gambling. See, for example, GO #37, s. 1965 (October 15, 1965), and departmental materials, 1968.

18. See OCCB Memo #1 (December 2, 1971) and PMD Order #2 (February 3, 1972).

19. Interviews with senior official, New York City, July 13, 1972 and May 14, 1973.

20. See OCCB Memos #9 (February 7, 1972) and #21 (July 14, 1972). To assist the OCCB's personnel and other members of the force in drawing up search warrant affidavits and processing applications in court, the department's legal division created a search warrant section. See TOP #358, s. 1972 (December 7, 1972).

21. Departmental materials, 1962 and 1963.

22. Departmental materials, 1964.

23. Departmental materials, 1967 and 1968.

24. Personal interviews with former superior officers, 1972.

25. See OCCB Memo #15 (April 5, 1972).

26. See Alexander Feinberg, "6 Police Captains to Work Full Time in Gambling 'War,'" *New York Times*, September 19, 1950, p. 1:1; Alexander Feinberg, "Deputy Inspectors Head Plainclothes Squads in Drive on Gaming, Vice," *New York Times*, October 20, 1951, p. 1:1; Department Directive #39, s. 1959 (February 23, 1959); Press Release #30, s. 1961 (May 2, 1961); GO #37, s. 1961 (June 12, 1961); and other departmental materials, 1954, 1961, and 1964.

27. See Patrolmen's Benevolent Association (PBA) Press Release of February 9, 1954; Press Release #14, s. 1954 (February 10, 1954); and departmental materials, 1961 and 1964.

28. Departmental materials, 1961.

29. Insp. Joseph L. Klein, "GO 34 and the Administrative Inspector," *Police Management Review* 6 (Planning Bureau, NYCPD, February 1964); and departmental materials, 1962 and 1965. In 1965, the GEIRB recommended that lieutenants who were being considered for plainclothes supervisory duties should receive a one-week course of instruction at the police academy.

30. Departmental materials, 1962-1964.

31. Departmental materials, 1963 and 1966.

32. Departmental materials, 1968.

33. *Rules and Procedures*, 1957 ed., Chapters 1, 3, 6, and 8, as amended.

34. Departmental materials, 1962, 1964, and 1966.

35. Department Directive #39-1, s. 1959 (March 17, 1959); Standard Operating Procedure #26, July 2, 1963, as amended; GOs #31, s. 1964 (July 23, 1964) and #37, s. 1965 (October 15, 1965); and departmental materials, 1966, 1968, and 1970.

36. Departmental materials, 1965.

37. See TOP #231, s. 1962 (May 10, 1962), and other departmental materials, 1962.

38. Evaluation reports covered in Chief Inspector Memo #50, s. 1965 (September 15, 1965) and TOP #82, s. 1967 (March 8, 1967).

39. Departmental materials, 1965, and personal interviews, 1972.

40. Ibid.

41. In 1964 a senior official reported to his superiors that supervisors in

gambling enforcement did not know what their people were doing or what information they were developing. Every time an inquiry was made, only the plainclothesmen could answer questions about investigations, the official said. Departmental materials, 1964.

42. Personal interviews, 1972.

43. Departmental materials, 1962-1965.

44. For a traditional discussion of "span of control," see O.W. Wilson and Roy McLaren, *Police Administration*, 3rd. ed., (New York: McGraw-Hill Book Company, 1972), p. 68; Departmental materials, 1968, and personal interviews, 1972.

45. Officials lacked incentives to become involved in dealing with problems of dishonesty and unethical behavior. Administrators in the early 1970s attempted to provide such motivation through several strategies.

46. See PMD Orders #1 (January 21, 1972) and #2 (February 3, 1972). Also see departmental materials, 1970-1972. A senior official stated that it was his practice to seek out good superior officers in other commands and, persuading them to work in OCCB but not drafting them.

47. OCCB Memo #1 (December 2, 1971).

48. OCCB Policy Memo #3 (April 26, 1972).

49. Interviews with plainclothesmen and field patrol observations, July 5, 1972. See also PMD Order #3 (February 4, 1972), which covered the updating of 328 known gambling combines.

In spite of official emphasis on "quality" investigations, statistics for 1974 reflected a decrease in felony gambling arrests (from 507 in 1973 to 419), with an increase in misdemeanor gambling arrests (from 160 in 1973 to 226). See *1974 Public Morals Division Annual Report* (January 8, 1975), p. 13.

50. Interviews with plainclothesmen, July 6, 1972, and field observations made the same day with plainclothesmen to observe routine surveillances of a gambling combine. See also OCCB Memos #31 (September 29, 1972) and #31-1 (March 19, 1973) which established detailed guidelines for executing search warrants.

In 1975 the OCCB reported two investigations of 23 and 18 months duration, involving undercover policemen posing as "cops on the take," who had been paid more than $22,000 to "protect" illegal activities, which resulted in numerous arrests of organized crime figures on charges of bribery and conspiracy. See *1974 PMD Annual Report*, p. 3.

51. Interviews with plainclothesmen, July 5-6, 1972.

52. Ibid. See also OCCB Memo #33 (October 9, 1972), which covered contacts with defendants or defense attorneys.

53. Although OCCB Memo #70 (June 17, 1974) mentioned the need for a "coordinated approach" in OCCB work, it stressed that investigations should be directed exclusively by superiors.

54. Departmental materials, 1961, 1962, and 1965.

55. *A Report of the Command Conference for Precinct Captains* (New York: Police Academy, April 6-9, 1965).

56. Departmental materials, 1966.

57. See *OCCB Functional Guide* (July 1973), pp. 1/6.1-7.1.

58. This was another facet of the broad strategy to decentralize responsibility for controlling corrupt practices.

59. See the OCCB's *Administrative Self-Inspection Manual* (1973) and the *Corruption Control Manual* (1973). Both manuals were issued after the police commissioner issued a general *Corruption Manual* to all commanding officers on April 24, 1973. See David Burnham, "Police Commanders Are Issued Manual on Corruption," *New York Times*, April 26, 1973, p. 38:1.

60. See GO #38, s. 1960 (August 26, 1960) and departmental materials, 1960 and 1965.

61. Departmental materials, 1966.

62. See GO #16, s. 1954 (March 30, 1954).

63. Departmental materials, 1955.

64. Departmental materials, 1964.

65. Ibid.

66. Departmental materials, 1963 and 1966.

67. See TOPs #251, s. 1970 (August 26, 1970) and #251-2, s. 1970 (September 18, 1970).

68. TOPs #250 through 250-4, s. 1970, also interview of senior official, New York City, June 15, 1972.

69. See TOP #73, s. 1972 (March 21, 1972), which completely reorganized the department's procedures for investigating corruption, revoking the series of directives in TOP #250, s. 1970. Officials also created a Special Task Force to investigate cases of possible corruption uncovered by the Knapp Commission. See Press Release #19, s. 1972 (March 7, 1972) and TOP #70, s. 1972 (March 17, 1972).

70. Departmental materials, 1960.

71. The unit was known as the Police Commissioner's Investigating Unit (PCIU) until approximately 1960, when its title was changed to Police Commissioner's Confidential Investigating Unit (PCCIU) during a reorganization.

72. See "Self Portrait," *Spring 3100* February, 1964, p. 3.

73. Growth of the PCCIU:

Manpower		Personnel in 1965			
Year	No. of Men				
1961	85	Supervising Assistant		Lieutenant	26
1962	86	Chief Inspector	1	Sergeant	15
1963	129	Deputy Chief Inspector	2	Detective	29
1964	143	Inspector	1	Patrolmen	48
1965	135	Deputy Inspector	3	Policewomen	4
1966	195	Captain	6		
				Total –	135

Source: New York City Police Department.

74. Departmental materials, 1954-1970.

75. Departmental materials, 1964-1966, and personal interviews, 1972.

In 1965, the Chief Inspector's Investigating Unit (CIIU) was divided into four sections: Administrative, Disciplinary, Enforcement, and Special Investigations. The CIIU's personnel included:

Asst. Chief Insp. (Commander)	1
Dep. Chief Inspector	1
Deputy Inspector	1
Captains	2
Lieutenants	15
Sergeants	9
Detectives	5
Patrolmen	26
Policewomen	2
Trainees	1

Source: New York City Police Department.

76. The PCCIU's authority to investigate corruption in the enforcement of gambling laws was mentioned in typewritten orders (not circulated to the entire force) first on August 7, 1947, and again on July 20, 1949. It was later published by the chief inspector on January 11, 1952 and remained in effect until it was renewed once more in Chief Inspector Memo #48, s. 1965 (September 7, 1965).

77. Departmental materials, 1965.

78. Departmental materials, 1966, and TOP #167, s. 1967 (April 26, 1967).

79. TOP #167, s. 1967 (April 26, 1967), and GO #15, s. 1969 (July 11, 1969).

80. See Press Release #89, s. 1968 (September 12, 1968), and personal interviews.

81. Alexander Feinberg, "Flath's Vice Squad Upset By Monaghan," *New York Times*, October 27, 1951, p. 1:2; "Tough Cop Named Top Aide to Adams," *New York Times*, January 13, 1954, p. 1:2; Jack Roth, "10 Policemen Lose Jobs For Defying Gambling Inquiry, Collusion in Numbers and Bookmaking Disclosed, Squad of 48 Shaken Up," *New York Times*, June 26, 1964, p. 1:1; "Special Jury Due to Press Inquiry on Police Graft," *New York Times*, June 30, 1964, p. 37:2; departmental materials, 1964 and 1965.

82. See TOP #397-1, s. 1967 (September 25, 1967) merging the PCCIU and the CIIU with the Chief of Patrol's Investigating Unit. Also see Press Release #63, s. 1968 (July 2, 1968).

83. Interview with senior official, New York City, July 14, 1972, and *OCCB Administrative Guide* (July 1973), pp. 1/6.1-7.1.

A new inspections program was also established within the Patrol Services Bureau to increase the effectiveness of the chief of patrol. In an effort to enhance the acceptance of this new program, commanders were no longer required to submit written explanations after an inspection of why departmental policy had not been followed. Instead the inspection report was to be used as a guide for needed changes, with "explanations" from commanders no longer required. See TOP #262, s. 1972 (September 12, 1972) and other departmental materials, 1972.

84. See OCCB Memos #62-1 (November 21, 1974), which discussed "up-dating photographs," and #73 (January 2, 1975), which established the command roster. In early 1972 administrators were considering the use of lie detector tests for policemen suspected of corruption, but they met strong opposition from employee organizations in the department. See David Burnham, "Lie Detector Tests for Police Weighed," *New York Times*, March 14, 1972, p. 47.

85. See the report of the first deputy commissioner, "Integrity Assessment," December 10, 1973, and *1974 PMD Annual Report*, p. 25. "Integrity tests" of the patrol force were also carried out. See Deirdre Carmody, "Nighttime Checks on Police Find Conscientiousness and Violations," *New York Times*, April 2, 1974, p. 1:1; "Coop Swoop: 124 Cops Off Base," *New York Post*, April 5, 1974, p. 13; and Deirdre Carmody, "54 Officers Facing Police Trial After 'Sleeping on Job' Inquiry," *New York Times*, April 19, 1974, p. 1.

86. See Press Release #104, s. 1971 (November 2, 1971) and other departmental materials, 1971.

87. Interview with senior official, New York City, August 1, 1972. See also David Burnham, "Brooklyn Police Face Indictments," *New York Times*, April 28, 1972, p. 45:1, in which the existence and scope of the Field Associate Program were made public.

88. Departmental materials, 1971.

89. "Integrity Assessment," p. 1.

90. Interview with senior official, New York City, August 1, 1972.

91. Ibid. Also Morris Kaplan, "24 Police Indicted in a Bribery Case," *New York Times*, May 3, 1972, p. 1:3. In 1974 nineteen of these plainclothesmen were dismissed from the force following "their conviction at a departmental trial on charges of bribe receiving and promotion of illegal gambling." See Press Release #64, s. 1974 (November 18, 1974), and "Codd Dismisses 19 Former Plainclothes Police Officers In Bribery Scandal," *New York Times*, November 19, 1974, p. 29:1.

92. OCCB Policy Memo #1 (March 10, 1972) and interview with senior official, New York City, August 1, 1972.

93. Personal interviews, Washington, D.C., and New York City, January 1975.

94. Press Release #56, s. 1974 (October 15, 1974).

95. Set out in *Rules and Procedures*, 1957 ed., Chapter 21, "Charges and Trials," as amended. See also Abraham Chess, "The Role of Administrative Discipline in The New York City Police Department." (unpublished master's

thesis, Baruch School of Business and Public Administration, The City College of New York, 1961). Also Press Release #39, s. 1954 (April 7, 1954); Department Directive #108, s. 1958 (August 7, 1958); departmental materials, 1966; and TOP #439, s. 1967 (November 10, 1967).

96. Departmental materials, 1964-1966. Announced officially on June 16, 1966 in Press Release #55, s. 1966, TOP #218, s. 1966 (June 16, 1966); and in GO #22, s. 1966 (July 12, 1966).

97. The "New Procedures For Handling Certain Minor Violations of the Rules and Procedures," known as the "Captain's Mast" was adopted in TOP #218, s. 1966 (June 16, 1966). The revised Command Discipline procedure was adopted in TOP #368, s. 1971 (October 5, 1971).

98. Interview with senior official, New York City, August 1, 1972. Also see note 91.

99. Interview with senior official, New York City, May 14, 1973 and December 11, 1973.

100. See *Gardner* v. *Broderick*, 392 U.S. 273, 1968.

101. Departmental materials, 1968. Also covered in TOP #251, s. 1970 (August 26, 1970), as amended, which contains the pertinent Mayor's Executive Memorandum of May 12, 1969 and the Mayor's Executive Order #21, of August 19, 1970.

102. See GO #19, s. 1957 (June 13, 1957), which amended resignation procedures; and GO #27, s. 1962 (July 26, 1962), which contained provisions of the Mayor's Executive Order #11, dated April 17, 1962, and the memorandum of September 21, 1962 from the director, Legal Bureau to the Police Commissioner.

103. Departmental materials, 1971.

Chapter 5
Achieving Organizational Responsiveness

1. See for example, H.H. Gerth and C.W. Mills, *From Max Weber* (New York: Oxford University Press, 1958), pp. 196-244; Frederick W. Taylor, *Principles of Scientific Management* (New York: Harper & Row, 1947); Herbert Simon, *Administrative Behavior*, 2nd ed. (New York: The Free Press, 1957). For a study of the evolution of the human relations perspective, see Charles Perrow, *Complex Organizations* (Glenview, Ill.: Scott Foresman, 1972), pp. 97-143.

2. See Rensis Likert, *The Human Organization* (New York: McGraw-Hill, 1967); and Douglas McGregor, *The Human Side of Enterprise* (New York: McGraw-Hill, 1960). Reprinted with permission.

3. McGregor, *The Human Side of Enterprise*, pp. 1-10.

4. Ibid., pp. 33-57.

5. Douglas McGregor, "The Human Side of Enterprise," paper presented at

the Fifth Anniversary Convocation of the School of Industrial Management, M.I.T., Cambridge, Mass., April 9, 1957. Reprinted in G.W. Dalton and P.R. Lawrence, eds., *Motivation and Control in Organizations* (Homewood, Ill.: The Dorsey Press, 1971), p. 311.

6. McGregor, *The Human Side of Enterprise*, p. 54.

7. Ibid., p. 42.

8. McGregor, "The Human Side of Enterprise," p. 310.

9. McGregor, *The Human Side of Enterprise*, pp. 49-52.

10. Ibid., p. 56.

11. Ibid., p. 42.

12. For some analyses of Theory X and Theory Y, see Saul W. Gellerman, *Motivation and Productivity* (Chicago: American Management Association, 1963), pp. 83-92; and Robert A. Ullrich, *A Theoretical Model of Human Behavior in Organizations* (Morristown, N.J.: General Learning Press, 1972), pp. 152-161.

13. *The Knapp Commission Report on Police Corruption* (New York: George Braziller, 1973), p. 1.

14. Ibid., p. 89.

15. Ibid., pp. 205-230.

16. Ibid., pp. 13-18.

17. Ibid., pp. 231-245.

18. McGregor, *The Human Side of Enterprise*, p. 42.

19. See James Q. Wilson, *Varieties of Police Behavior* (Cambridge, Mass: Harvard University Press, 1968), which describes the impact of three different sociopolitical environments on police.

20. For a discussion of how administrators can influence the legislative mandate that their agencies will subsequently enforce, see David B. Truman, *The Governmental Process* (New York: Alfred A. Knopf, 1971), pp. 439-446.

21. *The Knapp Commission Report*, pp. 71-72, and *Increased Legal Gambling in New York*, Hudson Institute Report to the New York State Gambling Commission (New York: January 1973). Also see Gerald Eskenazi, "Rise in Illegal Gambling Linked to OTB Climate," *New York Times*, January 10, 1974, p. 1:2.

22. See, for example, Herbert Kaufman, *The Forest Ranger* (Baltimore: The Johns Hopkins Press, 1967), pp. 75-80 and 203-209; Philip A. Selznick, "TVA and the Grass Roots," in Francis E. Rourke, ed., *Bureaucratic Power in National Politics*, 2nd ed. (Boston: Little, Brown, 1972), pp. 38-48; and Harmon Zeigler, "Administrative Policy Making Under Pressure," in *Interest Groups In American Society* (Englewood Cliffs, N.J.: Prentice-Hall, 1964), pp. 277-300.

23. For a description of the strategies that public bureaucracies can use to control their environment, see Aaron Wildavsky, *The Politics of the Budgetary Process* (Boston: Little, Brown, 1964), pp. 63-126.

24. For a discussion of the advantages of diversified constituencies, see

Frances E. Rourke, *Bureaucracy, Politics and Public Policy* (Boston: Little, Brown, 1969), pp. 12-24.

25. See, for example, *The Forest Ranger*, pp. 198-200, discussing the achievement of "voluntary conformity."

26. See, for example, Gellerman, *Motivation and Productivity*.

27. Problems in measuring "productivity" in our system of criminal justice are not limited to police. See Jerome H. Skolnick, *Justice Without Trial* (New York: John Wiley & Sons, 1966), pp. 167-176; Abraham S. Blumberg, *Criminal Justice* (Chicago: Quadrangle Books, 1970); David Burnham, "Police Officer's Study Alleges Men Work at 50% of Potential," *New York Times*, August 10, 1972, p. 1.

28. The process of substitution is not limited to gambling. Indeed, a more traditional area for misuse of statistics by police has been in enforcement of traffic laws. See, for example, Eric Pace, "Quota Precinct Writes 1,294 Tickets in Day," *New York Times*, January 20, 1972, p. 1; Edward Hudson, "Precinct Rescinds Its Ticket Quotas," *New York Times*, January 21, 1972, p. 1; and Jim Goodman, "Troopers Have Ticket Quota, Attorney Says," *The Sunday Times Advertiser* (Trenton, N.J.), April 14, 1974, p. 1.

29. Much of the material in this section is based on personal interviews with senior officials.

30. Early in 1974 the new police commissioner acknowledged that he was reassessing the department's priorities once again. "My predecessors . . . decided to attack the twin evils of crime and corruption by reforming the department's internal management as a preparation for improving field performance. Much was accomplished. But now the internal management techniques must prove their worth to the street. Since resources are limited we must re-examine all existing programs, and depending on their relative value for the street, drop some, suspend, modify, or continue others. What this city needs now are action programs to promote and ensure the public safety." Press Release #14, s. 1974 (February 13, 1974).

31. *The Knapp Commission Report*, pp. 6-7.

32. Interview with senior police official, New York City, June 8, 1973.

33. Ibid.

34. Ibid.

35. For another discussion of "resignation" as a phenomenon of administrative behavior, see Herbert Kaufman, *Administrative Feedback* (Washington, D.C.: The Brookings Institution, 1973), pp. 66-67.

36. McGregor, *The Human Side of Enterprise*, p. 246.

37. Interview with former senior official, Washington, D.C., May 23, 1973.

38. Report of the first deputy commissioner, "Integrity Assessment," December 10, 1973, with supporting materials.

39. Robert Presthus, *The Organizational Society* (New York: Random House, Vintage Books, 1962), p. 104.

40. For other discussions about fear as a motivating force in organizations, see Harold J. Leavitt, "Pressure and Coercion: A Second Model for Influence," in *Managerial Psychology* (Chicago: University of Chicago Press, 1972), pp. 146-151; Ullrich, *A Theoretical Model of Human Organizations*, pp. 101-106.

41. For a discussion of organizational change in the face of "pressure from external agents," see Anthony Downs, *Inside Bureaucracy* (Boston: Little, Brown, 1967), pp. 200-202.

42. "Integrity Assessment," with supporting materials. See also David Burnham, "Police Extortion Is Reported Cut," *New York Times*, December 28, 1973, p. 1:1.

43. Ibid., p. 4.

44. Ibid.; and supporting report of senior administrator in the Organized Crime Control Bureau, November 16, 1973.

45. Ibid. In a unique development stemming from this concern, the police commissioner in mid-1974 warned the department, "The rumor mill or the grapevine seems to be carrying a thought that I have relaxed department vigilance relative to improper practices–to be blunt–that I have gone easy on corruption. Nothing could be further from the truth. I have repeatedly said that I will assign whatever portion of the department resources may be necessary to root out corruption or to prevent its recurrence. And what is more, I have done so by assigning additional people or by providing added equipment wherever it has been needed. And we have continued to test our systems to detect inadequacies. Where deficiencies were discovered they were dealt with swiftly and positively, and I intend to keep that pressure on the system. You must lead by showing your personnel that you will accept only total honesty. Please do me, yourselves, and every member of the department a favor by carrying that message back." Press Release #32, s. 1974 (June 16, 1974). See also Selwyn Raab, "Codd Keeps Force Taut, if Not Wholly Happy," *New York Times*, January 10, 1975, p. 39.

46. The first deputy commissioner reported that it was "the opinion of the Task Force that no forms of organized corruption exist within the department." See the "Annual Report on the Integrity Level of the Department," November 25, 1974. Another Integrity Assessment was to be made in late-1975, but results were not available.

47. See, for example, Glen O. Stahl, "Liberating The Will To Work," in *Public Personnel Administration*, 5th ed. (New York: Harper & Row, 1962), pp. 197-222.

48. Kaufman, *The Forest Ranger*, pp. 161-200.

49. See, for example, U.S., Congress, Senate, Committee on the Judiciary, *Privacy and the Rights of Federal Employees*, Hearings before the Subcommittee on Constitutional Rights, 89th Cong., Second Session, September-October 1966, which describes surveillance practices of federal agencies.

50. See *Law and Order Reconsidered*, a staff report to the National Commis-

sion on the Causes and Prevention of Violence (Washington, D.C.: Government Printing Office, 1969), pp. 365-409; *The Urban Police Function* (New York: American Bar Association, 1973), pp. 144-170; and Alan A. Altshuler, *Community Control* (New York: Pegasus, 1970), pp. 37-44.

51. See, for example, Neil H. Cheek, "The Social Role of the Professional," in Mark Abrahamson, ed., *The Professional in The Organization* (Chicago: Rand McNally, 1967), pp. 9-16; Everett C. Hughes, "Professions," in Kenneth S. Lynn, ed., *The Professions In America* (Boston: Beacon Press, 1967), pp. 1-14; and A.M. Carr-Saunders, "Professions: Their Organization and Place in Society," in Howard Vollmer and Donald Mills, eds., *Professionalization* (Englewood Cliffs, N.J.: Prentice-Hall, 1966), pp. 3-9.

52. See Arthur Niederhoffer, *Behind the Shield* (New York: Doubleday, 1967), pp. 11-32; and James Q. Wilson, "The Police and Their Problems: A Theory," in James R. Klonoski and Robert Mendelsohn, eds., *The Politics of Local Justice* (Boston: Little, Brown and Company, 1970), pp. 161-174. Also see Emanuel Perlmutter, "P.B.A. Vote Upset Called Desire for a New Image," *New York Times*, June 10, 1974, p. 1:1.

53. For a typical description of the expertise model, see Gerald Astor, *The New York Cops* (New York: Charles Scribner's Sons, 1971), pp. 198-211.

54. See Frank D. Day, "Police Professionalism," *The Municipal Yearbook* (Washington, D.C.: International City Management Association, 1967), pp. 433-438; *Task Force Report: The Police*, pp. 126-128; *Police*, Report of the National Advisory Commission on Criminal Justice Standards and Goals (Washington, D.C.: Government Printing Office, 1973), pp. 369-379; and Charles B. Saunders, *Upgrading the American Police* (Washington, D.C.: The Brookings Institution, 1970).

55. See *Municipal Police Administration*, 4th ed., (Chicago: International City Manager's Association, 1954), pp. 483-499; Jerome H. Skolnick, *Justice Without Trial* (New York: John Wiley & Sons, 1966), pp. 235-239; and Patrick V. Murphy, "The Police: Corrupt Bureaucracy or Public Protector," speech at Princeton University, April 13, 1972.

56. In March 1958, the Law Enforcement Code of Ethics (see Exhibit Z in the appendix) was informally adopted by the police commissioner, who ordered copies of the code to be posted in all precincts and offices. See Department Directive #33, s. 1958 (March 17, 1958). In 1960 a different code of ethics, primarily concerned with conflicts of interest, was formally added to the department's *Rules and Procedures.* This code was subsequently amended in 1962 and again in 1970. See General Orders #13, s. 1960 (March 9, 1960) and #22, s. 1962 (June 8, 1962); and Temporary Operating Procedure #288, s. 1970 (September 25, 1970).

57. Herbert Packer found, however, it is these attitudes that underlie the "crime control" model of law enforcement—the antithesis of "due process." See *The Limits of The Criminal Sanction* (Stanford, Calif.: Stanford University Press, 1968), pp. 149-204.

58. See Abrahamson, *The Professional in the Organization*, pp. 24-30, 58-62.

59. Two such organizations, the American Academy for Professional Law Enforcement (founded in 1958) and the Law Enforcement Association on Professional Standards, Education and Ethical Practice (founded in 1970), merged in 1974. Their first joint conference was held in Washington, D.C., in January 1975; the conference topic was "Corruption and Its Management."

60. The Law Enforcement Assistance Administration, created in the Omnibus Crime Control Act of 1968, has provided billions of dollars in support of law enforcement. A considerable part of the expenditure has been aimed at professionalization, particularly through support of research and of programs offering higher education for policemen.

61. See Amitai Etzioni, *The Semi-Professions and Their Organization* (New York: The Free Press, 1969). Etzioni, however, does not list police as a "semi-profession."

Index

Index

About the Author

Allan N. Kornblum received the Ph.D. from the Woodrow Wilson School of Public and International Affairs, Princeton University, the M.P.A. from John Jay College of Criminal Justice, the J.D. from New York University of Law, and the B.S. from Michigan State University. He is an Attorney-Adviser for the United States Justice Department, Office of Policy and Planning. Dr. Kornblum has served as Director of Security at Princeton University, a Special Agent for the Federal Bureau of Investigation, an officer in the military police, a criminal investigator for the United States Treasury Department, and a patrolman for the New York City Police Department.